Different Societies, Shared Futures

Australia, Indonesia and the Region

The **Research School of Pacific and Asian Studies (RSPAS)**, a part of the **ANU College of Asia and the Pacific** at **The Australian National University**, is home to the **Indonesia Project**, a major international centre of research and graduate training on the economy of Indonesia. Established in 1965 in the School's Division of Economics, the Project is well known and respected in Indonesia and in other places where Indonesia attracts serious scholarly and official interest. Funded by the ANU and the Australian Agency for International Development (AusAID), the Indonesia Project monitors and analyses recent economic developments in Indonesia; informs Australian governments, business and the wider community about those developments and about future prospects; stimulates research on the Indonesian economy; and publishes the respected *Bulletin of Indonesian Economic Studies*.

The School's **Department of Political and Social Change** (PSC) focuses on domestic politics, social processes and state–society relationships in Asia and the Pacific, and has a long-established interest in Indonesia.

Together with PSC and RSPAS, the Project holds the annual Indonesia Update conference, which offers an overview of recent economic and political developments and devotes attention to a significant theme in Indonesia's development. The Project's *Bulletin of Indonesian Economic Studies* publishes the economic and political overviews, while the proceedings related to the theme of the conference are published in the Indonesia Update Series.

The **Institute of Southeast Asian Studies (ISEAS)** was established as an autonomous organization in 1968. It is a regional centre dedicated to the study of socio-political, security and economic trends and developments in Southeast Asia and its wider geostrategic and economic environment.

The Institute's research programmes are the Regional Economic Studies (RES, including ASEAN and APEC), Regional Strategic and Political Studies (RSPS), and Regional Social and Cultural Studies (RSCS).

ISEAS Publications, an established academic press, has issued more than 1,000 books and journals. It is the largest scholarly publisher of research about Southeast Asia from within the region. ISEAS Publications works with many other academic and trade publishers and distributors to disseminate important research and analyses from and about Southeast Asia to the rest of the world.

Indonesia Update Series

Different Societies, Shared Futures

Australia, Indonesia and the Region

edited by
John Monfries

ISEAS

INSTITUTE OF SOUTHEAST ASIAN STUDIES
Singapore

First published in Singapore in 2006 by
ISEAS Publications
Institute of Southeast Asian Studies
30 Heng Mui Keng Terrace
Pasir Panjang
Singapore 119614

E-mail: publish@iseas.edu.sg
http://bookshop.iseas.edu.sg

The responsibility for facts and opinions in this publication rests exclusively with the authors and their interpretations do not necessarily reflect the views or the policy of the Institute or its supporters.

ISEAS Library Cataloguing-in-Publication Data

Different societies, shared futures : Australia, Indonesia and the region / edited by John Monfries.
    (Indonesia update series)
    Based on the 2005 Indonesia Update Conference held at the Australian National University.
    1. Australia—Foreign relations—Indonesia.
    2. Indonesia—Foreign relations—Australia.
    3. National security—Indonesia.
    4. National security— Southeast Asia.
    5. Terrorism—Indonesia.
    6. Terrorism— Australia.
    I. Monfries, John.
    II. Indonesia Update Conference (2005 : Canberra, Australia)
    II. Series
DS644.4 I41 2005   2006

ISBN 981-230-386-3 (soft cover)
ISBN 981-230-387-1 (hard cover)

Cover: The cover illustration shows students in front of a newly rebuilt school in Aceh. The project was supported by the Australian aid agency AusAID. Photo courtesy of AusAID.

Copy editing and design by Beth Thomson, Japan Online
Printed in Singapore by Utopia Press Pte Ltd

In memory of Geoff Forrester (1946–2005), colleague and friend

CONTENTS

TABLES

FIGURES

CONTRIBUTORS

Richard Chauvel
Associate Professor, School of Social Sciences, Victoria University, Melbourne

Scott Dawson
Head, Secretariat, Australia–Indonesia Partnership for Reconstruction and Development, Department of Foreign Affairs and Trade, Canberra

Stephen Grenville
Fellow, Lowy Institute for International Policy, Sydney, and former Deputy Governor, Reserve Bank of Australia

Paul Kelly
Editor-at-Large, *The Australian*, Sydney

K. Kesavapany
Director, Institute of Southeast Asian Studies, Singapore

Noke Kiroyan
President, Indonesia–Australia Business Council, Jakarta

Jamie Mackie
Professor Emeritus, The Australian National University, Canberra

John Monfries
Former diplomat, and currently PhD candidate, Asian Studies Faculty, The Australian National University, Canberra

David Reeve
Associate Professor, Department of Chinese and Indonesian, University of NSW, Sydney

Isla Rogers-Winarto
Country Director – Indonesia, and General Manager – Network, IDP
Education, Jakarta

Rizal Sukma
Deputy Executive Director, Centre for Strategic and International Studies,
Jakarta

Hugh White
Professor of Strategic Studies, The Australian National University, Canberra,
and Visiting Fellow, Lowy Institute for International Policy, Sydney

S. Wiryono
Director General for Political Affairs, Foreign Ministry of Indonesia
(1990–93), and former Indonesian Ambassador to Australia

Richard Woolcott AC
Former Secretary of the Australian Department of Foreign Affairs and
Trade, and former Ambassador to Indonesia

ACKNOWLEDGMENTS

This book arises from the Indonesia Update conference on 'Indonesia, Australia and the Region' held at the Australian National University (ANU), Canberra, on 23–24 September 2005. As always with a book of this kind, many organisations and individuals should be warmly thanked for their support.

Firstly, the Australian Agency for International Development (AusAID) has been a consistent and generous sponsor of the Update over many years. Without its funding, the Update conferences and the books that stem from them would not see the light of day. We extend further thanks to AusAID for permission to use the photograph of an AusAID school rebuilding project in Aceh as our front cover illustration. We also thank the Department of Foreign Affairs and Trade for its interest and support, and for releasing Scott Dawson to deliver his valuable and informative paper on the Australia–Indonesia Partnership for Reconstruction and Development. The National Institute for Asia and the Pacific provided funding for the promotional aspects of the Update, while Sam Hardjono of the Australia–Indonesia Business Cooperation Council provided additional support.

The ANU's Research School of Pacific and Asian Studies (RSPAS), notably its director, Jim Fox, provided its traditional backing for the conference and for the book. Within RSPAS, the main point of contact and support was the Division of Economics headed by Hal Hill, and in particular the Indonesia Project. I would like to reiterate my personal thanks to the staff of the Indonesia Project for their splendid support over many months. I wish to thank especially Chris Manning, the head of the Indonesia Project, as well as Cathy Haberle, Trish van der Hoek, Elizabeth Drysdale and the volunteer helpers. (There were unfortunately too many of the latter to name individually.) Alison Ley of the Department of Political and Social Change efficiently organised the conference dinner, while Monika Doxey assisted with the media. To all the speakers and session chairs who did so much to make the Update a success, my sincere thanks for your efforts, especially to Jamie Mackie. I would like to give a special vote of thanks to the Indonesian speakers who took time out from their busy schedules to present papers at the Update, with special mention to Bill Liddle, who made the long trip across the Pacific despite teaching commitments immediately after the Update.

Thanks are also due to Beth Thomson for her pleasant and efficient approach to copy editing, designing and typesetting this book, and for the gentleness of her reminders to keep me to deadlines. It remains to thank Triena Ong and her staff at the Institute for Southeast Asian Studies for their professional cooperation in producing the book. I also thank the colleagues who took time to provide valuable and prompt comments and corrections in the process of peer reviewing the papers for the book. They include Ed Aspinall, Greg Fealy, Jamie Mackie, Bill Maley, Chris Manning, Ross McLeod, George Quinn, Budy Resosudarmo and Hugh White.

I am indebted to Louise Williams and the *Sydney Morning Herald* for permission to reprint the article accompanying David Reeve's chapter, and to Michael Leunig for permission to reproduce the cartoon that inspired its title.

John Monfries
March 2006

Opening Address

AUSTRALIA AND INDONESIA: A SHARED REGIONAL FUTURE IS A MUTUAL IMPERATIVE

Richard Woolcott AC

I want to thank the organisers of the 2005 Indonesia Update conference for inviting me to give this address this morning. Although I retired as secretary of the Department of Foreign Affairs and Trade in 1992, I am the founding director of the Asia Society AustralAsia Centre, which has twice hosted President Susilo Bambang Yudhoyono (SBY), and I maintain a close and continuing interest in Indonesia, not least because I have a married daughter and four grandchildren resident in Jakarta.

I would like to start by saying something about the Update itself. I know from the six years I spent representing Australia at the United Nations how agenda items, even those related to important issues, can become routine. I know some Indonesians consider that the Update has become something of a routine, in that it has tended to focus on shortcomings in Indonesian society such as corruption, a weak judicial system and violations of human rights. These are, of course, issues that need to be discussed and dealt with, primarily in Indonesia.

This, the 23rd Update, is, however, the first to deal specifically with the Australia–Indonesia relationship in a regional context. Our focus should be on how to maximise in the future the potential benefits of the relationship, how to reinvigorate it, rather than dwelling on past concerns.

In this forward-looking approach I intend to set out six guidelines, or markers, on how I consider Australians, including the Howard–Costello–Vaile government and the Opposition, should handle the relationship in the future.

The first and most obvious point is that Indonesia, a resource-rich nation of some 220 million people, consisting of a necklace of 13,600 islands stretching across our northern approaches and astride our main air and sea lanes, must always be a country of paramount importance to Australia. While there is a great focus at present in government, academic and media circles in this country on the opportunities for Australia provided by the booming economies of China and India, on the resurgence of the Japanese economy and on the established relationship with the United States, it would be foolish if Australians were to downplay the opportunities and potential offered by our immediate northern neighbour, as we did in the late 1990s.

The late 1990s and early 2000s were a period of upheaval for Indonesia. The East Asian economic crisis of 1997–98 had seriously damaged the Indonesian economy. The resignation of President Soeharto in May 1998 had opened the way to political change and three consecutive, erratic presidencies before the election of President Yudhoyono in 2004. The country had also experienced the bloody separation of East Timor in 2000 and the Bali bombings in 2002. Indonesia appeared to many Australians to be less stable, less predictable and generally less important to Australia – except for the need to cooperate in combating people smuggling and terrorism – than it had been throughout the 1980s and up to the mid-1990s. Such an attitude is short-sighted and mistaken, however. Our relationship with Indonesia will always be one of our most important relationships along with those with Japan, China and the United States. It is far too important to be allowed to drift.

Secondly, we should not expect too much, too quickly, from President Yudhoyono's government. When the former American deputy secretary of state, Richard Armitage, visited Sydney in 2005 he described Indonesia as 'a fantastic success' because it had become a democracy, because President Yudhoyono had close connections with America and because of the Indonesian government's opposition to Islamic extremism. The reality is, however, that SBY is a cautious consensus builder. He calculates what he can do politically and what he thinks would be too disruptive to attempt.

Indonesia is a fragile democracy. SBY's party holds only 55 seats in the Indonesian parliament, out of 550. His strength is derived from the size of his popular mandate rather than his parliamentary support. He received 60.6 per cent of the popular vote at the presidential election, but Golkar, led by Vice-President Jusuf Kalla, and the Indonesian Democratic Party of Struggle (PDI-P), still led by former President Megawati Sukarnoputri, can, if they combine, defeat legislation introduced by the president. This is why SBY has chosen to act on issues that can command wide parliamentary support, such as terrorism, gambling, drugs and corruption. As Prime Minister Howard said in New York recently, countries like Australia sometimes overlook how long it can take to fashion a stable democracy. He added that Indonesia deserved more credit than it had been given for the political reforms that have taken root in the last few years.

The third marker to which I wish to refer is Islam. The direction Islam takes in Indonesia is of enormous importance to Australia. The events of 11 September 2001 drew Australia much closer to the Bush administration but it did not change our geographic location in the East Asian region. We should remember that the United States is situated in a monotheistic hemisphere, which is nominally Christian from Canada in the north to Tierra del Fuego in the south. Australia's religious environment is totally different. In East Asia Christianity is a minority religion in a region of great diversity that includes very large Islamic, Buddhist and Hindu communities. By population, neighbouring Indonesia is the largest Islamic country in the world. Malaysia and Brunei also have Islamic majorities, while Singapore, the Philippines and Thailand all have substantial Muslim minorities.

While Australia needs to maintain firm opposition to Islamic extremism and continue to work with Indonesia in opposing terrorism, we need a more sensitive and sophisticated approach to religious issues in our region. President Bush's global 'war on terror', to which the Howard government has closely linked Australia, is sometimes seen, especially in the United States, as a politically expedient slogan that often serves to mask rather than define the real challenge.

What we are witnessing in much of the Islamic world, including Indonesia, is a struggle for the hearts and minds of Muslims, between the moderates and the modernisers on the one hand and, on the other, the conservatives and fundamentalists, including extremists who are prepared to use terror. It is vital to Australia that the moderates and modernisers prevail.

SBY, despite his strong opposition to terrorism and extremism, has been reluctant to respond to calls from Australia to ban the terrorist organisation Jema'ah Islamiyah because of the danger of radicalising many Indonesian moderates. As one prominent Indonesian said to me recently, 'If you mishandle the extremist minority, you could radicalise a number of the moderates, because they, like the extremists, share opposition to the American occupation of Iraq'. Moreover, since Jema'ah Islamiyah has the inclusive meaning in Bahasa Indonesia of 'Muslim Brotherhood', a blanket ban is difficult.

In respect of action against terrorism, we need also to draw a distinction between combating terrorist extremism – an objective that Indonesia shares – and the war in Iraq, which the Australian government supports but the Indonesian government opposed on the grounds that it would stimulate anti-Americanism throughout Indonesia, and would facilitate the recruitment of Islamic terrorists. Because the original invasion was led by the United States, the United Kingdom and Australia – all Western democracies – many Indonesians consider it to have eroded the moral standing of democracy and challenged the United Nations' founding principle of collective security.

The fourth marker I would like to put down is that Australians should not think of Indonesia as a threat. I suspect this is a manifestation of the uneasy feeling of many Australians that, historically, the country has felt under threat and needed the protection of a major power. First it was Japan. Then it was communist China. More recently some of these fears have unjustifiably been transferred to Indonesia.

According to a Lowy Institute survey in early 2005, only 52 per cent of Australians have a positive attitude towards Indonesia (Cook 2005). Other polls suggest that 30 per cent of Australians still see Indonesia as a threat to our security. This is presumably based on a mixture of fear, because of Indonesia's size, its proximity and the complexity of its society, as well as widespread ignorance and latent racism. Indonesia does not threaten Australia. Indonesia, unlike the Philippines, for example, is not a country of emigration. Moreover, its armed forces are relatively small and do not have the capacity to attack Australia.

Indonesia itself is a huge country in which the maintenance of law and order is a major preoccupation. As a senior Indonesian general once said to me when discussing this question: 'Indonesia has more than enough domestic problems with which to cope. The cure for indigestion is not to eat more'. I believe Australians should regard Indonesia as an opportunity, not as a threat; rather as the Howard government currently regards China.

Unfortunately, such concerns exist on both sides. Nationalism is a strong force in Indonesian politics. A number of members of the Indonesian armed forces and some members of parliament, including influential committee members, believe that Australia is a threat to Indonesia's territorial integrity. They see our support for the separation of East Timor as likely to be followed by support for the independence of West Papua and even Aceh, despite government and opposition denials. Our military expenditure is more than 10 times that of Indonesia and the clear superiority of our defence equipment and systems understandably troubles some Indonesian strategists. Only last week one of Indonesia's most senior generals, General Ryacudu, spoke in a public lecture of Australia as a threat from the South.

The fifth marker is the need to acknowledge that important policy differences remain, notwithstanding improved personal relations at the heads of government level. The stationery printed for the last Australia–Indonesia Ministerial Forum carries under the two crests the words 'Close Neighbours; Strong Partners'. The first is a fact. But the partnership, while growing stronger, is a work in progress. The election of SBY, Australia's very generous and prompt response to the tsunami tragedy and to the subsequent earthquakes in Nias and Sumatra, as well as growing cooperation in measures to combat terrorism, have created the opportunity to further improve bilateral relations. Indonesia strongly supported Australia's recent admission to the East Asia Summit, after we had belatedly agreed to sign the Treaty of Amity and Cooperation. But we should not forget the wise Malay proverb that makes the point that because the water is still, it does not mean there are no crocodiles below the surface. Important differences in policy remain.

I am not suggesting that policies that might cause concern to our regional neighbours should be avoided, especially ones clearly based on Australia's interests. We need to realise, however, that we are seen by many Indonesians as more closely aligned with the United States – or with the Bush administration – than ever before. This has nourished the perception of Australia's 'deputy sheriff' role.

While countries in the region generally welcome American involvement, there are still concerns that Australia is now a less independent voice than it was, and that we do not use our position to try to influence American decisions that may impact adversely on our region. Indonesia is concerned about Australia's plans to acquire and deploy missiles that will put Indonesia within range. The prime minister's support for a right to launch pre-emptive strikes, although since qualified, and the original decision to create a 1,000-nautical-mile surveillance zone, which would encroach on Indonesian territorial sovereignty, have also caused anxiety in Indonesia.

More importantly we need to recognise that Indonesians, including the president, the foreign minister and the defence minister, were all opposed to the invasion of Iraq. The invasion cannot be reversed and the situation it has created must be addressed. Nevertheless Indonesians remain concerned, as I have already noted, that the occupation has led to increased – not reduced – terrorism in the Middle East and that it has offered enhanced recruiting opportunities for Islamic extremists. Australia also needs to guard continuously against perceptions that racism and religious intolerance, especially in regard to Islam, are still prevalent in sections of the Australian community, and that our political leaders do not always show the leadership expected to oppose such sinister attitudes.

Unfavourable perceptions of our method of conducting diplomacy still linger. Our style is often seen as assertive, moralising and intrusive. What Foreign Minister Wirajuda has called 'megaphone diplomacy', often invoked for domestic political reasons, is unhelpful. There is also distaste for what is perceived to be jingoism, an excessive emphasis on military heroics and triumphalism in relation, for example, to our intervention in East Timor in 1999.

The sixth guideline I wish to stress is that although the Indonesian economy remains fragile – the value of the rupiah has fallen in recent months and foreign investment remains sluggish – we should expect that in the longer term and with stable government, Indonesia, with its some 220 million people, offers Australia considerable commercial and selective investment opportunities.

CONCLUSION

We need always to keep in mind, on both sides of the Arafura Sea, that the relationship between Australia and Indonesia is a complex and fragile one between two very different societies. It requires a continuing and special effort to sustain the relationship. With such an investment in it, the government should be able to avoid creating unnecessary misunderstandings and concerns, as it has sometimes done in the past, usually for domestic political reasons.

I consider it is imperative to strengthen further a close and cooperative relationship in the region, which we share. We must change perceptions of Australia in Indonesia, and perceptions of Indonesia in the wider Australian community. What steps can be taken to advance this cause? If I still had a policy-advising role, I would suggest the government take the following four steps.

Firstly, the government should ensure that adequately funded programs are provided for increased language studies, and for more people-to-people contacts – in both directions – between elected members of the Australian and Indonesian parliaments, academics, youth leaders, writers, journalists, moderate religious figures and other groups, to increase knowledge of each country in the other and to break down ignorance and prejudice.

It has been disappointing to note the sharp decline in Indonesian-language studies. I understand that there are fewer than 40 first-year university students studying Indonesian this year. The Australia–Indonesia Institute does valuable work in this regard. The Australian National University itself also makes a useful contribution through these Updates, the Indonesia Project and various study groups, but there is a need to do much more.

Secondly, we should consult more closely on important policy decisions that can affect either country. For example, we consulted Indonesia closely over our decision to participate in the first Gulf War in 1991 but we did not do so when we invaded Iraq in 2003.

Thirdly, Australia and Indonesia should work towards expanding defence cooperation through wider exchange programs and by reinstating, with Indonesian support, the 1995 Agreement on Mutual Security or some similar arrangement. We do share a region and have a common interest in its security.

Fourthly, in addition to working to strengthen our bilateral relations, we should continue to consult and cooperate with Indonesia whenever possible in multilateral forums such as the United Nations, the Post Ministerial Forum of the Association of Southeast Asian Nations (ASEAN), the ASEAN Regional Forum, Asia-Pacific Economic Cooperation (APEC), the World Trade Organization (WTO) and the Cairns Group. Even when we have different policies, it is helpful to ensure that the reasons for the differences are understood on both sides.

Indonesia faces a complex set of problems that most Australians cannot be expected to fully comprehend. Conversely, Australia enjoys a lifestyle that can only be imagined by most Indonesians. Seeking to build bridges between our very different societies is not something from which either side should shrink; rather, it is a national objective that should be seen as an exciting and worthwhile challenge. If we succeed, both Australia and Indonesia will benefit.

1   INTRODUCTION

John Monfries

The 2005 Update conference, the 23rd in the series, was the first to address specifically the relationship between Indonesia and Australia, in the context of the region in which both countries are located. Readers may wonder why it took so long for the subject to be covered, but the Update has usually focused on internal developments in Indonesia. Recent conferences have covered, for example, Indonesian history, environmental issues and women's issues.

THEMES AND ISSUES

After the decision on the topic was taken, two momentous events made the topic even more current and worthwhile. The first was the tsunami tragedy, which badly damaged many areas on the Indian Ocean littoral and wrecked Indonesia's northernmost province of Aceh, leading to a massive outpouring of sympathy and support from all round the world, including Australia. The second was the election of a new Indonesian president, Susilo Bambang Yudhoyono, to whom many hopes were attached. His visit to Australia in March–April 2005 contributed to a new and much more positive atmosphere in the bilateral relationship, after the tensions and crises of previous years, especially the East Timor-induced nadir of 1999. It was thus very timely to take the opportunity to consider and discuss the relationship in its broadest context, including its regional effects and implications.

In opening the conference Richard Woolcott laid down six important points (see pages xvii–xxiii). The first and most basic was the enduring importance to Australia of Indonesia, starting with, but not limited to, the obvious geographic factors. The second was the need to avoid exaggerated expectations of the new Yudhoyono government, given the new president's need to proceed cautiously and build consensus. The third point concerned the need for Australian sensitivity in dealing with the progress of Indonesian Islam, a point emphasised and elaborated by Jamie Mackie in the concluding chapter of this book. The fourth point covered the widespread popular delusion in Australia that Indonesia is some sort of threat, a delusion that needs to be dispelled. Fifth, Woolcott drew attention to the need to recognise and deal with the very real policy differences that remain, notwithstanding the better atmosphere of the relationship now. And finally, he stressed the commercial and investment opportunities offered by Indonesia over the longer term.

Subsequent sessions served to illustrate and expand on many of these points. Many speakers noted that relations at government level, including heads-of-government level, were indeed better than they had been for years, probably since the period of the Keating–Soeharto axis. Moreover, as Paul Kelly pointed out, the recent close identification of Prime Minister John Howard with improving the relationship with Indonesia was one of the more remarkable developments in Australian foreign policy in recent years. Kelly observed that two issues that had always plagued bilateral relations in the past, East Timor and Soeharto's authoritarianism, had nearly disappeared as complicating factors. As noted above, Australia's generous reaction to the tsunami disaster had a positive influence, although an Indonesian speaker, while recognising this, chided Australia for the excessively self-congratulatory tone of its press coverage.

But most speakers conceded that the level of public understanding in each country about the other was extremely poor, with the Schapelle Corby affair frequently cited as the most prominent recent example of this. David Reeve spoke in stark terms, but with considerable humour, about the level of ignorance and prejudice in some quarters in Australia. The difficulty as always is to discern how typical the more extreme views are and what should be done about them. It is probably the case that most Australians scarcely think about Indonesia from one month to the next. But when Indonesia is in the news, they can be led – or misled – by commentators with largely domestic agendas who lack specialised knowledge about the outside world, the outcome being a reinforcement of stereotypes and a drastic oversimplification of complex issues.

The extent of public distrust of Indonesia is shown clearly by the Lowy Institute survey (Cook 2005) quoted by several speakers, although Kelly cautioned against excessive alarm about this. It has been known for some time that many Australians regard Indonesia as the country posing the greatest threat to Australia, a sentiment that only reinforces the impression of popular ignorance and prejudice, underlining the heavy task in public education that lies before governments, educators and commentators if such misperceptions are to be dispelled.

Speakers inevitably drew attention to the deficiencies in the education system and government policy in Australia, leading to what must be accounted as a weak effort by Australia to understand its own regional environment. We have seen several ill-judged decisions in the area in recent years, such as the cancellation of funding for the National Asian Languages and Studies in Australian Schools strategy. The de-emphasising of Asia in Australian policy has also had an effect on students' perceptions of the importance of Asian studies, a de-emphasis now perhaps being reversed in gingerly fashion. A welcome recent development is the National Statement for Engaging Young Australians with Asia issued by all Australian education ministers after a high-level meeting in December 2005, but some practical follow-up will be needed.

Nevertheless, expectations need to be realistic. It is a legitimate and common complaint among interested academics and others that less than 3 per cent of university students are studying Asia-related courses now, even in relatively robust areas like Chinese language. But in discussing this, we need to define more closely what proportion of students we might expect *would* address Asian subjects. As was pointed out in discussion across several sessions, declining demand among students is part of the problem, exacerbated by security concerns and problems arising from the travel warnings issued by the Australian Department of Foreign Affairs and Trade. Given the funding constraints on all universities, the pressures to commercialise and the enormous emphasis on attracting fee-paying overseas students, we have to recognise that the battle for adequate levels of funding, Australian government attention and consequently greater public knowledge and understanding will always be difficult. This does not of course mean that it is not a battle worth fighting.

Needless to say, Indonesian perspectives on the relationship differ markedly from Australian ones. Australia does not loom large for Indonesian elites who normally look northward to Asia and eastward to the Americas. It is these regions that pose the large majority of strategic, political and economic challenges and opportunities for Indonesia. Nevertheless, it is very likely that the Indonesian elite's general familiarity with Australia exceeds any familiarity the Australian political elite may have with Indonesia. Few Australian politicians or senior business people will have visited or studied Indonesia, whereas an appreciable number of the present Indonesian elite have visited Australia many times, for study, for recreation or for medical reasons.[1]

BILATERAL AND REGIONAL LINKAGES

Conference participants generally seemed to agree, implicitly or explicitly, that Australia's standing in the region was affected by its success or otherwise in managing its relationship with Indonesia, and several speakers spent some time analysing the complex interplay between regional consultative multilateralism and the bilateral relationship. The Howard government's recognition of the importance of regional organisations was demonstrated by its strenuous efforts to secure a seat at the recent East Asia Summit, including its decision to accede to the ASEAN Treaty of Amity and Cooperation after previously declining to do so. A fascinating aspect of this diplomatic struggle was the considerable help given to Australia by Indonesia (along with Japan and Singapore). Apart from being very relevant to the Update theme, this is an example of the two countries' increasingly convergent interests, as Jamie Mackie points out in Chapter 13. Over the past 20 years Australia has established convincing credentials for its claims to a seat at regional forums, including its work on the Cambodia settlement, its contributions to multilateral efforts to soften the effects of the 1997 Asian financial crisis, and even its intervention in East Timor, notwithstanding the negative effects this had on Australia's relationship with Indonesia. Malaysian (largely former Prime Minister Mahathir's) opposition to Australian participation in the East Asia Summit was always unwise, even though it may perhaps have served short-term domestic political purposes. In the long term, there seems no rational reason to seek to prevent Australia from playing a constructive role in the region, and it is at least arguable that efforts to block Australia run counter to the region's own interests.

As is usual at such conferences, some worried discussion occurred about Islam and terrorism, ranging from Wiryono's reference to the 'struggle for the soul of Islam' to Harold Crouch's point that the influence of politically sectarian Islam in Indonesia seemed not to have increased since the 1955 elections. Wiryono pointed out the delicate task of the new Indonesian government in seeking to combat terrorism while taking care not to alienate the moderates, and while avoiding any appearance of subservience to the West, especially the United States. It was also emphasised, however, that sweeping phrases like 'Islamic terrorism' ran the risk of stereotyping. As Jamie Mackie indicates in his final comments in this volume, it is unhelpful for outsiders to try too conspicuously to put public pressure on the Indonesian government on this subject.

Nevertheless, a real problem remains. Kesavapany pointed to the shock felt in Singapore when an extremist group was uncovered there in 2001, and the adverse consequences, including economic ones, if the group's plans to attack a naval base had succeeded. During the discussion period, Kelly noted how dominant the terrorism issue had become for many leaders of Western democracies since the 2001 attacks in the United States, spurred by al-Qaeda threats to civilian populations and the perception that the terrorist menace has both a global and a regional dimension. While conceding the essentially moderate nature of mainstream Islam in Indonesia, Kelly pointed to the changes in Australian public perceptions of Indonesia arising (paradoxically enough) from the country's new openness. This meant that all the divisions and polarities of Indonesia's new democratic system were now on show, including the views of the extremist minority. This factor could and did influence Australian perceptions of the state of Indonesian public opinion and of the significance of extremism within it. Moreover, Kelly added, human rights was an issue of growing importance within Australia, and this was likely to affect Australia's foreign policy, especially in terms of greater scrutiny of the performance of our neighbours. Kelly linked this to persistent and troubling doubts in some quarters about the legitimacy of Indonesia's current boundaries.

Wiryono commented on the perceptions of injustice at the hands of the West that are feeding Islamic extremism, including within Indonesia. In relation to another contentious area, he referred to the fairly widespread suspicions in Indonesia about Australia's intentions with regard to Papua, bearing in mind the East Timor experience. Hugh White reinforced this point by speaking about the burning sense of grievance against Australia still felt in some military and political circles in Jakarta as a result of the East Timor experience, a factor of which most Australians are quite unaware. A proposed new security treaty that is said to include specific formal assurances of Australia's support for Indonesia's territorial integrity may be an important step in dampening the negative perceptions to which Wiryono referred. The possibility of such a treaty was mentioned during President Yudhoyono's visit to Australia, but at the time of writing it was unclear what stage negotiations had reached.

Discussion of the Papua issue at the Update conference revealed much uncertainty about the future of the Special Autonomy Law[2] giving Papuans a greater say in the government of their region, especially in view of what seemed to be a fading commitment by the central government to the autonomy process as a whole. Discussants mentioned the considerable mutual suspicions between the Indonesian political and military establishments on the one hand and the Papuan elite on the other, the difficulty of discerning the slightest feeling of commitment to Indonesia among leading Papuans, and the lack of enthusiasm for special autonomy even among moderate Papuans, especially because the Megawati government had undermined and negated the promises made by the previous Abdurrahman Wahid administration. The hope – certainly not the expectation – was that the Yudhoyono government might reverse the trend. Discussants saw little scope for Australia to play much of a role in the Papua issue, and in fact discerned some dangers in it even attempting to play a role.

An interesting question raised in discussion was the perceptible gap between Australian public attitudes towards Indonesia and those towards China. In addition to the obvious explanation that Indonesia is the geographically closer of the two, Kelly observed that, for historical reasons among other things, Australians have a more emotional attitude towards Indonesia than they do towards China; that they even have a feeling of Australian responsibility for Indonesian issues (very evident in the East Timor case), accompanied at times by the misguided belief that the Australian government can somehow solve the bilateral problems that arise. Such attitudes reflected a considerable overestimation of Australia's likely power in most cases, not helped by a highly 'dysfunctional' and ideological approach by the Australian media. One might add that the persistent tendency in some quarters to view Indonesia 'through the prism of East Timor'[3] can at times be an unhelpful factor in reaching realistic assessments of Indonesia.

THE ORGANISATION OF THE BOOK

For the first time in the history of the Indonesia Update volumes, this book does not contain the texts of the political and economic updates with which the conference always commences. These two opening papers, essential and interesting though they are, can often seem rather outdated by the time the Update book is published some months later. Accordingly, the political update by Bill Liddle and the economic update by Boediono have been published separately in the December 2005 edition of the *Bulletin of Indonesian Economic Studies* (Liddle 2005; Boediono 2005). I hope readers will forgive this pragmatic and – I think – sensible alteration to the normal procedure.

Richard Woolcott's opening address to the conference appears in the preliminary pages (see 'Opening Address'). Woolcott, a former head of the Department of Foreign Affairs and Trade and a former ambassador to Indonesia, has obvious and longstanding experience in this area. The remainder of the volume is divided into five parts. Part I gives contrasting Indonesian, Australian and regional views of the Indonesia–Australia relationship. S. Wiryono, the distinguished former Indonesian ambassador to Australia, provides an Indonesian perspective based on his familiarity with the relationship arising from his posting to Canberra (Chapter 2). The executive director of the Institute for Southeast Asian Studies in Singapore, K. Kesavapany, gives a regional perspective (Chapter 3) of the relationship, and senior journalist Paul Kelly offers an Australian perspective (Chapter 4).

Part II covers the security aspects of the bilateral relationship. Rizal Sukma discusses Indonesia's approach to terrorism in its regional context (Chapter 6), while Hugh White examines the bilateral security relationship in the broad, including the terrorism aspect but also looking forward to possible wider security cooperation (Chapter 5).

In Part III, on mutual perceptions and irritations, David Reeve comments on the highs and lows (especially the latter) of public images and mutual perceptions (Chapter 7). Isla Rogers-Winarto outlines recent developments in Australia's efforts to attract more Indonesian students in a highly competitive market, a topic influenced and often complicated by the periodic crises in the relationship, especially when mutual perceptions are negative (Chapter 8). Richard Chauvel provides a picture of the international aspects of the Papua issue (Chapter 9). This is an issue that has the potential to become a disruptive element in the bilateral relationship and, indeed, in regional affairs.

Part IV on economic, aid and business relations opens with an article by Scott Dawson on the new Australia–Indonesia Partnership for Reconstruction and Development, one of the more significant practical manifestations of the improved government-to-government relationship (Chapter 10). Stephen Grenville canvasses the broad sweep of regional economic arrangements and how Indonesia and Australia fit into them (Chapter 12). He also looks at the current state of Indonesia's economic reform agenda and how Australia can interact with this, with particular attention to the need for institution building. Noke Kiroyan outlines the generally cordial attitude of the business community to the Yudhoyono presidency, while acknowledging that it is too early to judge the success or otherwise of the new government's economic policies (Chapter 11). He indicates that Indonesian government initiatives – such as the two summits held in Jakarta to attract international investment in infrastructure projects – have the potential to provide good opportunities for Australian business.

Finally, the doyen of Australia's Indonesianists, Jamie Mackie, provides an overview of the conference as a whole (Chapter 13). He links together a number of important themes, such as ways of avoiding or minimising the crises that arise regularly in the relationship, and the less widely bruited need to exploit opportunities for policy coordination between the two countries on such subjects as policy approaches towards regional consultative organisations. He provides a useful historical context for the current bilateral relationship and canvasses a list of desirable policy priorities for Australia. A striking feature of the latter section is his clear exposition of Australia's many dilemmas in reconciling these objectives, all of which may seem desirable but which may quite often clash with one other. This strongly reinforces impressions of a complex, many-sided relationship which is not susceptible to simple (or simplistic) formulas.

I am aware that no single book can encompass all aspects of the complex bilateral relationship and its regional linkages. While some salient issues (such as illegal fishing, people smuggling and tourism) could not be treated here, I nevertheless hope that this volume will contribute usefully to debate on and understanding of one of Australia's most important and contentious external relationships.

POSTSCRIPT

The controversy arising from the arrival near Cape York of 43 refugees from Papua province, which occurred in April 2006 just as this book was going to press, further illustrates the ease with which cordial government-to-government relations can be disrupted by chance events. The kinds of complexes and knee-jerk reactions described by various contributors to this book were immediately on show on both sides, especially when 42 of the arrivals were granted temporary protection visas. While both governments tried to calm matters, with limited success, Indonesian parliamentarians made anti-Australian statements, a 'cartoon war' erupted in the press of both countries, small demonstrations were staged in several major Indonesian cities, and Indonesian importers threatened boycotts of Australian goods. While expressing amazement that Indonesians would dare to claim the moral high ground,[4] Australian critics of Indonesia pointed to the negative aspects of Indonesian rule in the province, sometimes using racial and cultural arguments about the differences between Papuans and mainstream Indonesians reminiscent of those used in the 1960s (see Chapter 9, this volume). These kinds of reactions dramatically showed up the gulf in basic perceptions between the two countries in some non-government circles.

Predictably enough, suspicion was widespread once again in Indonesia that the issue revealed Australia's true intentions towards Indonesia's sovereignty over Papua. Indonesia recalled its ambassador for 'consultations', a standard means of registering diplomatic displeasure, President Yudhoyono announced a 'review' of bilateral cooperation over people smuggling, and the Indonesian parliament said it would send an official protest delegation to Canberra. On the Australian side, government ministers reaffirmed Australia's support for Indonesian sovereignty over Papua and asserted (rather desperately) that the issue would not disturb good relations with Indonesia. They expressed praise for Yudhoyono's character and policies and reminded the public to give Indonesia credit for its efforts to establish democracy. The episode was a further reminder of the brittleness of the bilateral relationship, especially where popular feelings can erupt or be whipped up on both sides. It is not too hard to imagine how this spectacle looks from a regional perspective.

NOTES

1 Examples would include Hartarto, former industry minister in the Soeharto period and an Australian university graduate; former President Abdurrahman Wahid, a regular visitor before his brief presidency; Wimar Witoelar, Wahid's former adviser; Dewi Fortuna Anwar, a former foreign policy adviser to B.J. Habibie and still a senior civil servant; Mari Pangestu, the current trade minister; and Boediono, a speaker at the Update conference and a former member of staff at the Australian National University (who, incidentally, was appointed coordinating minister for economic and industrial affairs some weeks after the conference). Many of the elite have sent their children to Australia for schooling. On the Australian side, the only prominent figure who comes readily to mind in this context is former Deputy Prime Minister Tim Fischer. While a backbencher in the 1980s, he paid regular (almost annual) visits to Indonesia and several other Asian countries.
2 Law 21/2001 on Special Autonomy in Papua Province.
3 The phrase is the late Geoffrey Forrester's, quoted in Murdoch (1999).
4 See, for example, Brian Toohey in the *Canberra Times*, 5 April 2006.

PART I

Regional Viewpoints

2 AN INDONESIAN VIEW: INDONESIA, AUSTRALIA AND THE REGION

S. Wiryono

Despite many difficulties and tensions, the improved relationship between Indonesia and Australia offers opportunities in both the regional and bilateral context. A window of opportunity has opened for Australia to come closer to the Association of Southeast Asian Nations (ASEAN) as a dialogue partner, with Indonesian encouragement. For its part, Australia responded promptly and vigorously to the tsunami disaster in a way that was much appreciated in Indonesia. The visit of the Indonesian president to Australia further enhanced the relationship. Nevertheless, Australian public ignorance of Indonesia, and Indonesian public ignorance of Australia, remain all too evident. The disjuncture between official relations and public perceptions requires a major effort at public diplomacy, complemented by the efforts of private institutions, groups and individuals, if such misperceptions and misunderstandings are to be overcome.

INDONESIAN FOREIGN POLICY AND REGIONAL ARCHITECTURE

Although Indonesia comprises about 50 per cent of ASEAN by population, it will not be able to continue to play its traditional stabilising and leadership role in the region unless it is successful in addressing the internal imperatives of reform, social stability and economic growth. This may still take a few years to be realised. ASEAN, on the other hand, sees itself as part of a regional architecture in which one wing is composed of India and China and the other by South Korea and Japan. Australia, New Zealand and the United States serve as sources of additional support. Today, East Asia is dominated by China with its gigantic and overheated economy. The only challenge to China's economic dominance comes from India, but it has a long way to go before it will be able to match China in economic strength.

Indonesia sees the entire Asia-Pacific region as in need of a process that will ensure political and economic equilibrium in the area. This is not only because of China's dominance as an economic power but also because of its recent successes on the diplomatic front, which contrast with the massive erosion of the soft power of the United States in the region. Japan may seem to be locked into the role of chief ally of the United States in the region, but its influence continues to wane because of perceptions that it is not sufficiently contrite about its role as aggressor during the Pacific War. Indonesia bears little rancour at Japan's role during the war, but anger runs much deeper in China and South Korea. This does nothing to help promote regional harmony and cooperation.

In the 'flying geese' formation of East Asia, the perception has grown that Japan has lost its position as leader because its economy has been stagnant for such a long time. Recently, however, the Japanese economy seems to be turning around. The government is poised to carry out meaningful economic reforms following Prime Minister Junichiro Koizumi's landslide election victory on a platform of reform. The odds are that Japan, with its $4.7 trillion economy, will remain the world's second-largest economy for quite some time; China, with its $1.6 trillion economy, still has a great deal of work to do before it can overtake Japan as regional leader. Many observers now predict that once Japan has instituted the envisaged economic reforms, it will grow with a vengeance. But it will have to do more to endear itself to the rest of the region, and serve as a more effective promoter of regional cooperation.

Before the terrorist attacks of 11 September 2001 in the United States, cooperation in the Asia-Pacific had a double framework: the Asia-Pacific Economic Cooperation (APEC) process in the economic sphere and the ASEAN Regional Forum in the politico-security sphere. However, since the Asian financial crisis, and especially since 9/11, both APEC and the ASEAN Regional Forum have been losing steam. The APEC agenda has been diluted by the introduction of security-related items as a result of the preoccupation of member countries with the threat of terrorism. Moreover, APEC has not been able to advance its original agenda of promoting equitable multilateral trade. Instead of the Asia-Pacific region becoming a multilateral free trade area (FTA) as a result of the work of APEC, there has been a proliferation of bilateral FTAs which do not contribute to – and in fact work against – the development of a regional FTA.

Against this backdrop, it is relevant that an East Asia Economic Group was proposed by then Prime Minister Mahathir Mohammad of Malaysia in the early 1990s. The idea was promptly shot down, apparently because of objections by the United States, but has since been resurrected in altered form as the East Asia Summit. When Malaysia proposed an East Asia Summit in 2003, it had in mind as participants only the 10 ASEAN countries and their three northeast Asian counterparts, China, Japan, and South Korea. On the grounds that the East Asia Summit should not duplicate the ASEAN+3 process, Indonesia was able to persuade its ASEAN colleagues to include India, New Zealand and Australia. In an apparent escalation of inclusiveness, Malaysia then tried to bring in the United States and the Russian Federation as observers, but Indonesia successfully argued against this move as being premature.

The first East Asia Summit, which took place in Kuala Lumpur in December 2005, is projected to be the start of a process leading to the eventual establishment of an East Asian Community. It is envisaged that this would be simultaneously a security community, an economic community and a sociocultural community. As an economic bloc or FTA, the East Asian Community could be the world's largest. However, it will not be formed any time soon, considering the pace at which ASEAN, the pivotal component of the grouping, is known to move. At any rate, Indonesia is unlikely to support any quick developments in the East Asia Summit that will not also ensure the achievement of a more broad-based ASEAN security, economic and sociocultural community.

Within ASEAN and East Asia, Indonesia sees itself as a promoter of democratic values, doing so from the vantage point of its recognition as the world's third-largest democracy. At the same time, it is also projecting itself to the world at large as living proof that democracy and Islam can flourish together.

INDONESIA AND THE ASEAN–UNITED NATIONS LINKAGE

ASEAN prides itself on having been cited by the United Nations as one of the most successful regional organisations in the world. In September 2005, during the second ASEAN–United Nations Summit held in New York, the regional organisation once again sought UN assistance for the efforts of its members to achieve the Millennium Development Goals of the United Nations. It also once again sought assistance in building up its capacity for disaster prevention and management, and its ability to fight highly contagious diseases.

There is in fact a great deal of unspoken disappointment with the United Nations among ASEAN members, including Indonesia. Because they feel that the United Nations has not done enough for the region, ASEAN countries would rather focus on their relations with their northeast Asian and other dialogue partners. The lack of real warmth in the relationship between ASEAN and the United Nations is evidenced by the fact that the longstanding proposal for ASEAN to obtain observer status in the United Nations has not moved an inch despite being studied thoroughly.

AUSTRALIA AND THE REGION

Australia's participation in the East Asia Summit has opened a window of opportunity for Australia to move closer to ASEAN as a dialogue partner, although the Australian government would have done better not to hesitate so

conspicuously before agreeing to accede to the Treaty of Amity and Cooperation in Southeast Asia – for ASEAN, the litmus test of sincerity in any engagement with the region. Still, with Malaysia beginning to warm to Australia after
the departure of Mahathir Mohammad as prime minister, it should be possible
to start negotiations for an FTA between ASEAN and Australia. When such an
initiative is finally taken, Australia should be able to count on the full support of
Indonesia.

One reason why Australia may be drawing closer to its Asian neighbours is
that the heavy-handed approach of the United States to the use of its power has
lost support among many Australians. This is reflected in the findings of a Lowy
Institute survey in April 2005 showing that Australians had decidedly more positive feelings towards Singapore, Japan and China than towards the United
States (Cook 2005). Australians were also a great deal more worried about
American foreign policy than about the rise of China as a world power. Add to
these findings the fact that Australia's economic engagement with Asian countries has been so rewarding and the outlook for Australia's strengthening
involvement with Asia is even brighter.

AUSTRALIA AND INDONESIA

Unfortunately for Australia–Indonesia relations, the Lowy Institute survey also
showed that one country Australians liked *less* than the United States was
Indonesia. It is apparent that the excellent relationship between the Australian
and Indonesian governments is not matched by similarly positive feelings
between their peoples. This could be because Australians and Indonesians simply do not know enough about each other to sufficiently appreciate each other's
good qualities.

It is in the interests of the Asia-Pacific region for Australia and Indonesia to
be positively engaged with each other. This is not to deny that there are other
factors and relationships on which depend the peace, stability and prosperity of
the region. It is just as important for Australia to be economically engaged with
other Pacific-region powers like the United States, Japan and China, for example. But Indonesia will always be of great importance to Australia because it is
its 'Near North'. And Australia, even though it lies to the south of Indonesia, is
important to Indonesia because it belongs to the industrially developed North,
whose markets, technology and educational institutions can be of great help to
Indonesia in its march towards a more dynamic economy, a more mature
democracy and greater security.

For Australia, Indonesia's ability to strengthen its democracy, stimulate its
economy and ensure its own stability is important. Australia needs to understand
and support Indonesia's efforts to strengthen its capability in these areas.

Although the New Order government of former President Soeharto was unabashedly authoritarian, its achievement of 'stability' was hailed by former Australian Prime Minister Paul Keating as the single most important development for Australia at that time. The perception of a strong and stable Indonesia made Australia feel more secure. Despite the concerns of some Australians about a strong Indonesia, a weak and chaotic Indonesia would decidedly present a clear and present danger to Australia.

From the perspective of several decades, relations between Australia and Indonesia have always gone up and down like an elevator. They reached a very high level in the mid to late 1940s when Indonesia was waging a revolutionary war for independence and Australia gave its full, in-principle support to the fledgling republic. Relations declined in the 1950s when Indonesia waged a campaign to restore West Papua to the republic and Australia initially supported the position of the Netherlands in the dispute.

From 1967 to the early 1990s, relations between the two countries were largely defined by the imperatives of the Cold War. In the eyes of Australia and the Western world, Indonesia was a buffer against the encroachments of international communism. With the ascendancy of the Howard government, relations began to slide downhill and reached an all-time low with the political tumult leading to the separation of Timor Leste (formerly East Timor) from Indonesia.

In recent times, relations between the two countries have been improving steadily. Indonesia and Australia have had to work together to combat international terrorism. In the wake of the tragedies in Aceh and Nias, Australia responded promptly and vigorously in a way that was much appreciated throughout Indonesia. For its part, Indonesia was instrumental in helping Australia take its place at the East Asia Summit in 2005, along with New Zealand. The attendance of Prime Minister John Howard at the inauguration of President Susilo Bambang Yudhoyono and the recent visit of the Indonesian president to Australia took the relationship to an even higher level. Bilateral trade, stagnant between 1998 and 2001, picked up considerably in 2002 and has been growing at an encouraging rate of 15 per cent per year since then.

But even in these smoother times, the relationship between Indonesia and Australia has not been all plain sailing. The differences between the two countries in culture, political systems and levels of development are just too great for relations ever to be perfectly smooth. Indonesia may have no security concerns about Australia at present, but the usual irritants remain – often in the form of statements from the Australian side that spring from ignorance or, in the view of some Indonesians, arrogance.

Prime Minister Howard's statement that Australia had the right to make preemptive strikes against terrorists in other countries is still fresh in the public memory. The Corby case in Bali and the treatment of Indonesian Muslims in Australia are other issues that have aroused strong feelings in the public mind.

The commutation of the sentences of several Indonesians convicted of crimes in connection with the Bali bombings of October 2002 – in which a large number of Australians were killed – certainly did not sit well with the Australian public. What rankles in particular among many Australians is that, in their view, the Indonesian government has been soft on Abu Bakar Ba'asyir, the Muslim cleric who is the source of inspiration for, if not the actual leader of, Jemaah Islamiyah, the largest terrorist group in Indonesia.

Another irritant between the two countries is Australia's declaration of a 1,000-nautical-mile Australian Maritime Identification Zone covering a large slab of Indonesian waters, namely the Timor Sea, Sawu Sea, Banda Sea, Java Sea, Makassar Strait, Sulawesi Sea, Halmahera Sea, Moluccas Sea, Ceram Sea, Aru Sea and Arafura Sea. Indonesia sees this as an infringement of its sovereignty over its territorial seas, archipelagic waters, continental shelf and exclusive maritime zones. It holds that the Australian zone violates the United Nations Convention on the Law of the Sea of 10 December 1982, to which both Indonesia and Australia are a party.

The fact is that in both countries there will always be aggressive statements by members of parliament, and provocative opinion pieces in the mass media that militate against closer ties, no matter how closely the two governments may be working together on issues of common concern such as terrorism, illegal migration and money laundering. Indonesia and Australia have been cooperating closely in bilateral, regional and multilateral forums to develop initiatives to combat terrorism. Nevertheless, in the post-9/11 era, many Australians remain concerned about the possibility that Indonesia may become a source of terrorism and other transnational crimes. While the two countries are united in the fight against terrorist networks, they have entirely different national contexts in dealing with terrorism. Australia has been able to follow the lead of the United States in the war against terrorism, but Indonesia must be much more cautious. On the one hand, it must cooperate with other countries, including Western countries such as the United States and Australia, in counteracting terrorism; on the other, it must be careful not to be perceived as being in any kind of alliance with the United States and the Western world, which are regarded by a significant and activist section of the Indonesian population as being in conflict with the realm of Islam.

INDONESIA, AUSTRALIA AND ISLAM

Many international observers, including many Australians, find it difficult to understand why the government of Indonesia is 'soft' on Islamic militants to the point that it has so far resisted all suggestions to formally name Jemaah Islamiyah as the organisation behind the terrorist attacks in Bali. This becomes all the more difficult to understand in light of the fact that the Islamic militants represent a small minority of Indonesia's vast population, and that Muslim-based radical political parties have never been a major factor in national elections.

Leading Indonesian Muslim moderates and liberals hesitate to speak out against the violence being perpetrated by a few militants not so much because they have been physically intimidated (although some have indeed received death threats), but because they realise that this could be construed as support for American and Western aggression against the world of Islam. Although Australians naturally wish to see Indonesia's moderate Muslims win out over their militant counterparts, it does not help that Australian leaders openly urge strong measures against militant organisations and individuals. This only makes matters more complicated for the Indonesian government because it creates the impression that it is being dictated to. This is the case even if the Australian government is far from having such an intention and even though the Indonesian government would not allow itself to be dictated to by a foreign power.

The fact is that the Muslim countries in which the larger part of the population is radicalised are the very same countries that are seen to be indisputably pro-American or pro-Western. Examples are Pakistan, Saudi Arabia and Jordan. In contrast, in the Muslim countries that are regarded as more independent and definitely *not* in alliance with the United States or the Western powers, such as Malaysia and Indonesia, Muslim political parties have lost ground with the electorate. The Islamic Party of Malaysia (PAS) in Malaysia was trounced in the last national elections. In Indonesia the United Development Party (PPP) and the Crescent and Star Party (PBB) performed poorly in the series of national elections held in 2004. One political party with a Muslim connection, the Prosperity and Justice Party (PKS), fared surprisingly well, but only because it avoided references to its religious affiliation during the campaign, and emphasised its secular aspirations.

At least in part because it has not allowed itself to be seen by the public as a client of the Western powers, the Yudhoyono government has enjoyed tremendous public support in its attempt to crack down on terrorist networks. But it cannot defeat the challenge of terrorism by relying solely on military intelligence and police work, nor can it win the fight by itself. It has to work in partnership with other countries if it is to make headway in this fight, and one country that it must work with is Australia.

Australia has been of great help to Indonesia, notably in bringing the perpetrators of the Bali bombings to justice. Apart from technical help in investigative police work, Australia has helped by way of capacity building, particularly in the training of Indonesian police personnel. On the whole Australia has been most effective when it has extended its help without fanfare and when the cooperation has been carried out within a regional framework, as in the cases of the regional conferences on terrorism, money laundering, people smuggling and other forms of transnational crime.

One area in which Australia could be of further assistance to Indonesia in its fight against terrorism is in the promotion of interfaith dialogue as a way of empowering all moderates, but especially Indonesia's Muslim moderates. The Indonesian government believes that when its enormous silent majority of moderate and liberal Muslims finally find their voice and speak out, they will be very persuasive and influential. It is hoped that they will serve as an effective counterpoise to the militants, even if they do not actually manage to overwhelm them.

THE CULTURE GAP

Culturally, Indonesia and Australia continue to be strangers to each other. Misperceptions and misunderstandings are hindering the full flowering of the bilateral relationship. At a time when government-to-government relations are excellent and may actually be at a new peak, people-to-people contacts are suffering considerable erosion. There has been a decline in the number of Indonesians studying in Australia, and in the number of Australians taking up Indonesian studies in Australian schools.

The cultural gap between the two countries may be deep and wide but it is by no means insurmountable. The challenge is for responsible people in each country to close that gap; otherwise it may widen. Much of the problem could be ameliorated by the judicious practice of public diplomacy on both sides. It would be very constructive if Australia were to make up for the loss of Radio Australia as an instrument of public diplomacy. The Indonesian Department of Foreign Affairs, for its part, should increase the number of scholarships being offered to young Australians to come to Indonesia under its cultural scholarships program. An exchange program for Indonesian and Australian journalists could do wonders for the bilateral relationship. Also worth looking into is the possibility of Australia setting up a technology transfer program to extend help in the form of endowments to technical education institutions throughout Indonesia.

Now that the two governments have proven that they can work together effectively on issues such as terrorism, illegal migration and money laundering, it is time for them to plan and implement a program of public diplomacy precisely to increase mutual knowledge, understanding and appreciation between their peoples. But diplomacy is no longer the monopoly of diplomats, and it is also up to Indonesians and Australians themselves – including business people, academics, tourists and, above all, journalists and writers – to try to address the cultural gap.

In the years ahead, as the cultural gap narrows, as Australia engages itself more deeply with East Asia and is seen less as an extension of the United States in the region, and as Indonesia becomes more stable, prosperous and confident, there is bound to be a substantial improvement in bilateral relations. But without a deliberate effort at public diplomacy, complemented by the efforts of private institutions, groups and individuals, the achievement of that end result will take a great deal more time.

3 A REGIONAL VIEW:
THE GARUDA AND THE KANGAROO

K. Kesavapany

Much has happened since the last Indonesia Update conference in 2004. Indonesia has a new president; he has settled well into his challenging post, appointed his cabinet and launched a series of reforms, including the politically sensitive action of raising fuel prices in September 2005. More tragically, the December 2004 tsunami caused tremendous loss of life and extensive damage and destruction in Indonesia and several other countries. The president and the government of Indonesia have risen to the great challenge of rebuilding Aceh, and many countries, including Australia, have offered significant humanitarian help. Indonesia continues to battle acts of terrorism such as the latest bombing in Bali, with the help of other countries, but the threat keeps mutating along with the loose alliances of extremist groups. With so many political, economic, security and social changes, it is timely to reflect on a key bilateral relationship: that between Indonesia and Australia.

FACTORS IN REGIONAL VIEWS

There are several factors that influence national perceptions of the Indonesia–Australia relationship. While all members of the Association of Southeast Asian Nations (ASEAN) would acknowledge the salience of this relationship, geographic distance would diminish its importance for some members: the further away, the less its importance. Those ASEAN countries that share a land or maritime border with Indonesia, such as Malaysia, Philippines, Brunei and Singapore, would understand better the consequences of good or bad relations between the two giants to their south. There is, after all, an immediacy that adds reality to abstract notions of neighbourliness when two other neighbours start quarrelling on your doorstep.

A second factor is ASEAN solidarity; for better or for worse, when a fellow club member is engaged in a dispute with an outsider, one's immediate reaction is to express sympathy with the fellow club member. After all, if the same thing happened to us, we would expect regional sympathy and solidarity from other club members. The problem of course is this: what if, like Singapore, you are a member of several clubs, such as ASEAN, Asia-Pacific Economic Cooperation (APEC), the Commonwealth, the Non Aligned Movement (NAM) and the G77, and the numerous ties that link you to both sides pull you in opposite directions? The solution then might be to try and help settle the dispute and/or offer sympathy and support to both, without appearing two-faced. This is the essence of diplomacy.

The third factor is national interests: in the calculus of national interests that is ever ongoing, which has the higher priority – the national interest or the bilateral relationship? Should we not be offended by threats to our own independence and sovereignty when neighbours imply that we are a failed state, unable to safeguard our security by getting rid of terrorist bases and activities? Should we not be accorded some respect as a neighbour and friend? These are some of the questions and reactions that would occur to any self-respecting, fully independent state. Thus there is a need for extreme delicacy and careful deliberation in such matters, and it would be best to be very circumspect in what is a sensitive area.

The last factor is regional security and cooperation: when both Indonesia and Australia have warm and cordial relations, and both sides are cooperating in addressing issues such as terrorism, economic development and political dialogue, then this is beneficial for regional stability and security. All ASEAN members would appreciate and support such a situation. Conversely, when relations between Australia and Indonesia are bad, as was the case during the East Timor episode, other ASEAN members feel discomfited.

WHY ARE BOTH INDONESIA AND AUSTRALIA IMPORTANT TO ASEAN?

When one considers that Indonesia has half the total population of ASEAN, that its sea and land territories cover a sizeable proportion of the ASEAN area, that instability in Indonesia could be exported to the rest of ASEAN, and that Indonesia's prestige in NAM, the Organization of Islamic Countries (OIC) and the Organization of the Petroleum Exporting Countries (OPEC) is a useful asset to ASEAN – of which it is a founding member – then one realises that these are some of the factors that help explain the interest of the rest of ASEAN in the well-being of Indonesia. Then there is of course the sense of solidarity that ASEAN members feel towards a fellow member of ASEAN and fellow developing country. Indonesia was a leader of the struggle against colonialism, fighting a long and bloody war against the Dutch to win its independence. It thus has impeccable credentials within ASEAN, NAM and G77. Indonesia also controls vital sea lanes of communication that are essential to ASEAN trade, communications and energy supplies.

Australia is the nearest developed country to ASEAN, and was the first to start a dialogue relationship with it. Australia has a long and distinguished record of providing aid to many ASEAN countries, including defence cooperation with Malaysia and Singapore, both under the Five Power Defence Arrangements and bilaterally. Many ASEAN students have benefited from an Australian education, and ASEAN and Australian tourists have long enjoyed the hospitality of each other's countries. Bali/Phuket and the Great Barrier Reef/Bondi Beach are representative symbols of the natural wonders in our greater region. Once Australia had dropped its White Australia policy and started accepting Asian immigrants, the empathy between ASEAN and Australia grew, as there were now bonds of family and kinship. For all these good reasons, therefore, Australia is seen as the 'default Westerner', a kinder, gentler version of the European states.

But there is one specific reason why Australia is important to ASEAN, and in particular to Indonesia. The needs of Indonesia are very great given its efforts to recover economically from the Asian financial crisis and to democratise; as the only developed country in the region, Australia is able to play a key role in helping Indonesia in this process. Among all the countries in the region, Australia is uniquely placed to render assistance to its northern neighbour. It is not often acknowledged that Australia's GDP is equal to that of all the ASEAN countries added together. Thus Australia has the economic strength and resources to help Indonesia in times of need. It certainly has done much by way of the generous aid extended to Indonesia to help it recover from the tsunami. ASEAN thus understands the need for good and cordial relations between Australia and Indonesia. The point about Australia helping Indonesia was also made by Prime Minister John Howard when he visited Washington in July 2005 and said during a joint press conference with President George W. Bush: 'If Indonesia is a success story, it can be held up as an example to the rest of the Islamic world that the path forward is a path away from hatred and extremism'.

THE REGIONAL CONTEXT FOR AN EAST ASIAN COMMUNITY

In examining the state of Australia–Indonesia relations, the regional political context should also be taken into account, as regional politics affect bilateral relationships. In this regard, the East Asia Summit (EAS) held in December 2005 in Kuala Lumpur was a significant development. The purpose of the summit was to set up a new regional framework for discussion and cooperation on economic and security issues. The concept of an East Asian Economic Group was originally proposed by Malaysia, but membership of the new grouping has been expanded beyond that originally suggested. With India, Australia and New Zealand participating in this momentous event along with the ASEAN countries and South Korea, China and Japan, it may be useful to examine the regional context surrounding the EAS. A look at the Indonesian, Chinese and Japanese viewpoints may be instructive at this point.

The Indonesian view

Dr Edy Prasetyono, head of the Department of International Relations at the Centre for Strategic and International Studies in Jakarta, has expressed an Indonesian view of China's role in the EAS, as follows:

> Concerns over China are historically natural. Any new power coming to the front has always resulted in new adjustments of the international system, thus shaping a new balance of power in global politics. Whether or not China is a threat depends on how the international system creates space for China to get tuned in with the norms and values the system has developed. But it also depends on whether China understands their position as a superpower, with their responsibility to maintain global stability. A responsible superpower has to make compromises and sacrifices. ... The East Asia Summit to be held in Kuala Lumpur in December 2005 remains problematic in terms of agenda, membership and modalities; what makes it different from ASEAN Plus Three?[1] When some ASEAN countries demonstrated their reluctant acceptance to EAS to be held this year, what was in their mind was that ASEAN could be diluted by the big powers in the north, particularly China. ... ASEAN Plus Three should be the basis for regional integration in East Asia, that can be developed in stages comfortable to the member states. The fear of China's offensive diplomacy has been even more valid due to the fact that ASEAN itself has never consolidated its position to pursue an ASEAN Community, as outlined in the Bali Concorde.[2] An EAS could only cause a drift of some ASEAN member states away from achieving the ASEAN community (Prasetyono 2005).

The Chinese view

China's views on the EAS are clearly spelled out by Foreign Minister Li Zhaoxing in the following statement:

> The first EAS, which is to be held in Malaysia at the year-end, is something new in the process of East Asian cooperation. It will serve as an important platform for dialogue between East Asia and countries in other regions. The Chinese side attaches importance to the Summit, respects the consensus reached within ASEAN and supports ASEAN's leading role in the Summit. The Chinese side is of the view that the East Asia Summit will contribute to the solidarity of East Asian countries, 10+3[2] cooperation, the growth of [the] East Asian community and the common development of East Asia, Asia and the world as a whole (Zhaoxing 2005).

There are several possible interpretations of China's interest in promoting East Asian regionalism. The first is that China wants to build a bloc that it can dominate and lead, and use it as a power base to challenge the United States. The problem of course is that some members, such as South Korea and Japan, will never agree to or accept such a situation. A second theory is that China wants to co-opt those neighbours that may be negatively affected by its rising economic power, and extend its influence. A third version is that China may be trying to exclude the United States by building an Asians-only club. But again this is unlikely to work given that some states want the United States to continue to play a security and economic role in the region. Lastly, China may be trying to construct an East Asian club in which it has legitimacy and seniority. History will show which theory proves to be correct.

The reactions of regional states to China's efforts to build an EAS may be divided into those taking a neutral position, adopted by states that do not wish to be pressured by the United States, Japan or China; those taking a supportive position, adopted by those who stand to profit from such a stance; and those taking a negative position, adopted by those states that, for various reasons, fear that a China-led East Asia may not suit their national strategic interests.

Whatever the reactions of individual states, the rise of China will provide the impulse for East Asian regionalism. This is the single most important factor changing the political and economic dynamics of the region. Because of its huge size, enormous population and deep pool of talent, China will probably dominate East Asia in a matter of only 10–20 years. In comparison, Japan has a declining and ageing population, and is reluctant to accept immigration to reverse these trends. South Korea and the ASEAN countries are too small and weak to counterbalance the Chinese giant.

Thus, building an EAS – if India with its billion-plus population and fast-expanding economy is not included – in effect means creating a China-dominated community. China's population of about 1.4 billion would comprise about 75 per cent of such a community. Once India with its population of 1.2 billion is included, the proportions change radically: China would then comprise two-fifths; India another two-fifths; and ASEAN plus Japan, South Korea, Australia and New Zealand roughly another one-fifth. This is one reason why the EAS has now been expanded to include India, Australia and New Zealand. In contrast, the largest member in the European Union, Germany, is not as dominant in terms of population, economic strength or political influence as China would be in the EAS if India, Australia and New Zealand were *not* included.

Economic integration will be the force that drives Asian regionalism. The locomotive will be China, which is expected to become the world's largest economy by 2040. Over time, economic links between the regional economies will become stronger. East Asia has been the main beneficiary of China's booming economy: Japan, Hong Kong, Taiwan, South Korea and Singapore accounted for 47 per cent of Chinese imports in 2002, and provided 59 per cent of China's foreign direct investment (FDI).[3]

China has launched its own concept of peaceful development as a way of reassuring its neighbours that it will not cause any upsets as it grows, stating explicitly that it needs a peaceful external environment to promote domestic economic development. Chinese General Cai Bing Kui (2004) has stated that: 'China will not create obstacles or threats to anybody. It does not seek hegemony now, nor will it seek hegemony after it becomes powerful in the future'. China has also taken other measures to reassure ASEAN. These include issuing a declaration on the South China Sea;[4] offering to double ASEAN–China trade; signing the ASEAN Treaty of Amity and Cooperation; negotiating an ASEAN–China free trade agreement (FTA); and becoming ASEAN's first strategic partner in regional politics. It is also noteworthy that throughout 2005 China cleverly cultivated regional ties with countries such as Indonesia, Malaysia and the Philippines through high-level visits of leaders and offers of Chinese aid.

A critical question is what rules other members can negotiate with China to ensure that the EAS functions effectively, while not overly constraining China. The effort to seek a political and economic balance between China and the rest of the EAS has parallels in the history of the European Union, between larger members such as France, the United Kingdom and Germany and other, smaller, EU members. This process of accommodation would be doubly difficult if other member states were to become economic satellites of China. For ASEAN to insist on being the driver may be practical for the ASEAN+3 grouping, but in the case of the EAS, it remains to be seen whether China would accept such a situation in the long run.

The Japanese view

Japan's approach and strategy towards East Asian regionalism appears to be driven by rivalry and competition with China as both strive to assume the regional leadership. The tense relationship between the two countries was shown once again during the Asian Cup football matches held in China in August 2004 when Chinese fans booed the Japanese team, in the 2005 textbooks case, and in strong and negative Chinese reactions to Prime Minister Junichiro Koizumi's visits to Yasukuni Shrine in 2004 and 2005. Observers opined that China's proposed ASEAN–China FTA was aimed at strengthening its relations with the region while at the same time decreasing American and Japanese influence within ASEAN. Not to be outdone, Japan immediately proposed its own FTA with ASEAN; so too did India.

Japan's approach, after initial hesitation, of building a network of FTAs thus appears to be a counterstrategy to the rise of China as well as being motivated by concerns about being isolated. In January 2002, despite known difficulties over the agricultural sector, Prime Minister Koizumi announced that Japan would be willing to conclude an FTA with ASEAN, to be called the Japan–ASEAN Comprehensive Economic Partnership and to be realised by 2012. He also proposed an Initiative for Development of East Asia and called for the creation of a regional economic bloc or East Asian Community.[5] Japan has yet to flesh out its position on East Asian regionalism because of its difficulties with FTAs, especially with regard to agricultural and labour liberalisation. However, for Japan, ASEAN is a useful counterbalance to China's emergence as a great power.

The rise of China poses acute security and existentialist challenges for Japan. Never have the two powers been strong and powerful at the same time. Chinese nationalism and anti-Japanese sentiment have provoked corresponding feelings of nationalism and resentment in Japan. This was evident in Prime Minister Koizumi's remark in November 2005 that Japan's neighbours should stop playing the Yasukuni card. It seems that Japan has got used to the idea that it is the leader of the East Asian group, as indicated by the 'flying geese' model in which it plays the leading role, and cannot now accept taking second place to an emerging China. This explains Japanese resentment over what it sees as China using World War II issues to keep Japan forever in an inferior and apologetic posture. It has led Japan to make efforts to strengthen its security ties with the United States, become a 'normal' country with normal defence forces, strengthen its territorial claims in the East China Sea, monitor China's growing military power, tussle with it over energy and other resources, and so on. But the most acute dilemma facing Japan is its role in the EAS: should it accept a subsidiary role to China, or try to play an equal role with it?

Japan has become the significant 'other' against which Chinese nationalism can be focused. The defeat of Japan in World War II was central to the Communist Party's claim to have the right and legitimacy to rule China. Amid rising nationalism in both countries, and in response to provocative behaviour on both sides, public opinion has hardened in both Japan and China. Given the high level of mistrust and suspicion, each has tended to react negatively to the proposals of the other, especially if these have military implications such as the proposal to jointly police the Malacca Strait. The proposal to negotiate a trilateral FTA between China, Japan and South Korea also evoked a negative reaction from Japan. It would appear that by using the nationalist card against Japan, China is in danger of provoking Japan into displaying the very same nationalist response.

Prospects

The only political and economic force that can counterbalance China is the United States. It is likely to work with Japan to check the rise of China, exploiting issues such as Taiwan. Thus the key to building an EAS lies outside: in the triangular relations between China, Japan and the United States. I do not have the space or time to go into the details of these complex relations. Suffice it to say that if the triangular relations are good, the EAS will progress; if not, it will still progress, but with difficulty. The latest visit by Prime Minister Koizumi to Yasukuni Shrine in October 2005, followed later by a large group of Japanese MPs, was officially explained as a private visit but could be interpreted as a sign that Japan will not bow to pressure from its neighbours. In response, China postponed a visit by the Japanese foreign minister in late October 2005. Both China and Japan will need to reconcile the clash of their respective nationalisms and ambitions to lead the region.

As the world's dominant superpower, the United States is the price setter; as a rising power, China is still a price taker. The United States still sets the regional agenda. It can block or slow the efforts to build East Asian regionalism; after the Asian financial crisis, for instance, it blocked Japanese efforts to set up an Asian monetary fund along the lines of the IMF. All three great powers are acutely aware of these political realities. China too understands the nuances. As a rising power, its current behaviour is different from that of a risen power. At present it needs friends and will be willing to accommodate the interests of others.

The prospects for building an Asian regional community are therefore mixed. On the one hand power rivalry between the great Asian states is endemic, as shown by the competitive relationships between China, Japan and India in their offers to negotiate various FTAs with ASEAN. All three are entering uncharted waters in their bilateral relations with each other. The most problematic relationship is that between Japan and China. Japan is not used to taking second place after being ahead of China for so long in the development race. But with a declining and ageing population, Japan may have no choice but to reconcile itself, as graciously as it can, to being overtaken by a rising China, and reinvent a new role for itself.

Japan's position is similar to that of Britain when it was overtaken by the United States at the end World War II. Britain decided to face reality and join the European Union. Later it chose to stress its special Anglo-Saxon ties with America, and became a very close ally of the United States. It is clear that Japan faces a similar series of choices: whether to become part of the new Asia; and whether to accept and live with rising Chinese influence or remain within the US sphere of influence. Another choice could be to run with the US hound while also running with the Chinese hare.

Australia faces similar dilemmas. As long as the United States and China are not at loggerheads, for instance over Taiwan, both Japan and Australia should be able to balance the pulls of competing allegiances. Trying to build an Asian community against the background of a tense Sino-Japanese relationship will be an interesting process to observe. Against this evolving regional background, Australia's relations with ASEAN, and particularly Indonesia, become doubly important.

AUSTRALIA–INDONESIA RELATIONS

The cultural divide across the Arafura Sea

Just as the Wallace Line divides the flora and fauna of Indonesia and Australia/ Papua New Guinea, there is also a clear and distinct cultural division between Indonesia and Australia. Indonesia is an ancient civilisation with its roots in Hindu, Buddhist and Islamic culture. With such ancient precedents, it is no wonder that Indonesian culture highly prizes stylised discourse, the virtue of restraint, the art of politeness and refined behaviour, the qualities of humility and compromise, the language of indirect allusions and so on. These are qualities that are also found in other ancient Asian civilisations, from the Middle East to India, China and Japan.

Across the Timor Gap, Australia is a new and young immigrant culture in an ancient continent. It retains much of the feisty, frontier ethic, even though most Australians are urban dwellers. Thus there is stress on speaking openly and frankly, on giving as good as you get, on values like mateship, independence, self-reliance, ruggedness and toughness. Then there are the added values of human rights and democracy, an open society and individualism that Australia shares with other Western societies. In short, Australia is as different as can be from Indonesia. It is not surprising, therefore, that both frequently find the other incomprehensible or alien. The cultural discourse is simply too divergent.

Australia marches to a different security drum

Another point of difference between the two countries is their divergent security perceptions. Indonesia lies on Australia's northern security perimeter and is the source of Australian security concerns about illegal migrants, fishing in its territorial waters, environmental pollution and terrorism. Seen from the Indonesian perspective, Australia is Indonesia's southern frontier; it is the source of many criticisms about human rights and democracy in Indonesia, and of intrusions into Indonesian domestic matters such as West Irian (now Papua province), Aceh and East Timor. This reversal of views shows that what you see depends on where you stand, and what you say depends on where you sit.

In addition, Australia is seen by some observers to be marching to a different drum, an American one. Australia is a treaty ally of the United States. As a member of the US-led 'Coalition of the Willing', it committed troops to Afghanistan and Iraq. Indonesia, as the world's largest Muslim country, has an opposing view of the conflicts in Iraq and Afghanistan. In Indonesia there are high levels of anti-US sentiment. The terrorists who bombed the tourist spots in Bali deliberately targeted Westerners, and 88 of the 200 casualties were Australian (while another 33 were Indonesian). It is no coincidence that another terrorist bomb attack in Jakarta was aimed at the Australian embassy. The furore over Prime Minister Howard's alleged 'deputy sheriff' remarks illustrates the intense Indonesian sensitivities on this issue.[6] While the public image of the United States and Australia has improved as a result of the generous post-tsunami aid given by both countries, a bitter aftertaste lingers.

There thus needs to be improved sensitivity and respect for the independence and sovereignty of ASEAN countries, particularly since these are new and vulnerable countries. When a country has just suffered a near melt-down, it feels very upset, insecure and prickly; this is a time when friends and neighbours must be acutely aware of its fragility and sensitivities.

The relationship in context

Australia–Indonesia relations do not occur within a vacuum but operate within a regional context. Thus it may be useful to discuss some of the parameters affecting and defining the relationship.

A rising China

Both Indonesia and Australia are being affected by the needs of a rising China, as well as by economic competition from China. China needs resources, such as tropical products and minerals, from both countries. While China is a good market for Australian mineral exports, Indonesia is being adversely affected by competition from cheap Chinese products and labour as well as competition for FDI. Thus, while Australia is prospering from increased exports, Indonesia is finding it more difficult to generate badly needed jobs and investment because of relentless competition from China. Furthermore, the spread of Chinese influence within Southeast Asia may not be welcomed by Indonesia. Aware of this ambivalence, during President Susilo Bambang Yudhoyono's visit to China in July 2005, the Chinese gave him a warm welcome, signed several agreements – such as one that will boost bilateral trade from $14 billion to $20 billion – and sought to put substance to the strategic partnership between the two countries.

During a visit to Washington in July 2005, Prime Minister John Howard stated that:

> My approach is to build on the things we have in common and not become obsessed with the things that make us different. We have a good relationship with China, not just based on economic opportunity. We are unashamed in developing our relations with China.

Australia will, nevertheless, need to address three key questions concerning its China policy. First, how far is Australia willing to go in accepting Chinese leadership in Asia? Second, what role does it want the United States to play in the new balance of power in the region? And third, where do other regional powers, such as Japan and India, fit into the picture? These are questions that Indonesia, Singapore and other ASEAN members will also have to answer.

Religious differences

To the cultural fault-line that runs across the Arafura Sea, we can add the religious division that exists between Islam and Christianity, the majority religions in Indonesia and Australia respectively. I am not saying that these religions are at loggerheads at present, but if the terrorist organisation Jemaah Islamiyah (JI) should ever succeed in creating an Islamic caliphate in Indonesia, how would Australia coexist with such a polity? It is not only terrorist organisations like JI that are committed to installing an Islamic state in Indonesia; so are a number of Islamic parties such as the Prosperity and Justice Party (PKS). According to the Pew Global Attitudes Project (2005), a sizeable 15 per cent of Indonesians still think suicide bombings are 'sometimes' justifiable (down from 27 per cent in 2002) and 35 per cent support Osama bin Laden (down from 58 per cent in 2003). While the trends are downward, the absolute numbers are high and give cause for concern.

Democracy and human rights

Indonesia is now a functioning democracy, having successfully organised legislative and presidential elections in 2004. Its legitimacy and credibility as a democracy have been rising with each successful, free and fair election. President Yudhoyono stressed in a speech in Singapore in February 2005 that his mission was to advance democracy and reform in Indonesia. Australia has assisted by sending observers and providing some funds. Within the context of respect for Indonesia's independence and sovereignty, Australia now has to deal with Indonesia as a fellow democracy, equal in the club of democracies. Indonesia is, after all, the world's third-largest democracy. So how best can Australia help a fellow democracy fight terrorism and institute effective policing while not alienating the Indonesian National Army (TNI)? How best can it help Indonesia achieve better governance, fight corruption and implement effective economic reforms, all sensitive issues, while respecting fully Indonesian independence and sovereignty? These sensitive issues require a sure hand and a light touch.

INDONESIAN VIEWS OF AUSTRALIA

Australians have written numerous articles and books on Indonesia–Australia relations. The views of Australians are ably and eloquently expressed in speeches and statements by politicians from the prime minister downwards, including a very comprehensive parliamentary report (Foreign Affairs Subcommittee 2004); in papers by eminent scholars such as Dr Stephen Sherlock and Dr Carlyle Thayer, and by the Australia–Indonesia Institute; and in various Australian media articles.

Three contributions by Indonesians – all written in English – bring an Indonesian perspective to this topic. First, former Indonesian Ambassador to Australia Imron Cotan has noted the long history of interactions between Indonesians and Aborigines, as well as the fact that Australia supported and assisted Indonesia in its struggle for independence (Cotan 2005a). He points out that bilateral trade between Indonesia and Australia totals about $5 billion; Australia is the eighth-largest export market for Indonesia and its sixth-largest source of imports. Cotan states that Indonesia will support Australian participation in the EAS in Kuala Lumpur in December 2005.

In another speech, Cotan describes relations between the two countries as being 'characterised by peaks and troughs; seldom has there been the stable, friendly and cooperative long-term relationship that some would expect of close neighbours' (Cotan 2005b). He identifies Australia's involvement in East Timor as a major turning point; the excellent bilateral relations up to then nose-dived to the extent that Indonesia decided in September 1999 to abrogate the security pact with Australia signed in December 1995. Indonesia also postponed, delayed, or abandoned altogether important official contacts, including the Indonesia–Australia Ministerial Forum.

Two incidents in particular – the Tampa ship incident in 2001 involving illegal immigrants trying to enter Australia, and the Bali bombings on 12 October 2002 – brought the two countries closer together. The improvement in bilateral relations has been evident in closer cooperation on a number of fronts. In the area of terrorism, initiatives have included the Bali Regional Ministerial Meeting on Counter-terrorism in February 2004 and the establishment, with Australian funding, of the Jakarta Center for Law Enforcement Cooperation. In the area of religion, the governments of Australia and Indonesia co-sponsored an International Dialogue on Interfaith Cooperation, held in Yogyakarta in December 2004. And in response to the tsunami, the generous aid given by Australia to tsunami victims – involving a A$1 billion aid package from the government in addition to A$800 million raised by the public – is being distributed through the jointly supervised Australia–Indonesia Partnership for Reconstruction and Development (see Chapter 10).

Finally, Cotan stresses the need for more consultation by Australia on matters such as travel advisories, the need for pre-emptive strikes, missile defence systems and the recently introduced Australian Maritime Identification Zone. The former ambassador's remarks provide a good insight into Indonesia's areas of concern about Australia.

Wimar Witoelar, an Indonesian commentator writing after Schapelle Corby was sentenced to 20 years' jail for possession of 20 kilograms of marijuana, makes the following observations:

> The Corby case is not a case of bilateral relationships, but the sad story of an individual. Yet many refuse to accept the independence of the two aspects ... Australian perceptions of Asia are based on its insecurity, not on the realities in the Asian countries. ... [The] Indonesian perception of Australia is based on popular fears and myths. Social and political changes in 1999–2005 are changing our perception of Australia because our confidence as Indonesians is growing. ... It is not easy to imagine the triggers for animosity, but discomfort always pervades in the [Australia–Indonesia] relationship. ... We feel we have achieved a lot since 1999. ... Yet these attempts by Indonesian society to reform itself are not always recognized in parts of Australian society, who isolate cases of injustice and feel targeted as victims. This is unfortunate when it is the Indonesian people who have been the most severe victims of the failings in our system. ... When a bomb goes off in Jakarta, there is recrimination towards our people. We forget that Indonesians are the victims, not the perpetrators. The new society of Indonesia is proud of its achievements, but its confidence needs reinforcement from the outside world. ... Australia cannot escape from its identification with U.S. policy because of the loudly proclaimed loyalty of the Australian government to the U.S. government. We will continue as neighbours to have a love and hate relationship between our two societies, just as there are love and hate relationships within our own society (Witoelar 2005).

THE FUTURE: WHITHER AUSTRALIA–INDONESIA BILATERAL RELATIONS?

With the election of President Yudhoyono, the good start created by his successful visit to Canberra in April 2005 and the momentum generated by Australia's assistance to tsunami victims and in counterterrorism, it is possible to envisage an upturn in bilateral relations for a considerable period of time. In a sensitive, non-intrusive manner, Australia should seize this opportunity to help President Yudhoyono implement his reform program and his economic reconstruction and anti-corruption efforts.

Given that bilateral relations in the past have gone up and down like a yoyo, ranging from excellent to disastrous, much effort must be made to keep relations stable and progressive. Particular incidents like the Corby case should not be allowed to derail good bilateral relations. Australia can do much to help Indonesia in various ways. Such help could take the form of military training and the provision of defence material, which Indonesia badly needs. Australia could help in the effort to professionalise the TNI by providing advanced staff-college training, perhaps in the context of an Australia–ASEAN Defence College. In the field of education and human resource development, the University of New South Wales Asia's establishment of a Singapore campus in 2007 will create an excellent opportunity to start a third-country training program, wherein Australia and Singapore jointly provide scholarships for Indonesian students to study in either country.

In conclusion, Australia well understands that there are not only cultural, religious and developmental divisions between Indonesia and itself, but psychological differences as well. Reading the words of the two Indonesians quoted above, one is struck by the sensitivity, prickliness, feelings of inferiority, complex emotions of resentment, victimhood, colonial hangovers and so on expressed therein. The gap between Australia and Indonesia is not only economic, developmental, cultural and religious, it is also a civilisational divide, like that between the European Union and the Arab states, the United States and Mexico, or China and Russia. It is therefore vital, for the sake of stability and progress in the region, that the leadership and people in both Australia and Indonesia continue to develop the relationship as a major focus of their attention.

NOTES

1 ASEAN+3 = the 10 ASEAN countries plus China, South Korea and Japan.
2 That is, ASEAN+3.
3 According to Oxford Analytica, <http://www.oxan.com/>, 7 July 2004.
4 China and ASEAN signed a Declaration on the Conduct of Parties in the South China Sea during the ASEAN Summit in Phnom Penh in November 2002. This agreement was intended to prevent further tensions over the Spratly Islands and reduce the risks of military conflict in the South China Sea.
5 Japan was thus the first to propose an East Asian Community. It should not be confused with the EAS: the latter is a broad political process whereas the East Asian Community is a proposal for an economic community.
6 Some Australians also had reservations about these remarks. In 2002, former Prime Minister Paul Keating said:

> I believe the government's problems with foreign policy stem from its own insecurity; from a defensive and uncertain view of Australia and its place in the world. A sense that we should know our place; that we shouldn't get ideas above our station. A government that has little faith in Australians or what they are capable of.
>
> We saw it clearly in John Howard's agreement to the assertion that Australia's role in the region was to be the Deputy Sheriff (Keating 2002).

In an article for the *Sydney Morning Herald*, retired diplomat Bruce Haigh wrote:

> The TNI was also upset with John Howard over his assertion in 1999 that Australia was the US deputy sheriff in the region and with his statement in late 2002 that he was prepared to use a pre-emptive strike against terrorists and their supporters in the region ('Fiddling with Iraq, as fundamentalists creep into the backyard', 29 April 2003, <smh.com.au>).

4 AN AUSTRALIAN VIEW: THE OUTLOOK FOR THE RELATIONSHIP

*Paul Kelly**

History suggests that this may be a dangerous time in Australia–Indonesia relations. We have now reached another high tide in government-to-government relations. I remember the two previous such occasions – in the early 1970s under Prime Minister Gough Whitlam and President Soeharto, and in the 1990s under Prime Minister Paul Keating and President Soeharto. Both these high tides ended in tears and recriminations because the relationship lacked a sufficiently firm foundation or, to use former Foreign Minister Gareth Evans' word, 'ballast'. On both occasions East Timor was the trigger for significant setbacks.

It is a reminder that bilateral relations are hostage to the latest chapter in this complex story of Indonesian nationhood and the response of Australian public opinion to the Indonesian project. I am not predicting that the current high tide will end in tears and recriminations. However, I expect relations will oscillate between their good and bad phases and that Australia–Indonesia ties will be subject to more volatility and unpredictability than any of Australia's other main relationships.

In these remarks I have six potentially contradictory points to make. First, government-to-government relations in 2005 revealed, again, the crucial role of a personal relationship between the heads of government. John Howard and Susilo Bambang Yudhoyono (SBY) have such a personal relationship and mutual trust. This rapport is important in helping to set the tone for their respective governments. While the significance of such heads-of-government ties can be exaggerated, history suggests they are pivotal.

When President Yudhoyono visited Australia in April 2005, he said relations were getting 'stronger, closer, better'. In a sophisticated speech he conceptualised relations the way Australia likes to see them. He acknowledged the need for better people-to-people links – a critical defect in the relationship. Yudhoyono was, however, very ambitious for the relationship, far more ambitious than any previous Indonesian president. This is a very encouraging sign. Without doubt, he is the best Indonesian president for Australia. But this is also a trap, since there is no guarantee that his successor will be as enthusiastic or ambitious about ties with Australia.

The scale and speed of Howard's response to the tsunami that struck Indonesia testifies to this bond. This response transcended a generous humanitarian impulse on Australia's part. Howard's reaction was also a deeply political response, and for a prime minister who often misjudges the region, he managed this issue with statesmanship. It showed a sensitivity towards Indonesia and a bonding with its leader that took some observers by surprise. Howard acts with the confidence of a leader who has put his own stamp on the relationship and sees SBY as a counterpart with whom he can do business.

Second, the network of shared interests between Australia and Indonesia is deepening. This is reinforced by Indonesia's gradual return to economic health after the crisis of 1997–98 (per capita income in Indonesia returned to its pre-1997 crisis levels only in 2004). It is encouraged further by the evolving democratisation of Indonesia and the shared interest in police cooperation to combat the terrorist threat. The more that business, educational, cultural, security and political links are buttressed, the more they operate as a long-term stabiliser. The quest for such stabilisation is basic to this bilateral relationship.

Third, for Australian public opinion there have been two path-breaking events on Howard's watch – the independence of East Timor and the shift to a new democratic constitution in Indonesia after Soeharto's demise. These events removed the two-generation-long critiques successfully advanced by the Australian media to limit ties with Jakarta – that it sponsored an illegal, brutal invasion and that it was an authoritarian state reliant on military force.

One of Foreign Minister Alexander Downer's prime motives in changing Australia's East Timor policy in 1998 and 1999 was to achieve a more sustainable basis for long-term relations. The two former Australian prime ministers who had sought to get closer to Indonesia, Whitlam and Keating, were stung because their policy inevitably meant getting closer to Soeharto. Other Australian leaders were wary of Indonesia precisely because of the Soeharto issue and its domestic political risk for them. When President Yudhoyono visited Australia he came as the symbol of a new Indonesia. There were no complaints about him or his trip, whereas Soeharto felt unable to come at all after his visits in the 1970s and, if he had tried, the criticism would have been thunderous. The resolution of the East Timor question and Indonesia's move towards a democratic polity are long-term markers that create a better foundation for relations.

Fourth, we need to realise that the cultural gap between the nations is deep and permanent and that it will lead to frequent tensions and occasional firestorms. Such tensions are built into the differences between the Australian and Indonesia polities. I believe, however, that shared interests are more important, ultimately, than cultural differences. History suggests that shared interests are usually acted upon by governments, and Australia's national interest will dictate sound relations with Jakarta.

For Australians, the proper approach towards the cultural gap is a renewed commitment to cultural awareness and skills in our dealings with Indonesia and Asia. Australia needs to see engagement as an intellectual and cultural exercise, and that demands a nation that is equipped with language and broader cultural skills to manage this challenge. This is where the Howard government has sent the wrong messages.

For Indonesians, however, there are also lessons from the Howard government's complex saga with Indonesia over a decade. The main lesson is that Australia's engagement with Asia and with Indonesia is a national project. It is a feature of Australia's existence. It is permanent and bipartisan. It transcends changes of government in Australia and changes of policy in Australia. Different Australian governments will engage in different ways, with shifts in emphasis and priorities. The reality, however, is that no Australian government will abandon the engagement project, and Indonesia should realise the debate in Australia is not over the basic policy but the details.

Fifth, public opinion in Australia towards Indonesia remains ambivalent, confused and reluctant to embrace the idea of a changed Indonesia. It senses the three great movements – a rising profile for democracy, Islam and nationalism – but it cannot integrate them into a meaningful picture.

I believe it is wrong to say that public opinion drives the relationship from Australia's perspective. Yet public opinion is critical because it imposes limits and constraints upon what is achievable. Indonesia has changed a lot in recent years but Australian attitudes towards Indonesia have changed very little.

Indonesia's transition to a democratic constitution has a dual impact – it offers a better basis for long-term understanding yet it complicates relations by exposing the complexity and mysteries of Indonesia to the Australian community. This is a test for both nations. As their democratic publics discover more about each other, will relations improve or deteriorate?

I think we should not become too alarmed about recent polls showing that only slightly more than 50 per cent of Australians have positive feelings about Indonesia (Cook 2005). Frankly, this is not too bad after 30 years of a media campaign in this country depicting Indonesia as a military dictatorship that brutalises its people. We need to remember that for nearly three decades Indonesia has been a bad news story in Australia. The contrast with China and Japan is illuminating because these countries had a narrative saga that was appealing to popular sentiment: China learnt the error of Marxist economics and began its conversion to capitalism, while Japan realised its World War II folly and devoted its energy to constructing a peaceful and prosperous society. There is no such appealing, integrating narrative that explains Indonesia to Australians.

Australians have been ill served by the media coverage of Indonesia. Australia's media has created two stereotypes: Indonesians as innocent victims, for example through the tsunami and military repression, who deserve compassion and support; and Indonesia as an intolerant, corrupt and brutal nation too ready to use military force to impose its will. Such stereotypes distort and deny. How often have you ever read, for example, that President Habibie authorised the self-determination ballot in East Timor, that the military allowed the transition to democracy, or that the Bali court being attacked over the trial of Schapelle Corby was the same court that tried and convicted the Bali bombers who killed so many Australians? Australians seem to love Indonesian justice when it is applied to Indonesians who seek to kill us, but attack the same court when it imposes punitive penalties on Australians for drug crimes. This problem is not confined to the tabloid newspapers and television in Australia. It is also embedded in much of the so-called quality media.

Sixth, there are signs emerging of Australia and Indonesia as regional partners. The most recent evidence was the strong Indonesian support for Australia to become a foundation participant in the East Asia Summit. This reflected an Indonesian view of the region that Australia should be included and not excluded – and this view was put to contradict China. The rise of China is changing the strategic calculations in the region and this is working to Australia's advantage. As nations think about the need to balance China, there are more possibilities and challenges opening up for Australia. The old arid debate about whether 'Australia is part of Asia' is fading as practical decisions are taken to reflect the reality of Australia's deep engagement.

Indonesia is pivotal to Australia's diplomatic success in Asia. Indonesia's support was essential for Howard to win Australia's entry into the East Asia Summit in 2005, just as Indonesia's support in the early 1990s was essential for Keating to realise his ambitions for the Asia-Pacific Economic Cooperation process. Australia forgets that Southeast Asia often judges us according to our relations with Jakarta. If these relations are in disrepair then it is futile to believe there will be no wider impact in the region.

Let me conclude by looking at what could go wrong, because some things almost certainly *will* go wrong.

Perceptions of Islam in Indonesia will be fundamental to the Australian relationship. If terrorism continues or escalates with more Australian casualties, and Islam is identified in Australian eyes with growing violence, then relations will be put under great strain. Nearly 90 Australians were killed in Bali in 2002, and in 2004 the Australian embassy was attacked. If Jemaah Islamiyah or other terrorists groups launch more attacks and claim more Australian casualties in greater numbers, then the relationship will begin to be defined by disorder, trauma and violence. In this situation Australian governments might feel compelled to demand that Jakarta launch security crackdowns and take more con-

certed action against terrorists. Friction would grow between the two governments over how to contain such violence.

Perhaps the most serious risk lies in the rise of secessionist movements,
notably in the province of Papua. It is imperative that Australia supports the
integrity of Indonesia as a sovereign nation, and this is the firm position of both
the Coalition and Labor. Yet Australian public opinion is likely to respond with
sympathy to the idea of a people seeking independence and being denied it by
Jakarta. Much depends on Indonesia's success in managing such political
issues; it was Jakarta's failure to manage East Timor effectively that finally precipitated the crisis. If the Papua issue gains traction in our politics there are
some certainties: elements of the right and left will back independence as a
moral issue; every act of violence by Indonesian authorities will attract media
coverage; the conflict will be presented as a re-run of East Timor; and there will
be significant partisan support from the Australian media for the independence
cause.

There is also, I suspect, a deeper issue at stake – the reluctance within certain sections of Australia's political and media systems to accept the legitimacy
of the Indonesian nation as presently constituted. According to this view, independence movements should be encouraged and the separation of some
provinces is seen as a desirable outcome. I do not want to exaggerate the extent
of this sentiment. Yet it exists and it will resurface if there is a new crisis over
Papuan independence.

NOTE

*   By arrangement with the organisers, Paul Kelly delivered an informal paper, speak-
    ing from notes. This text is a summary of his remarks.

PART II

Security Aspects

5 THE NEW AUSTRALIA–INDONESIA STRATEGIC RELATIONSHIP: A NOTE OF CAUTION

Hugh White

> *Oh wad some power the giftie gie us*
> *To see oursels as others see us!*
> *It wad from monie a blunder free us,*
> *An' foolish notion.*
> Robert Burns, 'To a louse', 1786

A NEW START?

No one watching relations between Australia and Indonesia in 2005 can have failed to notice a new sense of promise – at least as viewed from Canberra. For the first time since 1996, Indonesia has seemed to offer Prime Minster John Howard's government more opportunities than problems. The problems have been real enough of course: not only the second Bali bombings, but the trials of young Australians on drug charges which have generated a lot of attention and a little reflex hostility towards Indonesia among Australians, and reciprocal prickliness from Indonesians in return. But at the national level serious commentators have observed that the atmospherics of the relationship have regained a little of that sense of possibility that we last saw in the time of former Prime Minister Paul Keating.

Two factors seem to have contributed to this. The first is Indonesia's new president, Susilo Bambang Yudhoyono (SBY), whose effect on the relationship was most clearly demonstrated by his visit to Australia in April 2005. This was the most successful visit here ever by an Indonesian leader. SBY is the first Indonesian leader who can connect directly with Australians. Indonesia's previous leaders by contrast have all been more or less incomprehensible to us, both as politicians and as people. Moreover, SBY's predecessors have evidently made little effort to understand Australia. In this too SBY is different, as Opposition Leader Kim Beazley said soon after the president's visit:

> There's no politician as substantial as President Yudhoyono who has so clearly understood this country, understood our fears, understood our sensitivities, understood the contribution that we want to make and comprehended the value of the relationship. He is a totally different leader. He wants to understand Australians; what makes us tick, what we stand for and our hopes and fears for the future (Beazley 2005).

John Howard's words of welcome at a parliamentary lunch during the visit, in which he described President Yudhoyono as 'a man I respect and like a great deal', suggest that he too feels that Indonesia's new leader is someone he can do business with (Howard 2005d).

For Australians at large, however, the event that seems most clearly to mark an upturn in Australia–Indonesia relations is not the election of SBY, but the Boxing Day tsunami. Australians responded spontaneously and generously to the tragedy, and Howard, reflecting the national mood, was keen to appear concerned and generous on Australia's behalf. He seems to have seen the tragedy as a circuit breaker for public perceptions of Indonesia in Australia, which have been dominated for years by negative images of East Timor, illegal immigrants, terrorism and drug trials. He has frequently referred to the tsunami, and Australia's response, as a turning point in the relationship (Howard 2005d). Here, he seems to be saying, is the opportunity to turn the page after a decade in which, notwithstanding some useful achievements, the atmosphere has been tepid at best, and sometimes much worse.

But of course we need to ask whether this Australian optimism is justified, and whether Indonesians necessarily view things the same way. While everything that John Howard and Kim Beazley have said about SBY may be true, we should not underestimate the complexity of SBY's political situation, or view him as simply and unambiguously 'pro-Australian'. That would court disappointment. He is evidently committed to a good relationship, but that commitment will not always over-ride other imperatives in the complex political landscape of democratic Indonesia. Likewise we should not assume that Indonesia sees Australia's response to the tsunami in quite the same way we do. No one likes to need help, and gratitude is usually tempered by unease, even resentment, at being placed in the position of supplicant. The tsunami reprised an image of the relationship with Indonesia which Australians find comfortable: Australia rich and powerful, and Indonesia weak and in trouble, looking for our help. But we should not be surprised that Indonesia finds this image less congenial. When SBY responded to John Howard's welcome in Canberra in April 2005, he thanked Australia warmly and graciously for its tsunami assistance, but he also argued forcefully that the relationship should not be shaped by an image of Indonesia as a country in strife:

> I hope you see beyond such snapshots and see a nation that, given our seemingly endless natural disasters, has been down on luck lately, but remains high in spirit and strong in will. I hope you see a resilient people that continues to beat the odds, a

nation that continues to bounce back even stronger no matter how hard and how many times we are hit. I hope you see a vibrant democracy that continues to mature, a promising economy that continues to grow, a dynamic people that is eager to fulfill its potential (Yudhoyono 2005a).

EVEN FOR DEFENCE?

The response to the tsunami has been seen as particularly important in providing the opportunity to rebuild the defence relationship. No element of Australia's connections with Indonesia has been harder hit by the vicissitudes of the past few years than defence links. Though both governments can point to a range of positive developments in security cooperation in recent years, especially against terrorism, the defence relationship has hardly recovered from the deep trough into which it was plunged by the angry response from both sides to the East Timor crisis of 1999. For over 20 years until then, the two sides had worked to build a highly institutionalised bilateral defence relationship involving a relentless program of visits, exercises, joint working groups and collaborative projects. There had been interruptions along the way, as in 1986 when the relationship was rocked by the 'Jenkins articles'.[1] But these successive ructions quickly passed, and the relationship readily picked up from where it had temporarily been left.

This all culminated in the bilateral Agreement to Maintain Security (AMS) signed in 1995. The AMS marked the apogee of the relationship thus far: a confident affirmation that Australia and Indonesia shared basic strategic interests, and were prepared to cooperate closely to promote and protect them. As such it was a significant policy departure for both governments – and especially for Indonesia, which had long championed a strict non-alignment that abjured security alliances. It reflected the personal commitment of Keating and Soeharto, and presupposed that the level of trust they had developed with one another could become institutionalised in the wider relationship.

In September 1999, as Australian-led forces landed in East Timor, Indonesia abrogated the AMS, and the wider defence relationship virtually ground to a halt. This was not just Indonesia's doing. Anger in Australia, including within the Australian Defence Force (ADF), at the conduct of the Indonesian National Army (TNI) in East Timor raised doubts about the value of the defence relationship – reflecting unrealistic expectations about the purpose of the relationship, fanned by government claims that close ADF cooperation with the TNI would improve its respect for human rights. In this atmosphere most of the structure of contacts, activities, visits and meetings was abandoned. The depth of the freeze, and the hopes that the tsunami might provide the start to a thaw, is indicated by the fact that throughout his terms as chief of army and as chief of the defence force, from mid-2000 on, General Peter Cosgrove never visited Indonesia until,

in January 2005, he went to see the Australian forces deployed to Aceh to help
with tsunami relief. The tsunami has seemed to provide an opportunity to get the
ADF and the TNI back together again in something like the old spirit. Since the
tsunami, the first bilateral combined exercises since 1999 have been held (Hill
2005), and more high-level visits have taken place. Also in 2005, the two governments started to explore the possibility of negotiating a new bilateral security agreement, to replace the AMS which was torn up in 1999. It seems that the
defence relationship is at last looking more positive again.

BARRIERS REMOVED

In many ways a revived defence relationship would make a lot of sense. The circumstances seem much more auspicious now than they did in the heyday of
defence contact in the early 1990s. Back then the relationship was constrained
by two seemingly perennial limitations. First, Indonesia had an authoritarian,
military-backed political system which differed sharply from Australia's. This
raised continual problems of divergent expectations, attitudes and approaches,
as well as profound differences in practical interests and experiences between
the apolitical ADF, limited to a very narrowly defined role in national affairs,
and ABRI (as the Indonesian military was called then), which was engaged in
all aspects of Indonesian national life. Second, Indonesia's incorporation of East
Timor, and the TNI's operational and political role there, made the defence relationship a perennial political pressure point on Australian governments for Australian domestic lobby groups, and were a source of constraint in the
relationship between the militaries themselves.

     Today, of course, these restraints have largely been removed. Jakarta has
relinquished East Timor. Indonesia has emerged as a thriving democracy, and
the TNI has adapted to a more limited role in Indonesian politics and national
life. The conditions for a fuller and deeper defence relationship would therefore
seem to be very promising. The wider strategic context seems more propitious,
too. Those who believe that militant Islamic extremism poses the key strategic
challenge of the age will note that terrorism has already provided a fruitful field
for closer cooperation between Jakarta and Canberra. But those who place
greater weight on more traditional strategic concerns about the future power balance in Asia can also see reasons for closer cooperation across the Arafura Sea.
Australians and Indonesians have always recognised that their strategic interests
converge most naturally in their shared desire to limit the potential for intrusion
into our shared region of potentially hostile great powers. Australian and
Indonesian strategic objectives converged after 1965 because, most fundamentally, we shared a desire to limit communist Chinese influence in Southeast
Asia. Now, as the question of China's role in the region becomes once again the

primary strategic question, the natural convergence of our interests and objectives might be expected to underpin the renewal of our strategic and defence relationship.

All good arguments. But frankly, I am cautious about the prospects for Australia and Indonesia to build a close, effective and durable defence relationship. However the defence relationship develops, we should not assume it will look much like the one we were trying to build in the years before 1999. And above all we should be careful not to allow ourselves to be swept up in the moment and push for progress at a speed that cannot be sustained. The history of the defence relationship traces a sawtooth trajectory: short periods of rapid development, followed by sharp and painful reverses, then another dizzying climb, followed by another letdown. We have a record of overpromising and under-delivering. This time, let's be more circumspect. We should build slowly, carefully and modestly, remembering what difficult ground we are building on.

STRATEGIC AMBIVALENCE

No one should make big plans for the defence relationship with Indonesia without starting from the simple fact that, on Australia's side, it will always be based on a deep ambivalence, in the literal sense of that word. Indonesia impinges on Australia's deepest strategic preoccupations in two ways. It is the only large country within easy range of Australia; because of its proximity and sheer size, it has the strategic potential to pose a serious military challenge to Australia directly. And it is also the only one strong enough to help defend our neighbourhood against an intruder. Whether it is strong or weak, Indonesia therefore offers both potential protection and potential threats to Australia. A strong Indonesia can threaten attack and offer protection against others. A weak Indonesia offers less threat directly but more danger that others could attack us via Indonesia. This is the ambivalence reflected in the phrase Paul Dibb used in his *Review of Australian Defence Capabilities* 20 years ago: that Indonesia is the country *from or through* which a direct threat to Australia would most likely emerge (Dibb 1986: 48). When Australian strategists have looked at our neighbourhood in isolation, as a self-contained strategic system, a strong Indonesia looks like a liability. But when we look at our neighbourhood as an element of the wider Asia-Pacific strategic system, it looks like an asset. Australia has this kind of strategic ambivalence towards no other country.

This ambivalence makes the development of a stable, coherent and close defence relationship a very complex matter of policy for Australia. For many years the questions seemed rather easier from the Indonesian side. It goes almost without saying that for most of the time since 1945 Australia has impinged much less on Indonesia's strategic preoccupations than vice-versa. If they had ever thought about it in these terms, Indonesian leaders might have thought that a strong Australia to their south was a strategic asset in helping to protect the neighbourhood from hostile intrusion, but it has hardly been a central tenet of their strategic policy. Had they thought about it, they would probably have realised that Australia would be very likely to provide air and naval forces to help defend Indonesia should it ever come under attack from a major external power. But notwithstanding tensions over West Irian and Indonesia's policy of 'Confrontation' towards Malaysia, it has – until recently – been hard to detect any consistent anxiety in Indonesia about a potential threat from Australia. Again, had they thought about it, Indonesian leaders would probably have concluded that Australia would only be inclined to use force against Indonesia if Indonesia was threatening one of its neighbours: Malaysia, Singapore, Papua New Guinea or perhaps the Philippines. For this reason, Australia's acquiescence in Indonesia's incorporation of East Timor was important for reasons that went well beyond East Timor itself.

This difference in some ways reflects the geography and the strategic psychology of the two countries. Australia as a relatively homogeneous continental state has always been preoccupied with attack from outside. Indonesia as a very diverse archipelagic state has been more focused on internal cohesion. As long as Australia posed no threat to Indonesia's national cohesion, there was little enough for Jakarta to fear from us. And until 1999 Indonesia felt it had little to fear from Australia in that regard. But our role in East Timor in 1999 changed Indonesia's strategic perceptions of Australia in a way that Australians – including perhaps our government – do not seem fully to understand.

A MUTUAL SENSE OF GRIEVANCE

Rebuilding the defence relationship with Indonesia, or building it anew, will be harder than most Australians think, because the events of 1999 have changed Indonesian strategic perceptions of Australia in what seem to be deep and lasting ways. Both countries came out of East Timor's transition to independence with a sense of grievance against the other. Australians passionately believe that Indonesia, and especially the TNI, was deeply in the wrong in allowing and fomenting the violence and dislocation that marked East Timor's separation from Indonesia. But we are much less aware of the grievance on the other side – the sense in Indonesia, even among those who deplored the TNI's conduct, that Australia actively set out in 1998 and 1999 to damage Indonesia, taking advantage of its weakness after the economic collapse of 1997 and the fall of Soeharto in 1998, and behaving in a way that was actively hostile and even threatening. The fact that Australia had for so long accepted and even promoted Indonesia's incorporation of East Timor made this seem an especially sharp betrayal. I do not agree with any of these views. By launching the Interfet force,

I think that Australia did no more than was absolutely necessary and proper in the circumstances of September 1999. But I also think Australians need to take much more seriously the fact that many Indonesians evidently hold quite different views, and that these affect Indonesian attitudes towards Australia. This is an important new factor which we need to take into account in the management and development of the relationship.

Moreover, I can understand *why* Indonesians think the way they do about Australia's role in 1999. We contribute to it ourselves by the way in which we describe the events of 1999. The Australian government tends to present East Timor's passage to independence in 1999 as the result of a deliberate policy initiative by Australia. In July 2005, in a newspaper article, Minister for Health and Ageing Tony Abbott used the word 'liberate' to describe what Australia did for East Timor in 1999. 'It is inconceivable that governments between Whitlam and Keating would have had the self-confidence to liberate East Timor …', he wrote (Abbot 2005: 62). I have heard other ministers – even the prime minister – use the same word in the same context. By using this word they imply that Australia took the initiative and deliberately set in train the course of events that led to East Timor's independence.

This seems to me to be simply untrue. First, until after the ballot in August 1999, Australia did not want East Timor to become independent. In fact it was Canberra's strong preference that East Timor should remain part of Indonesia, as John Howard made clear after his meeting with President Habibie in Bali in April 1999 (Howard 1999). Second, the decision to allow the East Timorese to vote on their own future, and to acquiesce to independence if that was their choice, was Habibie's. If anyone deserves the credit for liberating East Timor, it is Habibie, even while he must also take some of the blame for not preventing the tragedy that followed the ballot.

In reality, then, Australia's leading role in the events in East Timor emerged only after the August ballot, and came about by accident. We did not seek East Timor's independence, nor did we seek a prominent role for the ADF in the process of transition. These were both outcomes we wanted to avoid if possible. For understandable political reasons the government has retrospectively constructed an image that casts its statesmanship in a more favourable light. It also seeks to counteract the views of those who, equally inaccurately, think that Australia's policy in the months leading up to the ballot was shaped primarily by a desire to avoid offending the TNI and so hold the government responsible for the disasters of September.

SEEING AUSTRALIA AS A THREAT

But in Indonesia, I fear, talk of Australia's 'liberation' of East Timor confirms Indonesians' deeply-held new worries about their strange southern neighbour.

We in Australia have forgotten the bellicose atmosphere of September 1999, when the *Sydney Morning Herald* argued that Australia should put troops into East Timor, even without UN endorsement or Indonesian acquiescence. That memory is still vivid in Indonesia. We have forgotten, or perhaps never fully realised, the impact on a weak and vulnerable Indonesia of the plain threats of economic retaliation and military intervention that were issued on Australia's behalf by the United States to ensure Indonesia's compliance with the wishes of the United Nations. That memory too still seems to be strong in Indonesia. Many Indonesians, now and at the time, agreed that East Timor should be let go, understood the wrongs that had been done by the TNI before and after the ballot, and accepted that international intervention was the only way out of the mess after the ballot. But even they could still feel resentment at the way Australia had behaved, and fear that we might do so again.

Indonesian concern that the East Timor crisis of 1999 showed a new and more dangerous neighbour can only have been confirmed by much that has happened since. In 2000 the government produced a new white paper that greatly increased defence spending and placed a major new emphasis on the ability of Australian forces to project power into our immediate neighbourhood. Since then it has ordered new long-range stand-off weapons. It has, without any clear strategic justification, placed a major new emphasis on amphibious forces, planning to double the size of new amphibious ships from 12,000 tonnes to over 24,000 tonnes. And of course it has apparently adopted and maintained a new policy of strategic pre-emption against threats in Australia's neighbourhood.

As a matter of fact I think it is quite mistaken to view any of these developments as directed against Indonesia. The new role for the army in the 2000 white paper was driven primarily by concerns about the South Pacific, not Indonesia. Long-term funding increases reflected the need to update air and naval forces, not to bolster intervention capability. New long-range missiles are designed to maintain our strike capability as the F-111s retire from service. The new enthusiasm for large amphibious forces seems to have no coherent strategic purpose at all. And John Howard's advocacy of pre-emption is simply an artefact of domestic politics. But they all amplify the message that Indonesians read into the events of 1999, and they resonate with the deeper roots of Indonesia's ambivalence about Australia – roots that go back to Indonesian perceptions of Australia's colonialist past.

One can see how, viewed from Indonesia through the lens of the East Timor crisis, all this could raise anxieties about Australia's future intentions towards Indonesia. These worries are directed most specifically towards West Papua. The state of separatist sentiment in West Papua and the nature of Jakarta's response to it are critical questions in themselves. But my interest here is the way that concerns about Australian policy towards West Papua have become the focus of Indonesian fears about Australia's new, post-Interfet militant regional activism. I have heard theories from Indonesian friends and acquaintances about how Australia intends to 'liberate' West Papua as it did East Timor. The details in some of these theories are lurid to the point of being ludicrous – of secret government committees in Australia dedicated to achieving West Papuan independence through Australian military intervention, and plans by the TNI to launch counterattacks. I have responded with the most earnest and detailed rebuttals, citing Australian support for Indonesia's territorial integrity and our interest in avoiding the emergence of yet another weak and vulnerable state on our doorstep. My comments have been met with the same unanswerable response: 'But that is what you Australians said about East Timor'.

So a new element has been brought into the strategic relationship between Canberra and Jakarta – the fact that some Indonesians now see Australia as a threat. We Australians have a real problem of self-perception in responding to this. We find it hard to take seriously the idea that another country – especially one as big as Indonesia – regards us as threatening. Indeed, this is I think the first time in our short strategic history that we have ever been regarded in this way by anyone. We have not worked out how to respond. Indeed we are not sure how seriously to take it. It is easy to dismiss Indonesian concerns about Australia as a political ploy, designed to win points in domestic politics, or to put Australia on the back foot internationally. No doubt there is an element of each of these at work in Jakarta. But we should not allow ourselves to be too complacent. My sense is that beneath the politics there is a real concern about Australia's strategic objectives towards Indonesia. Look, for example, at the words of Indonesia's highly articulate – and Australian National University educated – foreign affairs spokesman, Marty Natalegawa, speaking in Vientiane in July 2005 about Australia's decision to accede to the Treaty of Amity and Cooperation. He is reported to have said:

> From Indonesia's perspective, if Australia was to accede to the Treaty of Amity and Cooperation, this is extremely important, not only symbolically but also substance-wise about Australia's peaceful intent and interaction with the region. I can think of no other instrument the Australian Government can accede to that shows, in an absolutely clear manner, that Australia is a country that is interacting peacefully with the region and has no hostile intent whatsoever (quoted in Kerin 2005: 2).

What is striking about this comment is that even someone as intelligent and well-informed about us as Natalegawa apparently believes that Australia's peaceful intent towards the region – and specifically towards Indonesia – cannot be taken for granted. Perhaps he does not really think this himself but is simply warning us that others may. Either way we should pay attention to this new and potentially dangerous factor in what is anyway a rather complicated bilateral relationship. One of the biggest challenges in strategic policy always is to understand how others – especially potential adversaries – see one's actions, attitudes and motivations. This can take a little work. On emotive issues there is a natural tendency to resist acknowledging the other's point of view. In a polarised environment it is discouraged by peer pressure. Understanding the other's point of view can seem like sympathising with them, or even agreeing with them. But it is worth the effort, because understanding the way others see us is a vital piece of data for framing our own policy. So we need to acknowledge the fact that Indonesians still feel, however wrongly, a deep sense of grievance about what happened in 1999, and a real sense of anxiety about Australia's future intentions.

REBUILDING TRUST

Indonesia's new-found anxieties about Australia will make it both harder and more important to build a new defence relationship. Much was claimed on both sides in the 1980s and 1990s about the benefits of the relationship that was constructed in those years, and most of it was highly exaggerated. But it did have two valuable effects: it provided Australia with reassurance about Indonesia's intentions, and it fostered personal contact between ADF and TNI officers, which helped to prevent a clash between the ADF and the TNI in 1999. Both of these benefits are worth looking for again. Probably one reason why Indonesians have grown more suspicious of Australian intentions over the past few years is simply that we have seen less of one another because of the collapse of the defence relationship after East Timor. That has meant there has been less opportunity for Australians to explain, and for Indonesians to see for themselves, what we are up to. Building a new defence relationship that allows more contact must help.

How about the idea of a new security agreement? I have a hunch that Indonesia's interest in negotiating a bilateral security agreement is largely motivated by its fears of Australia's future strategic intentions. If so, it may seek language in the agreement that tries to limit Australia's actions in some future crisis. That would make agreement hard to reach. It may be counterproductive for Australia to resist such language, because that would only reaffirm Indonesian suspicions about our intentions. But if Canberra accepted such language it would be strongly criticised in Australia's domestic political debate. So it would probably be a mistake to try to use a new security agreement as a key instrument in addressing Indonesian concerns. On balance, this is probably an idea whose time has not yet come. Trying and failing to produce a substantive agreement might only make matters worse. Reaching an unsubstantive one is not worth the effort.

What is needed instead are frank exchanges on the specific issues that are causing concern between the two countries. Of these the most obvious is West Papua. This is indeed a difficult and potentially dangerous question between

Australia and Indonesia. No one should doubt Canberra's sincerity when it says that Australia supports Indonesia's territorial integrity and West Papua's place within it. But equally, Indonesians are right to wonder how an Australian government would react if separatist activism grows, if that activism provokes violent repression by the TNI and if international opinion starts to be mobilised by vivid press reporting of that repression. I think most Australians involved in the management of the bilateral relationship would agree that this is the most dangerous credible scenario we could face. Many Indonesians would suspect that Australia was supporting any separatist movement. As evidence of repression grew, any Australian government would come under huge pressure from domestic opinion to provide such support. Escalation to a full-blown crisis could happen quite quickly.

Of course the prime responsibility for avoiding this kind of disaster lies with Jakarta. The effective management of separatist sentiment in West Papua is Indonesia's challenge. It will take patient and generous statesmanship, of the kind that seems to have helped achieve a settlement in Aceh. We can only hope, as SBY has hinted, that the Aceh settlement will provide a model of sorts for West Papua. But Australia has a big stake in the success of such a settlement, and our policies and approaches may influence its chances. In particular, if Indonesian policy makers and opinion leaders suspect – as some seem to – that separatist sentiment in West Papua is at least in part the result of Australian agitation, they will be less likely to take seriously the grievances that underpin that sentiment, and more likely to resort to harsh and oppressive measures. We urgently need to find ways to persuade them that whatever the merit of separatist grievances, they are not simply an artefact of Australian interference.

One way to help do that is to straighten out our account of what happened concerning East Timor in 1998–99. The most potent source of misunderstanding between Australia and Indonesia in the years since 1999 has been the way in which Australia's distorted version of what happened – our 'liberation' of East Timor – has reinforced Indonesia's own distorted version of events. To counteract that, we in Australia need to give a more honest account which explains that we did not set out to secure East Timor's independence, nor did we ever want to deploy the ADF to take over the province. Our account needs to acknowledge frankly that President Habibie deserves more credit for East Timor's independence than any Australian, and that Interfet succeeded so well in large part because Indonesia – in the end – allowed it to succeed. This revision of what has started to become a cherished national myth in Australia would be no easy task.

Another step we could take to counteract Indonesian anxiety would be to explain better the direction of our broader strategic policy. There has been no comprehensive explanation of the purpose and direction of our defence planning since the defence white paper in 2000. Even close study by well-informed analysts leaves real doubts about why we are building some new capabilities, and how we see our future role in the region. The government's sudden adoption in recent years of a new policy of more active intervention in the South Pacific, while eminently sensible in its own terms, may have added to the uncertainty among those who observe our policies from afar, and with an incomplete understanding of our interests and priorities. There would be real merit in Canberra making a special effort to explain to Indonesians what all this means and how it fits together. Plenty of Australians would be interested too.

POLITICAL CONSTRAINTS

It is only sensible to recognise that nothing can be done to help reduce Indonesian suspicion of Australia, and to start rebuilding trust, without both sides being willing to make a substantial effort, to take some real political risks and to pay some real political costs. Today this is as true in Jakarta as it is in Canberra. One of the new dynamics in the relationship is the democratisation of Indonesian foreign policy, in which Australia has become one of the key political footballs. Any Indonesian leader who tries to reshape negative perceptions of Australia will pay a political price. The good news is that SBY seems to be willing to pay at least part of that price.

I am less confident that the same can be said of Australia's leaders. For many years the relationship, including the defence relationship, between Australia and Indonesia was supported by a bipartisan consensus in Australia. That consensus recognised that the relationship would never be popular among Australian voters, but that it was important nonetheless. The consensus collapsed in 1998, led initially from the Labor side of politics by Laurie Brereton as shadow foreign minister, and followed enthusiastically enough by the government. As is usual in such cases, a retreat to populism was presented as a triumph of plain commonsense over elitism. The longer-term cost will become clearer now, if the government decides it is serious about rebuilding a defence relationship with Indonesia. So far there has been little sign that it is willing to pay a serious political price by trying to lead public opinion on the value and importance of a good defence relationship with Indonesia. Without that we will get nowhere. So unless we are willing to take the kinds of steps I have outlined above to start alleviating those suspicions, it may be better to leave things as they are. Raising false expectations may only make things worse.

We should not, however, repeat the mistakes of last time. The defence relationship with Indonesia has long been plagued by unrealistic expectations. Those involved on the Australian side have too often believed – and too often encouraged others to believe – that the purpose of the relationship was to provide a means by which we could remould the TNI in the image of the ADF. This was always unrealistic: the TNI is too strong an institution, too deeply embedded in its society, to be shaped by the kind of passing impressions that its contacts with the ADF might make. To think otherwise is naive and narcissistic. A new defence relationship should keep its feet firmly on the ground. It will be enough if we can get back into the humble but vital business of helping each side to understand the other's policies, and our respective views of how our long-term regional goals and policies intersect.

Despite the difficulties I have mentioned here, the prospects for doing this modest work are quite favourable. In SBY we have an Indonesian leader we can work with, and who can speak directly to Australians in a way none of his predecessors have ever managed. In John Howard we have a leader whose credentials as a defender of Australia's interests in the region, especially in relation to Indonesia, make it easier in many ways for him to sell to Australian voters the need to work effectively with our big neighbour. In Indonesia we have seen the remarkably swift and so far peaceful evolution of democratic government. And in our wider region we have major strategic and security dynamics which affirm the essential congruence of our enduring strategic interests. That is not a bad start.

NOTE

1 In 1986 *Sydney Morning Herald* journalist David Jenkins reported on the wealth that President Soeharto and his children and cronies had amassed while he was in office. The Indonesian government responded by cancelling the visa-on-arrival agreement between Indonesia and Australia, issuing a blanket ban on all Australian journalists and cancelling automatic rights for Royal Australian Air Force planes to fly over Indonesian territory. Relations between the two countries suffered a major setback.

6 THE WAR ON TERROR: THE PRIMACY OF NATIONAL RESPONSE

Rizal Sukma

Until the late 1980s, the Association of Southeast Asian Nations (ASEAN) was often described as a success in managing regional security. However, this positive image changed quickly with the end of the Cold War, and ASEAN was soon seen as a regional organisation in need of new meaning and relevance. Talk about the declining role of ASEAN – in terms of both intramural cooperation and extra-mural relations – began to grow stronger and louder after the region was swept by financial crisis in 1997. With the world now confronting the challenge of overcoming terrorism, ASEAN is under even greater pressure to prove itself as an organisation worthy of existence, and still relevant.

As a regional organisation in a part of the world that has been dubbed the 'second front' in the war against terror, ASEAN is understandably expected to play an important and active role in combating terrorism. However, it is precisely on this front that current criticisms of ASEAN have been directed. It has been asserted, for example, that 'the ASEAN approach against international terrorism might be viewed as slow, incremental, and turgid particularly in addressing and containing the growth of Islamic extremism in the region' (de Castro 2004: 208). It has been stated also that 'ASEAN as an organization has done relatively little to coordinate the substantial counterterrorism efforts of its member states' (Dillon and Pasicolan 2002: 1) And 'even after the bombing of the Sari Club in Bali in October 2002, there was little substantial counterterrorism cooperation among the ASEAN states' (Chow 2005: 302). In short, criticism of ASEAN since 11 September 2001 has focused on 'the lack of meaningful and substantial cooperation' in the war against terrorism at the regional level, which 'would not only strengthen the currently operating terrorist organizations, but also open up the possibility for new organizations to operate from Southeast Asia' (Swanström 2005: 11).

Some of this criticism is valid. Because terrorism is often transnational in nature, it seems logical to argue that the response would be much more effective if it were undertaken collectively at the regional level. For that reason, ASEAN is expected to 'do more' on a collective basis. The reality, however, is that the national response still has primacy in the war on terror. This chapter argues that while regional cooperation is clearly necessary, the central role of national response should not be overlooked, given constraints on regional cooperation due to the nature of terrorism in the region, domestic sensitivities and the nature of ASEAN cooperation itself. Observers therefore need to be realistic in expecting ASEAN to do more on a collective basis.

The discussion is divided into three sections. The first section looks at ASEAN's response to the threat of terrorism since September 11. The second section discusses the limits of regional cooperation in combating terrorism and analyses the effects of the war against terror on ASEAN and regional security in Southeast Asia. The third section explains why the national response to terrorism, given the difficulties posed by the lack of a common regional strategy, serves as an important element in the war on terrorism in Southeast Asia.

ASEAN'S RESPONSE TO TERRORISM

As an organisation, ASEAN's coordinated response to the problem of terrorism began in the context of the need to counter transnational crime, a problem that had become an increasingly important focus of ASEAN security cooperation since the end of the Cold War. In December 1997, ASEAN issued a declaration on transnational crime (ASEAN 1997) and instituted regular ministerial meetings to coordinate the work of the region's law ministers and attorneys-general, national police chiefs and other ASEAN bodies. Terrorism, while included, was not given special attention, because at the time ASEAN was more concerned with problems such as people and drug trafficking, arms smuggling and piracy. Indeed, no mention was made of terrorism either in the ASEAN Vision 2020 promulgated in December 1997 or in the 1998 Hanoi Plan of Action (Chow 2005: 304). In 1999, ASEAN adopted an ASEAN Plan of Action to Combat Transnational Crime, to implement the declaration on transnational crime.

The terrorist attacks on 11 September quickly changed regional perceptions on the issue. In November 2001, at the Seventh ASEAN Summit in Brunei, ASEAN leaders signed a Declaration on Joint Action to Counter Terrorism which acknowledged terrorism as 'a profound threat to international peace and security' and as posing 'a direct challenge to the attainment of peace, progress and prosperity of ASEAN and the realisation of ASEAN Vision 2020' (ASEAN 2001). The leaders called for a series of measures to combat terrorism, includ-

ing closer cooperation among law enforcement agencies, early signing/ratifica-
tion of or accession to all relevant anti-terrorist conventions, exchange of information and intelligence on terrorist organisations, and the development of
capacity-building programs to enhance the capability of ASEAN members to
investigate, detect, monitor and report on terrorist acts.

These measures were then incorporated into the terrorism component of the
work program adopted by ASEAN governments in Kuala Lumpur in May
2002, as an integral part of a joint communiqué on transnational crime
(ASEAN 2002). Under the work plan, ASEAN agreed that cooperation would
focus on six areas, namely information exchange, legal matters, law enforcement, institutional capacity building, training and extra-regional cooperation,
with progress to be reviewed at subsequent meetings of the relevant ASEAN
ministers.

The ASEAN declaration on terrorism laid out what needed to be done by
ASEAN, without providing specific guidance on how this would be achieved.
Chow (2005: 313) notes, for example, that 'the declaration did not address ...
the methods for combating terrorism through multilateral cooperation'. This
clearly suggests differences of opinion among ASEAN countries on how the
war on terror should be tackled at the regional and global levels. While
acknowledging the need for 'concerted action' to combat terrorism, the declaration and subsequent communiqué was framed with two important qualifications.
First, the joint communiqué makes it clear that 'the sovereignty, territorial
integrity and domestic laws of each ASEAN Member Country shall be respected
and upheld in undertaking the fight against terrorism' (ASEAN 2002). Second,
the declaration on joint action to counter terrorism affirms that 'at the international level the United Nations should play a major role in [combating terror-
ism]' (ASEAN 2001). This latter point signals the differences among ASEAN
countries regarding the role of the United States in the war on terror (Chow
2005: 309).

The pace of regional cooperation in combating terrorism began to accelerate
after the Bali bombings in October 2002. Meeting during the Eighth ASEAN
Summit in November 2002, ASEAN leaders condemned 'the heinous terrorist
attacks in Bali' and declared that they were 'determined to carry out and build
on the specific measures outlined in the ASEAN Declaration on Joint Action to
Counter Terrorism'. They also promised 'to intensify our efforts, collectively
and individually, to prevent, counter, and suppress the activities of terrorist
groups in the region'. The Bali bombings served as a wake-up call for the region
and provided an impetus for ASEAN members to step up their counterterrorism
measures. However, intra-ASEAN cooperation remains limited to areas previously agreed on by member states, mainly information and intelligence exchange, training, seminars and law enforcement.

THE LIMITS OF REGIONAL COOPERATION

The discussion of ASEAN's response to terrorism in the previous section is not meant to overlook the regional body's achievements on this front. Much has been accomplished through the cooperation of members. Intelligence exchange, for example, led to the arrest of Singaporean citizen Mas Selamat Kastari, head of the Jemaah Islamiyah (JI) network in Singapore, by Indonesian police in February 2003. A number of training courses run by Singapore in 2003 on aviation security, intelligence analysis, post-blast investigation, and bomb and explosive identification have also improved the capacity of law enforcement agencies to conduct counterterrorism operations (Singh 2003: 214–15). While some see ASEAN's issuance of various declarations as nothing more than rhetoric, within the context of the organisation itself they are a significant way for members to register their political commitment towards one another. More importantly, the place of terrorism in the ASEAN agenda has shifted from being merely a domestic issue to being a common regional problem.

To go beyond what has been done so far would require a new kind of commitment and level of cooperation from ASEAN members; it would require not only the transformation of ASEAN from a 'diplomatic community' to a 'security community', but also the consolidation of democracy in key ASEAN member states. In other words, as matters stand at present, there are limits to the collective efforts to combat terrorism that can be carried out. These limits to regional cooperation are defined by the nature of terrorist threats in the region, domestic sensitivities regarding terrorism, and the nature of ASEAN cooperation itself.

The nature and characteristics of terrorist threats in Southeast Asia

The problem of terrorism in Southeast Asia is certainly not new. Especially in the 1950s and 1960s, some regional states faced the threat of insurgencies in their respective countries. In the late 1970s and early 1980s, elements of radical Islamic groups seeking to destabilise the authoritarian New Order government carried out a string of terrorist attacks in Indonesia. However, the magnitude of the threat posed by contemporary terrorist networks is far greater than anything experienced so far. The capacity of the terrorists to inflict damage, in terms of both loss of life and physical destruction, is unprecedented in the history of terrorism in Southeast Asia. This was demonstrated by the Bali bombings in October 2002, the Marriott Hotel bombing in Jakarta in August 2003 and the bombing near the Australian embassy in Jakarta in September 2004, as well as a series of bombings in Manila and other parts of the Philippines.

In the immediate aftermath of September 11, terrorism experts engaged in a vigorous debate on the nature and characteristics of the terrorist threat and terrorist organisations in the region. Debate centred on the question of whether the terrorist networks in the region were part of an al-Qaeda-linked global network or were home grown. Due to the destructive capacity displayed by the terrorists in a number of attacks, many experts concluded that Southeast Asia had become a home for the global terrorist network of al-Qaeda. Huang (2002a), for example, claimed that 'what one finds in Southeast Asia is an international terrorist network as well-grounded, well-supported, far-reaching and threatening as al-Qaeda', and that 'many terrorist organizations in the region in fact have close and long-running connections not only with each other, but to Osama bin Laden's al-Qaeda as well' (Huang 2002b). The international media has depicted the region as a safe haven for terrorists and a hotbed of terrorism and terrorist groups. An article in *The Age*, for example, claimed that 'the United States believes dozens, possibly hundreds, of al-Qaeda fighters have slipped out of Afghanistan into Indonesia' (Alcorn 2002).

Others, however, saw the presence of transnational links of global proportion in Southeast Asia as mere speculation without compelling evidence. Tim Dodd of the *Australian Financial Review*, for example, said that 'in Indonesia, the extent of links with Al Qaeda are unclear' and that 'there is still no hard evidence that Al Qaeda exists there in an organised way' (Dodd 2002). It has also been argued that the terrorist groups in Southeast Asia are locally oriented, mainly pursuing domestic political agendas, and are not necessarily the local or regional arms of an al-Qaeda global terrorist network. Most governments in the region, while acknowledging the threat of terrorism, would also dismiss the accusation that their country had become a base for an al-Qaeda network.

While debate on the extent of al-Qaeda's presence in Southeast Asia continues, few would disagree that the threat of terrorism in Southeast Asia is real and alarming. None would disagree that some forms of linkages among national terrorist groups, and between them and the global terrorist networks, may exist. However, while the regional links are evident in the case of the JI network, the nature and extent of global links – especially those with al-Qaeda – remain difficult to determine.[1] Reports by the International Crisis Group on JI, for example, suggest that the network is regionally directed and largely autonomous (ICG 2002, 2003b). In other words, the nature of the 'link' between national, regional and global terrorist networks, whether inspirational, ideological or operational, cannot easily be defined.

The difficulty of determining the precise nature of terrorist groups in Southeast Asia – national, regional or global – reflects the complex characteristics of the problem of terrorism in the region. Indeed, it is even difficult for Southeast Asian states to agree on which groups can be regarded as terrorist. ASEAN member states agree on the existence of JI as a key regional terrorist organisation and support the decision by the UN Security Council to enter this organisation on the list of banned terrorist organisations.[2] However, they differ as to which other groups should be declared terrorist organisations. While some ASEAN countries regard Indonesian groups such as Laskar Jihad and Majelis Mujahidin Indonesia (Council of Indonesian Mujahideen) as terrorist organisations, for example, Indonesia continues to view them as legitimate organisations. In the Philippines as well, the government is reluctant to brand Moro separatist organisations, especially the Moro Islamic Liberation Front (MILF), as terrorist organisations.

Part of the difficulty stems from the fact that it is not easy to establish the connections between Islam and terrorism. Reading and understanding Islam through a prism of terrorism will be misleading. Such an approach distorts the reality of important nuances between radicalism and terrorism, which in turn could lead to wrong policy prescriptions in dealing with the problem of terrorism. As Professor Ahmad Syafii Maarif of Indonesia's largest modernist Islamic organisation, Muhammadiyah, has made clear, radicalism 'refers to a set of attitudes and ways to express [a political belief], the latter clearly embraces criminal acts for political purposes' (Maarif 2002). He also sees radicalism as 'an intra-religious problem that should be dealt with by the Muslim community itself'. Despite all the publicity and flurry of interest in the media surrounding radical groups such as Laskar Jihad and Front Pembela Islam (Islamic Defenders Front), the motives and actions of these groups remain anchored in domestic Indonesian politics.[3] Suggestions that these groups have maintained close links with al-Qaeda remain unsubstantiated. In this regard, it has been pointed out, correctly, that 'without making a distinction you drive all of these [Muslim] groups to be more radicalised, to be more extremist because they thought that you are attacking the practice of their religion by accusing all of them of being terrorists' (Calvin Simms, journalism professor at Princeton University, quoted in Krastev 2002).

The most problematic aspect of terrorism in Southeast Asia is the presence of a religious, especially Islamic, dimension to the problem – problematic because the terrorists themselves try to make a connection between Islam and their terrorist acts. The problem is especially acute in countries such as Indonesia where Islam constitutes the majority religion. The Bali bombers, for example, made extensive use of religious quotations to justify their evil acts.[4] Moreover, many of those who have been accused of being terrorists, or who are seen as potential terrorists, are associated in some form or other with Islamic institutions. The use of religious arguments and the link with Islamic institutions could have a psychological effect on the wider Muslim community, which could easily construe the war on terror as a war against Islam itself.

The problem of terrorism in Southeast Asia is concentrated in certain countries only, leading to varying degrees of concern within ASEAN. Terrorism poses the most serious challenge in the five original ASEAN countries, namely Indonesia, Malaysia, the Philippines, Singapore and Thailand. When the religious dimension is factored in, then it is terrorism in Indonesia, and to a lesser degree the southern Philippines and southern Thailand, that raises most concern. Again, the concentration of the problem in just a few countries reinforces the unwanted perception of a link between Islam and terrorism. Consequently, there is a tendency within Southeast Asia to see the problem of terrorism as largely a problem of Islam. In such circumstances, it is hardly surprising that ASEAN member states are concerned about a possible division emerging within the association along Muslim/non-Muslim lines.

Domestic sensitivities

Terrorism is a major source of domestic sensitivities in ASEAN member states, especially in countries where the threat of terrorism is relatively serious and where Islam constitutes the majority religion (as in Indonesia and Malaysia) or in countries with significant Muslim minorities (as in the Philippines and Thailand). These domestic sensitivities involve two main concerns. First, there is concern in some countries that the war on terror may affect domestic stability, because of a possible alteration in national power relations, a deterioration in inter-religious relations or growing feelings of alienation among the Muslim minority. Second, there is concern about the possible direct involvement of an extra-regional power, especially the United States, in the war on terror in Southeast Asia.

Indonesia, for example, has been caught by the need to preserve and maintain vulnerable domestic power relations in the post-authoritarian era. The main challenge for the government is to balance the need to maintain security (by combating terrorism) against the need to preserve liberty. An aggressive policy which ignores such a balance would face challenges from both the country's Islamic forces and its secular pro-democracy forces. Indonesia's government was, and still is, worried that such a policy could easily be construed as an attempt to discredit Islamic political forces, which have become an important player in domestic politics since the collapse of the New Order regime in May 1998. Similarly, an aggressive policy is opposed by the secular pro-democracy forces, which see such an approach as a return to authoritarian methods. In combating terrorism, Indonesia's government must also avoid giving the impression that it is merely serving the United States and following the US-led war on terror.

Concerns about the effects of terrorism on inter-race relations are more visible in Singapore. The uncovering of JI networks and the arrest of several terror suspects in Singapore in 2001–02 clearly pointed to the participation of some Singaporean Muslims in regional terrorist networks. The government has therefore taken special care to assure the Malay population that the war on terror in the country is not directed against Islam. The sensitivity of the problem in Singapore is reinforced by the fact that the country has been a staunch supporter of the American-led war on terror.

In Thailand and the Philippines, the primary concern is how to deal with terrorism in Pattani and Mindanao without alienating the Muslim minority in the southern part of each country. The insurgency in southern Thailand clearly poses a serious challenge for Bangkok in maintaining harmony between Pattani Malays and the rest of the population. The government is worried that any involvement by external actors would exacerbate the problem, so it has strongly maintained that the problem is an internal one that will need to be resolved by Thailand alone. The Philippines is facing similar problems with the MILF in Mindanao; the army has conducted counterinsurgency operations against the MILF, but at the same time the government is maintaining the hope for a political solution.

Concerns about the involvement of an extra-regional power, especially the United States, in the region are strongly felt in Indonesia and Malaysia. They both tend to see the problem of terrorism in their respective countries as a domestic problem with a regional dimension, and therefore dismiss the possibility of links with al-Qaeda. It is likely that both Indonesia and Malaysia are concerned that if such links do exist, then the United States may be pressed to get involved directly in eradicating such terrorist groups. Their wariness about the direct involvement of the United States in a war on terror in Southeast Asia was clearly demonstrated when the two countries 'disapproved' of the presence of American forces in the Philippines to 'advise' the Philippine army on counterinsurgency operations against the Abu Sayyaf Group.

The nature of ASEAN cooperation

The limits of regional cooperation in combating terrorism are also shaped by the nature of ASEAN cooperation itself. For more than a decade since the end of the Cold War, ASEAN has been struggling to redefine its role in order to reaffirm its relevance and efficacy in responding to a new security environment. Since then, it has been trying to resolve persistent traditional security issues such as rivalry among major powers, intra-ASEAN territorial disputes, territorial disputes in the South China Sea, and some members' traditional suspicions of other members. At the same time, ASEAN has actively directed its efforts to address the increasing importance of non-traditional security challenges in the region, by expanding ASEAN's membership, creating an ASEAN Regional Forum as the principal forum for security dialogue in Asia, strengthening the ASEAN Secretariat and other institution-building measures.

The post-September 11 security environment – at the national, regional and global levels – has certainly increased the magnitude of the security challenges facing ASEAN. The rise of terrorism as a lethal new threat clearly adds to the security burden of ASEAN. While some key member states remain preoccupied with internal conflicts such as communal violence in Indonesia and separatism in Indonesia and the Philippines, the problem of terrorism clearly highlights the interconnectedness of national problems on the one hand with regional security and stability on the other. The threat of terrorism in the region serves as the latest reminder to all member states that security interdependence has become an undeniable reality in Southeast Asia. What happens in one country certainly does have an impact in others.

Despite the growing magnitude of the threat of terrorism, ASEAN's approach to security has never been driven by an over-riding preoccupation with a single issue. Since its inception in August 1967, ASEAN has always approached security matters in a comprehensive manner. For Southeast Asian countries, security has always encompassed a wide array of issues on the social, cultural, economic, political and military fronts. Problems in those areas – especially within the domestic context – are seen as having the potential to destabilise nation-states and thereby regional peace and security. Based on this conception of security, ASEAN has always made a distinction between what we now conceptualise as traditional and non-traditional threats. Until very recently, ASEAN countries tended to see non-traditional security issues primarily as the domestic problem of a member state requiring a national solution. The growing salience of non-traditional problems since the end of the Cold War has forced ASEAN to recognise the important of cooperation between states in dealing with such issues.

In resolving regional security issues, ASEAN has from the outset taken two inter-related approaches. First, non-traditional security threats have been left to individual member states to resolve, especially through nation-building measures. Second, to assist individual states to resolve such problems, regional cooperation has been seen as necessary to create a peaceful external environment so that states will not be distracted from domestic priorities. These approaches later evolved into a strategy of building regional resilience, a concept influenced by Indonesian thinking on *ketahanan nasional* (national resilience). Such thinking postulates that

> if each member nation can accomplish an overall national development and over-come internal threats, regional resilience will automatically result much in the same way as a chain derives its overall strength from the strength of its constituent parts (Wanandi 1984: 305).

In other words, ASEAN believed that the management of relations between states in the region should be founded on the sanctity of the national sovereignty of member states. Regional cooperation was sought in order to reinforce, not erode, sovereignty.

In the context of the war on terror, however, it has been pointed out that:

> combating international terrorism at the regional level calls not only for coordination of policies, but also for the abandonment of some sovereignty in favour of trans-regional cooperation. The principle of non-intervention needs to be dealt with, as it

creates immense problems for regional cooperation over terrorist conflicts (Swanström 2005: 9).

In reality, it is unlikely that these two requirements – the abandonment of some sovereignty and non-intervention – would be fulfilled by ASEAN. When coupled with domestic sensitivities, deep regional cooperation to combat terrorism becomes even more difficult. This was clearly demonstrated during the ASEAN Summit in Phnom Penh in November 2002, when ASEAN officials maintained that member countries would not pressure Indonesia to take tougher action in the fight against terrorism despite the fact that the summit took place only a few weeks after the Bali bombings.[5] Indonesia's sensitivities were also evident in the angry response of its government and people to a comment by Senior Minister Lee Kuan Yew of Singapore in February 2002 that Indonesia had become 'a nest of terrorism'. The comment was seen by many in Indonesia as interference in Indonesia's internal affairs. Indonesians were also irritated by various remarks by Malaysian officials that it had not done enough to combat terrorism.

NATIONAL RESPONSE: THE CASE OF INDONESIA

The three factors discussed above – the nature and characteristics of terrorism in Southeast Asia, domestic sensitivities on this issue and the nature of ASEAN cooperation – serve to limit what ASEAN as a unit can do to combat terrorism. In the absence of comprehensive and deep regional cooperation, the national response to terrorism becomes a significant element in the war on terror in Southeast Asia. Therefore, it is imperative that more attention be paid to strengthening the efficacy of the national response in combating the threat of terrorism in the region. This is particularly important in the case of Indonesia, where counterterrorism measures have been seen as inadequate.

In an Indonesian context, there are at least four main advantages to be gained from a national response to terrorism. First, the national government would be able to disrupt terrorist networks despite the absence of a regional consensus on what terrorism means and who the terrorists are. This would simplify the measures required by each individual country and allow them to focus on the need to take action against suspected terrorist groups or individual members of terrorist networks. Second, a national response makes it easier for the government to avoid the impression that it is cracking down on terrorism only to fulfil the agenda of a foreign country, especially the United States. Through a national response, the government can demonstrate and convince the public that it is merely responding to the growing threat to national security. Third, because a national response is less associated with foreign agendas, the national government is better placed to forge national support from mainstream groups in dealing with terrorist groups that justify their acts in terms of Islamic teachings. Fourth, as the problem is also related to domestic sensitivities within the Muslim community, a solution can be sought within the domestic Muslim community itself.

What needs to be done is to strengthen the national capacity to deal with terrorism. Indonesia, for example, needs to strengthen its capacity to address the underlying causes creating a favourable environment for terrorism. The country's intelligence capacity and professionalism are still weak and there has been a lack of coordination among the state institutions responsible for disrupting and undermining terrorist networks. An improvement in these two areas is badly needed. The capacity and professionalism of law enforcement agencies, especially the police and the legal system, also need to be improved. Reform of the police force needs to be deepened and accelerated so that it can function as a truly professional institution within a democratic order. Over the longer run, Indonesia will need all the support it can get to consolidate its democracy and accelerate economic recovery.

Cooperation between Indonesia and Australia serves as one illustration of a national response that is helping to build a more effective framework to combat terrorism. After the Bali bombings in October 2002, the Indonesian and Australian police forces worked effectively together to investigate the attacks, hunt down the perpetrators and bring them to justice. Since then, cooperation beween the two countries in combating terrorism has intensified significantly. One of the most important joint initiatives in this regard has been the establishment of a counterterrorism centre, the Jakarta Center for Law Enforcement Cooperation, to which Australia is contributing A$36.8 million over five years. Australian assistance has also extended to other areas of counterterrorism, including a greater focus on travel security, the strengthening of airport, immigration and customs capabilities, and the development of a capacity to disrupt terrorist financing. Australia has contributed A$4.7 million for the establishment of a transnational crime centre in Jakarta; it will serve as a focal point within the Indonesian police force for the prevention, identification and dismantling of all forms of transnational crime, including terrorism. Indeed, Indonesia's counterterrorism capacity has improved significantly due to the support and assistance of the Australian government.

To be fully effective, however, such support must be backed up by a significant improvement within Indonesia itself. It has often been argued that the crux of the problem is instability and a socioeconomic crisis in Indonesia, and the absence of state authority in dealing with these problems. The emergence of radical Islamic groups in Indonesia, for example, is better understood within the context of grievances against the oppressive state policy during the New Order period, a backdrop of social and economic problems, and perceived and actual injustices in society. Many of these groups are the product of decades of bad governance and an absence of democracy; they are home-grown groups with a domestic rather than international focus. As a perceptive scholar has aptly stated, 'dealing with [militant groups] intellectually is the task for moderate Muslims' (Schulze 2002a: 10). When such groups resort to violence in expressing their demands, the problem should be dealt with through the corridor of law enforcement rather than through the use of military might.

The possibility of an increase in the number of Indonesians attracted to and sympathising with the ideology and worldview of radical Islam should not be discounted entirely. The appeal of radical Islam will increase if the state fails to bring about a speedy economic recovery, and if it fails to consolidate its democracy. Indeed, it has been acknowledged that the real threat to Indonesia:

> lies not in Indonesian Islam and Islamic politics, but in continued economic fragility, lawlessness and inadequate law enforcement, on-going corruption, badly managed decentralization, inattention to past abuses and inequalities, an unresponsive power-focused political elite, and the incapacity or unwillingness of armed services and police to deal with lawlessness and internal conflicts while respecting fundamental human rights' (Dagg 2001: 5).

A failure by the Indonesian state to address these challenges would cultivate a deep distrust in the merits of the non-theocratic nature of Indonesia's current political and economic system. Islam as conceived by radical groups might then be seen as an alternative remedy to the current social, economic and political ills plaguing the nation. In that context, the ideology and worldview of radical Islam might have greater appeal for a frustrated population. As Jones (2002) argues, such a scenario can be prevented 'not merely by cracking down on radical Muslims, but by providing alternatives to the way of life they offer'. These alternatives clearly include the ability to ensure democracy works effectively. The growth of radicalism, which creates a favourable environment for terrorism, can be checked if Indonesia manages to accelerate its economic recovery and establish a solid democracy, based on the rule of law, that guarantees freedom for every citizen. Oppression is not the answer to radicalism, and will only lead to more radicalism. The experience during the three decades of New Order rule clearly demonstrated this. Despite all the difficulties and challenges the country is currently facing, no Indonesian would want a return of New Order authoritarianism in which personal and communal rights are curbed in the name of the ideology of *stabilitas* (stability) and *pembangunan* (development).

NOTES

1 For an excellent analysis on this topic, see Hamilton-Hart (2005).
2 Despite this, government officials and leaders in Indonesia have avoided acknowledging the existence of JI in public.

3   See, for example, Dagg (2001: 3–4), Schulze (2002a: 12, 2002b) and Emmerson
    (2001: 5).
4   See, for example, Samudra (2004).
5   'ASEAN won't pressure Indonesia over terrorism', *Sydney Morning Herald*, 5 Nov-
    ember 2002, <http://www.smh.com.au>.

PART III

Mutual Perceptions and Irritations

7   STRANGE, SUSPICIOUS PACKAGES

David Reeve

'There's a worrying emotional element in Australia's relations with its biggest neigh-bour. It's difficult to portray Australia as racist ... Australia has easily accommodated a large number of Asian and other migrants. But the assumption of cultural superior-ity ... from an earlier historical period is too general for the relationship to become easy' (Rosihan Anwar 2005b).

'It's a different story to the official one when Australians and Indonesians talk ... The message that came out of the talks was stark. Whereas at the top levels of Australia's relationship with Indonesia the feeling might be one of increasing closeness and co-operation, as the politicians keep telling us, below that surface there lingers deep mis-understanding and suspicion on both sides' (Banham 2005).[1]

This chapter endorses and underlines recent analyses that have suggested a dan-gerous disjunction between elite and popular perceptions towards Australia and Indonesia, within the two countries. There is much goodwill and cooperation at senior levels of government on both sides; there are sound and increasing people-to-people contacts. But as Patrick Walters wrote in *The Australian*:

A strange paradox continues to afflict Australia's bilateral relations with Indonesia.

While people-to-people links strengthen year-by-year, opinion polls show a steadily increasing proportion of Australians now nominate Indonesia as our princi-pal long-term security threat. ...

They demonstrate that Australian governments still need to address lingering pop-ular perceptions about the long-term direction of Indonesia.

The number of Indonesian students studying in Australia has more than doubled in the past decade. ...

Yet by contrast, the number of Australians studying Indonesian at schools and uni-versities continues to fall in the wake of government funding cuts to Asian studies in schools (Walters 2004).

What Patrick Walters wrote in 2004 has been emphasised by events in 2005, including the reactions in both countries to the media circus of Schapelle Corby's trial.

Meanwhile, a sign of high-level goodwill was the delight of the Australian press with the visit of Indonesian President Susilo Bambang Yudhoyono (SBY) on 3–5 April 2005. Most commentators followed SBY and Australian Prime Minister John Howard in proclaiming a new era, a landmark deal, a comprehensive partnership, a remarkable growth in relations, a lasting bridge, a truly historic visit. This sense of a breakthrough, the warmest reporting on Indonesia in a decade, is part of a striking recent enthusiasm for 'Asia' in the Australian media. No longer is Asia the arc of instability and crescent of crisis.

The Australian press also admired SBY himself. When SBY spoke of the often trivialised and caricatured picture of Indonesia in the Australian media, the *Sydney Morning Herald* said: 'If any individual can change the perception, this looks like the man to do it … It was not hard to share his optimism. This is a very impressive, serious man' (Seccombe 2005). *The Australian* spoke of SBY as 'a class act … obvious warmth and charm … the most competent individual to hold that post … A gifted politician, a moderate reformer, a competent technocrat' (Sheridan 2005).

As Patrick Walters has written, there is a group of well-to-do Indonesians who look on Australia positively for its education system, its medical services and its real estate opportunities. The cooperation between Australian and Indonesian police has been much strengthened. A new regional security centre has been established in Semarang with considerable Australian assistance and involvement. Australia's response to the tsunami was received positively in Indonesia, even if not as positively as one might believe from reading the Australian press coverage. Indonesia's role in helping the Australian government obtain a seat at the East Asia Summit in December has been very pleasing to both parties. There is an expanding network of people-to-people contacts. But these have not lessened the deep suspicions in parts of Indonesian and Australian society. In the following discussion I have used many quotations, to give a more accurate sense of the flavour of the opinions.

INDONESIAN PERCEPTIONS OF AUSTRALIA

Indonesians' suspicions of Australia are regularly expressed in the letters section of the Indonesian media. Five issues of concern to Indonesians are well known in Australia: East Timor, Afghanistan, Iraq, Australia's 'deputy sheriff' role in the region and its claim to have the right to make pre-emptive strikes. These were never going to win the approval of the Indonesian public, except perhaps among sophisticated members of the foreign policy elite who secretly welcome a long-term American role in the region as a stabilising counterweight to the rise of China.

There are four more irritants that are less well known in Australia: Australia's treatment of traditional Indonesian fishermen; its alleged involvement in bugging the Indonesian embassy; suspicions that Australian NGOs in Papua are at least gleaning intelligence, at worst preparing for another East Timor in Papua; and, most recently, Indonesian astonishment over Australian reactions to the Corby verdict.

A complex web of suspicion surrounds Australia's actions in East Timor in 1999. No detailed explanation of these actions has been mounted in Indonesia. Probably Australian officials were relieved enough when the first waves of anger died down in October 1999. I certainly felt that at the time, living in Yogyakarta amidst rising anger. Once the atmosphere of crisis had passed, it may have seemed best to let sleeping dogs lie. But it meant that Australian actions and views, fears and idealism, were not canvassed, and our motives remained suspect. The TV coverage showing large Australian soldiers pointing guns at militia who were forced to lie on the ground looked terrible on Indonesian TV, even when the coverage came from Australian cameras.

The most extreme (but fairly commonly canvassed) interpretation is that 'Australia' conspired to break part of Indonesia away, for territorial or strategic reasons, to gain access to oil reserves, from a wish to weaken Indonesia or out of hostility to Islam. At another point on the continuum is the view that John Howard played domestic politics with Indonesia's interests; at another, that whatever the rights and wrongs of the East Timor issue, 'Australia' was just too loud, too pushy and too provocative in a situation where 'Indonesia' was already embarrassed and vulnerable. All agree that 'Australia' was duplicitous in reversing its earlier understanding of Indonesia's role in East Timor.

Fears in Indonesia about a worldwide conspiracy against Islam are more widely held than most Australians realise. Since in Australia these seem to be fringe conspiracy theories, Australians can find it hard to believe that sensible Indonesians might take them seriously. They do. There are hard and softer versions of these views. Some Indonesians are convinced of a Jewish–Christian conspiracy and war against Islam, with Afghanistan and Iraq seeming to prove the point. Softer versions of these views are suspicion – or at least doubt – about the truth behind the 9/11 bombings in America and the Bali bombings in Indonesia. Could those accused have had the technical skills needed to carry out these acts? The crucial question, they say, is 'Who benefited?' They doubt the existence of Jemaah Islamiyah and dispute the role of its purported spiritual leader, Abu Bakar Ba'asyir; these are said to be a 'ghost' created by falsified American information, 'American fiction', the CIA and its allies.

Some of these views are evident in the articles below.[2]

'Australia's sins towards Indonesia'

In an article entitled 'Australia's sins towards Indonesia', Herry Nurdi (2005) touches on several of the themes that reoccur frequently in letters to the editor in Indonesia. He says:

It's on record that Australia has repeatedly wounded Indonesia's sovereignty as a free nation. From small issues up to problems that can't be brushed aside. Indonesia cannot remain silent. Don't let Australia become increasingly strident and ill mannered.

Five major Australian 'sins' are canvassed in this article. The first is the deaths and alleged ill-treatment of Indonesian traditional sailors/fishermen while in Australian custody. The article contains accusations of inadequate treatment, frequent deaths, Australian duplicity in taking over Sand Island (part of the Ashmore/Cartier group) since 1970, and special incentives for Australian water police to hunt traditional sailors. Almost 50 per cent of the article is taken up with the issue, indicating its prominence in discussions of Australia's failings.

Australia's second sin is to export 'forbidden goods' to Indonesia:

> Another currently hot issue is the many forbidden goods flying from that southern continent into Indonesia, especially Bali … Although these criminals have been found guilty, it's clear that there are still efforts to interfere by the Australian government, to free or at least lighten the punishment of those who are damaging the Indonesian younger generation with the forbidden goods they bring. … Bali is indeed a paradise for these carriers of illegal goods, most of which come from Australia.

'There are also political sins, even conspiracies', the article continues, citing as an example the bugging of the Indonesian embassy in Canberra, uncovered in 2004. An Australian intelligence body had allegedly bugged the workroom of the ambassador. 'Strangely', even after its discovery, the bug could not speedily be removed, as the embassy was required to get the permission of the Australian police to remove it. Major General Nachrowi Ramli supposedly confirmed the bugging, and that Australia had 'dared' (*berani*) to bug Indonesia's Palapa satellite. The bugging had apparently gone on since 1991.

Australia's fourth and 'peak' political sin has been its 'active involvement in encouraging East Timor to break away from Indonesia'. John Howard's famous letter to President Habibie was 'the first step in undermining Indonesia's sovereignty … And after that, we know how it went'. It ended with East Timor's independence.

> But in fact there are many contradictory stories about the active involvement of large nations like America and Australia in bringing active terrorist cells to life in East Timor to fan the flames of opposition to Indonesia at that time. Australia certainly seemed persistent in its involvement in the Timtim [East Timor] case. We have to understand, that the Timor Gap … is said to contain many rich energy sources.

Australia's fifth sin is to violate Indonesia's national sovereignty through its declaration of an Australian Maritime Identification Zone that extends into traditional Indonesian fishing areas:

> After improving its war technology, what is now a hot issue is that Australia has put forward its wishes to join in controlling Indonesia's waters …

> Especially after the Bali and Kuningan Bombings, which are widely said to be high-level manipulations, Australia is increasingly tightening its national security … Indeed, it is perfectly natural to secure the nation's own territory. But what is forbidden is when those activities threaten another nation's sovereignty, in this case Indonesia. And that cannot be allowed to go on for too long.

This is a straightforward piece of writing. The main attributes of Australia are: *dosa, lancang, kurang ajar, haram, durjana, merusak, konspiratif, berani, merongrong, ngotot* (sins, loud, disrespectful, forbidden, criminal, destructive, conspiratorial, brazen, undermining, perversely stubborn). Not a pretty list.

An Indonesian analysis

Asked during a radio interview to comment on reactions in Australia to the Corby verdict, Krishna Sen said that 'the attention of the Indonesian media has been on the Australian media' (Aedy 2005). This is evident in three articles written by veteran journalist Rosihan Anwar for *Waspada Online*. They draw heavily on Australian press statements and editorials and on analysis from the *New York Times* (Raymond Bonner) and the *International Herald Tribune* (Philip Bowring).[3] There can hardly be an Indonesian journalist more distinguished, seasoned or mainstream than Rosihan Anwar. A combination of summary and quotes from his articles is given below:

'Results of the Corby verdict'

The tone of Rosihan Anwar's column of 6 June 2005 is generally dispassionate and analytical. He comments on reactions in Australia and Indonesia as follows:

> The reaction of the Australian people towards Corby's verdict is very fierce. Not just threats but an attempt to kill Indonesian diplomats in Canberra.[4] …
> [In Indonesia] the case has aroused astonishment, questions and accusations that Australia has intervened in the Indonesian judicial system in ways that would not be tolerated by Australians if others did the same to them (Rosihan Anwar 2005a).

He cites an editorial in *The Australian* saying that beneath the hysteria and striking out at Indonesia lies an element of racism in Australia, and a broad view that Indonesia is a nation of corrupt politicians and Islamic terrorists.

'Australia's bad character'

On 13 June 2005, Rosihan Anwar comments that this is not the first time that drug-related arrests of Westerners have become a problem:

> But the popular reaction in Australian circles suggests that they expect special rights when they are overseas. … The Australian reaction will not please all its neighbours, who expect to be treated as sovereign nations (Rosihan Anwar 2005b).

Australians' generous response to the tsunami is noted and appreciated. 'But what is less admirable is the self-satisfaction', the proclamations of 'how generous we are'. Rosihan Anwar notes that newspaper headlines in Australia had stated that Australia had 'taken over leadership' in the Acehnese operations ... and dismissed Indonesia's own efforts or those of neighbours Singapore and Malaysia'. He adds:

> Fortunately very few people in the countries that received aid ever heard this boasting and big-mouthing. But this attitude clearly depicts Australia's problem in treating its neighbours, above all – but not only – Indonesia, as equals.

Another reasoned and serious article. Still, no reader could come away without feeling the force of the first and final phrase of the article: 'Australia's bad character'.

'Bang Bam'

Rosihan Anwar's third article, published on 20 June 2005, presents an overview of Australian reactions, including calls for a tourist boycott of Bali and for tsunami aid to be stopped (Rosihan Anwar 2005c). He describes a four-colour work of graffiti painted on the walls of the state parliament in Perth, which included the words 'Invade Indo' and 'Bang Bam' (referring to President Bambang Yudhoyono). He cites the role of tabloid journalism and shock jocks in further inflaming tensions.

'Australia's obsession with the Corby case is easy to see, but difficult to explain', he says. The common explanation is that Corby is 'one of us', in contrast to Australians of Asian descent in other Southeast Asian jails.

Rosihan Anwar traces Australia's antipathy to and fears of Asia to its nineteenth-century past, and the arrival of the Chinese. Until 20 years ago an Asian face was still relatively rare in Australia. Now Australian cities are a melting pot of Asian and other races, but 'it's very difficult to get rid of stubbornly persistent attitudes'. The article describes the attempts of Tim Lindsey, director of the Asian Law Centre at the University of Melbourne, to explain Indonesian law to Australians, and the flood of hostile emails he received in response to these attempts. It also reports the comments of Allan Gyngell, executive director of the Lowy Institute for International Policy, including the comment that Australians consider Indonesia as the greatest security threat to Australia, even ahead of China. The article summarises the views of Alan Dupont, senior fellow at the Lowy Institute for International Policy, on Indonesia's lack of capacity to threaten. In the article, Rosihan Anwar stresses how 'inward looking' Indonesians are.

The article argues that the relationship between Indonesia and Australia has always been marked by friction, but that in the first half of 2005 both governments took steps to improve it. It concludes with a quote from Sian Powell,

Jakarta correspondent for *The Australian*, suggesting that certain 'disgusting' Australians should think again and shut up.

Opinion pieces and letters to the editor

This section draws together half a dozen quotations from opinion pieces or readers' letters in two major newspapers, *Kompas* and *Jawa Pos*, during the period 3–17 June, all in response to Australian reactions to the Corby verdict. Three of the correspondents – two students, one lecturer – come from major universities, and one is a graduate of the Australian National University (ANU).

The first extract is from an opinion piece called 'Corby, Australia and us' by P.L.E. Priatna. He says he has lived in Melbourne and claims an interest in international affairs. Here the importance of the issue of Indonesian traditional fishermen is underlined:

> The Australian reactions [in the Corby Case] seem both emotional and irrational, accompanied by a feeling of hostility towards Indonesia. The cases of the death of Muhamad Heri[5] and the burning of Hok Doen Heng[6] with his ship are unable to touch the conscience of that section of the Australian public angry at the Corby case. From these two different cases … there's a sense of exaggerated nationalism … and xenophobia in symbols of identity, which have drowned out the human feelings of the Australian public (*Kompas*, 3 June 2005).

The writer of the second excerpt is Eby Hara PhD, identified as a social and political sciences lecturer at Jember University, and an ANU alumnus. The title is 'Corby and the Indonesian stereotype'.

> The pattern of Australia–Indonesia relations is strange. When it is good, it is very good, like siblings. When things go wrong, it's like two enemies. The question left from the Corby case is: Has Australia done enough to promote a better understanding of the Indonesian people and the systems of Indonesia? (*Jawa Pos*, 8 June 2005).

In 'Australia and the terrorist threat from the south', Farid M. Ibrahim inverts the usual 'threat from the north', identifying Australia as the threat. He gives the following advice together with an admonition against arrogance:

> Australia should throw away its Eurocentric perspective. This is the only way to make the Australian public understand that world civilisation at the beginning of this 21st century is not just the result of Western progress alone but is also due to the large contribution of what is called 'the East' (*Kompas*, 9 June 2005).

The writer of the fourth excerpt, an opinion piece called 'Cutting off one's nose to spite …', is Zamaahsari A. Ramzah, identified as a social and political sciences student at Muhammadiyah University, Yogyakarta. Here the central accusation is of racism, with the fishermen drawn in as a proof and a comparison.

> Now Australia has put its foot in it. The terror in Canberra aimed at the [Indonesian] embassy has clearly badly damaged Australia's good name in the eyes of the world as the nation most free from terrorist action. …

The attitude of Australian citizens towards [the Corby verdict] is very much out of proportion and emotionally coloured. I see RACE discrimination from Australians towards its own nationals [the 46 non-white Australians in Asian jails].

Meanwhile, in the case of Muhammad Heri, the Indonesian fisherman who died after being detained at sea for 10 days, and Hok Doen Heng, who was burned with his boat in mid-April near the Darwin Sea, the Australian public remains silent (*Jawa Pos*, 10 June 2005).

In 'Corby and media exploitation', Supriyanto, identified as an international relations student at the University of Indonesia in Depok, makes some bitter remarks about Australian celebrities. Australian racism and lack of sympathy are key themes of this opinion piece.

Don't ask Russell Crowe or Pauline Hanson about the Indonesian judicial system. They surely don't know. You would only get a gladiator reaction or racist comment that would be very unsympathetic toward Indonesia (*Jawa Pos*, 11 June 2005).

The last excerpt, by Bintaro of Surabaya, is from the letters to the editor section of the *Jawa Pos*. In 'The Australian albino mentality', he locates the causes of current Australian attitudes in the country's convict past. The letter contains several enduring themes found in emotional Indonesian reactions against Australia. It ends with a warning.

As a protest against the 20-year sentence for Schapelle Corby, the terrorist actions towards the Indonesian embassy in Canberra are tied to the mentality of Australians, who are, it is said, descended from criminals. After Cook's discovery of the continent … it was claimed as a colony by the English crown. In later developments, this continent thousands of miles from England was made a rubbish tip for heavy-grade convicts. It was these convicts who bred and became the ancestors of the current Australian nation.

History records that the treatment of the Aboriginals by white Australians was just as bad as the treatment of Indians by white Americans. The Aboriginals were hunted, slaughtered, and their lands and natural wealth seized from them.

What is even more hurtful for Indonesia is that Australia is a racist country that disparages and looks down on Asian culture. Former Malaysian Prime Minister Mahathir Mohamad used to get enraged at Albino Australia's behaviour. Mahathir said that Australia cannot possibly understand Asia, much less become part of Asia.

So, for Indonesia, there is no choice but to take a tougher attitude, if we are to have any self-respect. Although we are neighbours, if they don't respect us, we are not obliged to be nice to them (*Jawa Pos*, 17 June 2005).

Views of the foreign policy elite

In April 2004 the *Bulletin* interviewed the new Indonesian ambassador, Imron Cotan (Daley 2004). The ambassador criticised Australia's role in Iraq, and contrasted Australia's portrayal of itself as a hero in Iraq with its attempts to make Indonesia feel like a 'second-class country' for invading East Timor.

Most relevant here, Cotan said that while helping the Indonesian Department of Foreign Affairs assess new applicants for diplomatic positions in 2003, 'it emerged that 95% of the 6000 aspirants held anti-Australian views', and 'he and others in his department were shocked to discover the depth of anti-Australian sentiment in the Indonesian community as evidenced by the views expressed by the applicants to become diplomats'. He agreed that there were some people in the military and diplomatic establishments who held deep anti-Australian views – a logical consequence of the East Timor 'hiccup'.

The ambassador said:

> So, 95% of those 6000 have anti-Australian sentiments. They have nothing to do with the [Indonesian] military, they have nothing to do with the Department of Foreign Affairs. This is a fact that we really should take into serious consideration. And I think generally speaking – I don't know whether it is because of the media or because of other factors – but definitely, generally speaking, Indonesian people – the Indonesians – they have to some extent these sentiments ...
>
> [T]hey saw that Australians are all so arrogant, trying to impose values upon us in the region (*Bulletin*, 20 April 2004: 36–7).

Daniel Novotny, a doctoral candidate at the University of New South Wales researching Indonesian foreign policy and 'balance of threat' theory, recently returned from Indonesia where he interviewed 45 members of the foreign policy elite.[7] His findings are fascinating. For example, he discovered that Australia is presently seen as the second-biggest external security threat to Indonesia, though lagging far behind the United States. And this is among the foreign policy elite! He found considerable concern about Australia, ranging from unease to suspicion, among younger diplomats, particularly those who had lived and studied in Australia. Even the diplomats who liked Australians saw danger in Australia's fears of Indonesia. They were worried that these fears might result in a miscalculated and irrational reaction, including a military strike – a fear made more acute by Australian statements about pre-emptive strikes. What is going wrong with the experience of living and studying in Australia?

AUSTRALIAN PERCEPTIONS OF INDONESIA

This section focuses on two major events in mid-2005: the publication of an Australian Strategic Policy Institute (ASPI) report on Australian perceptions of security threats (McAllister 2005), and the sustained Australian reactions to the trial and verdict in the Schapelle Corby drug case in Bali. This is not to say that Australian perceptions of Indonesia are singularly negative. A set of very positive perceptions can be seen on the website of the Australian Consortium for In-country Indonesian Study (ACICIS), the consortium of universities that places Australian students in Indonesian universities for a semester or a year.[8] ACICIS has been operating for just over 10 years, and has placed around 600 Australian students in Indonesian universities in Yogyakarta and Malang. The responses could hardly be more positive: 'fantastic', 'wonderful', 'the best year of my life'. Semester after semester, 95 per cent of the students strongly endorse the program to fellow students. The positive effects of personal experience and people-to-people contacts could hardly be more plain.

The Australian Strategic Policy Institute report

In June 2005, ASPI published a report entitled 'Representative views: Mass and elite opinion on Australian security' (McAllister 2005). In canvassing popular views on security, the report found that 29 per cent of voters identified Indonesia as the most likely threat.

> Which countries are seen as most likely to pose a security threat to Australia? ... [T]he answer from voters is unambiguous: Indonesia. The popular belief that Indonesia is a threat has increased substantially since the mid 1970s, and it has largely replaced China as the country in our region regarded as most threatening to Australia ... The proportion of voters mentioning Indonesia as a threat reached one in five after the Dili massacre in November 1991, and increased to three in 10 after the events in East Timor following the referendum in August 1999. In 2004, 29% of voters identified Indonesia as 'most likely' to pose a threat to Australia in the future, a slight decline from the figure of 31% recorded in 2001 (McAllister 2005: 13).

Turning to electoral candidates' perceptions of security, the report has this to say:

> Although Indonesia remains the country most likely to be mentioned as a threat by candidates, the proportion nominating Indonesia has been declining since 1996, in contrast to the pattern among voters. In 1996, 17% of major party candidates mentioned Indonesia – a figure that declined to 12% in 2001 and 10% in 2004 ... By contrast, the proportion of voters mentioning Indonesia has increased, peaking at 31% in 2001 and averaging about three in 10 voters during the period following the referendum and resulting turmoil in East Timor. The relatively benign elite opinions about Indonesia have undoubtedly been influenced by government efforts since 1999 to mend bilateral relations. These efforts have, however, gained less visibility among voters, who still regard Indonesia as a significant potential security threat to Australia (McAllister 2005: 15).

On the need to close the gap between politicians' and the public's perceptions of the threat posed by Indonesia, the report says:

> There is talk again of a security agreement between Australia and Indonesia, spurred in part by a new warmth between the political leadership. However, the [security treaty of 1995] demonstrated that the public needs to be taken along in any new negotiations, and that the final form of any treaty needs to reflect a shared vision. As Prime Minister Howard recently observed, we should not 'make the mistake of benchmarking the relationship according to whether or not we have a treaty'. Governments should remember that treaties without strong foundations and broad sup-

port can too easily become hostage to single issues in the bilateral relationship. The merits of a new treaty are debatable, and the public needs to be part of an informed debate (McAllister 2005: 15).

This is a carefully conducted survey, and it confirms the findings of an earlier ASPI survey (McAllister 2004).

Early in 2005, during a visit to the University of Wollongong, Ambassador Cotan thought it important to address Australian fears of Indonesia. He said that Australians had no reason to fear his countrymen: 'Australia does not need to worry about Indonesia. The majority of our population is Muslim, but they are moderate in nature. The fanatics are in the minority'. He said that Australians have a three-point guarantee against an Indonesian threat: 'Firstly, we are governed by a democracy and every decision is checked through parliament. Secondly, we don't have any intention to threaten Australia; and thirdly, we do not have the means to threaten Australia' (*Illawarra Mercury*, 2 February 2005: 18).

The Schapelle Corby trial

The public interest in and responses to the trial of Schapelle Corby in Bali were particularly strong in May and early June 2005. The case received intense media coverage. An event in a foreign country was treated like an item of domestic politics; there was a media scrum, much comment by shock jocks, and wide radio, television, print and internet coverage. Emotions were intense; 'Nation's fury', said the *Daily Telegraph* on 28 May 2005. Indonesian consulates and the embassy were threatened and attacked. The network that had paid for Corby's story campaigned vigorously on the basis of her innocence. Newspapers wrote about 'our Schapelle'.

No doubt theses will be written on this extraordinary event, in which such passions were licensed and encouraged. The ABC's Sally Loane was amazed by the 'avalanche' of emails and text messages, and astonished by those claiming that Indonesia would invade Australia and that this was a first step.

On the one hand a number of senior journalists, correspondents and academics tried to put the affair into a sensible perspective, as Rosihan Anwar has noted. Tim Lindsey was reviled for his efforts. On the other hand, a more populist viewpoint was represented by the shock jock Malcolm Elliott, as recorded and quoted by the ABC television program Media Watch (2005).

> 'I believe right now Bambam Yodhoyono is sitting up there and his hands are tied because it's a legal matter. Wham Bam Thank You Mam Yiddi-yono is going to be called into all of these — well, that's what he is, isn't he — have you ever seen them? Whoa, give them a banana and away they go ...'
> – Malcolm T. Elliott, Radio 2GB, 15 May 2005'

'And that's Malcolm being restrained', commented Media Watch presenter Liz Jackson. 'Here he is on the judges who are hearing Corby's case:'

'Malcolm: The judges don't even speak English, mate, they're straight out of the trees if you excuse my expression.

Caller: Don't you think that disrespects the whole of our neighbouring nation?

Malcolm: I have total disrespect for our neighbouring nation my friend. Total disrespect. ...

And then we get this joke of a trial, and it's nothing more than a joke. An absolute joke the way they sit there. And they do look like the three wise monkeys, I'll say it. They don't speak English, they read books, they don't listen to her. They show us absolutely no respect those judges.
– Malcolm T. Elliot, Radio 2GB, 15 May 2005'

Elliott then turns his attention to the former Indonesian president, Megawati Sukarnoputri.

'What about that little midget woman who was up there, what was her name? Midget. Who was the president? Megawati. Megawati midget, yeah. Goodness.
– Malcolm T. Elliot, Radio 2GB, 15 May 2005'

A more moderate response, but in its way just as rejecting of Indonesia, is this letter to the editor from reader Gordon Drennan of Burton, South Australia:

I suspect the reason why most Australians don't much care if the relationship with Indonesia is damaged is that they don't see any reason we should have one.

They don't see any reason we should pay them billions of dollars, apologise for every perceived slight and pretend not to notice what their military gets up to.

We don't share culture, history or religion. We don't trade much. Our political systems don't have much in common. And our legal systems certainly don't. Okay, they're on the people-smuggling route to us, and they have a cheap tourist resort, but about all we have in common is an accident of geography. That doesn't mean much these days. Indonesia, if we were talking about people who lived in our street, would be the sort of neighbours you'd nod politely to in passing, and give a hand to if they needed it, but not pretend you had much interest in being best friends with (*Weekend Australian*, 4–5 June 2005: 18).

There is much more to say on the Corby case. By late June the fuss had quietened down, but the deeper popular emotions could easily be aroused again. Some of the best commentary came from our political press cartoonists, who presented Australian reactions in a witty and sardonic manner, a tribute to the capacity for reflection and self-mockery. Among these cartoonists was Michael Leunig, from whose cartoon the title of this chapter is borrowed.[9]

DOES IT MATTER?

I believe there is a hard-headed view in Canberra that so long as relations between the two countries are managed by a skilful elite, the vagaries of public opinion are inconsequential. This view can be found among politicians, bureaucrats and the military. And of course it is not necessary for populations to 'like' each other, as a glance at the histories of England and France will show.

The metaphor of nice neighbours is also unhelpful. Disputes between neighbours can be intense, as we see so often in local councils and the courts. At the international level, in 2005 tensions ran high between Malaysia and Indonesia over the island of Ambalat. Being neighbours creates friction; that should not surprise or alarm us. Perhaps popular emotions can be managed relatively easily.

How wide are the negative perceptions in each country? In Australia they have been surveyed, and ASPI provides a figure of 29 per cent (McAllister 2005). Presumably this is a Hansonite slice of the population: older, less educated, more rural; although the negativity could spread widely and quickly if encouraged. In Indonesia, the surveying has not been done. Probably most Indonesians neither know nor care much about Australia; they have more pressing issues to deal with. However, I think among the urban newspaper-reading public, as measured by letters and articles, there is considerable suspicion, and it probably spreads out into the wider populace through Islamic schools critical of US and Australian actions in Afghanistan and Iraq. Indonesian suspicions of Australia probably reach higher, too, further up into the bureaucratic, diplomatic and military elites.

I believe that perceptions such as these do matter, and that governments should have broad popular backing for important policies that have a major

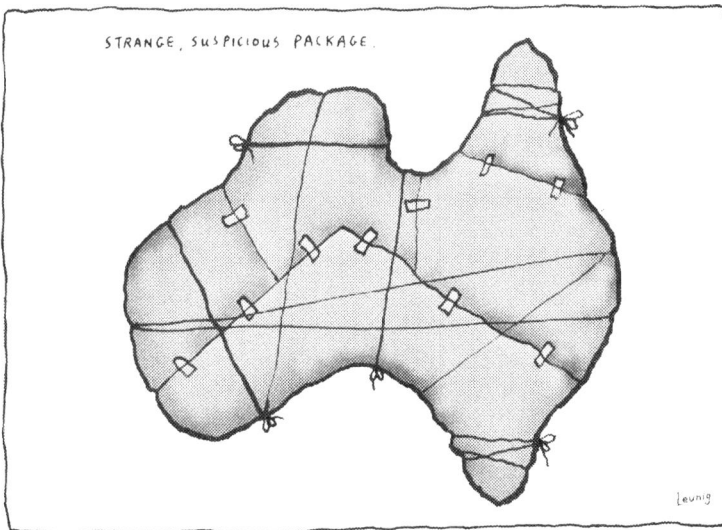

First published in The Age *on 3 June 2005.*
Reprinted by permission of Michael Leunig.

effect on our future. Reasoned public debate is important. Popular opinion based on prejudice is dangerous. The Australian government realised that matters were getting out of hand in the Corby case in early June, and took quick action. A statement by Australian Foreign Minister Alexander Downer suggests he is thinking again about the importance of increasing popular knowledge of Asia (AEF 2005: 17–20).

My recommendations are:

1   Exchange Schapelle Corby and perhaps others for the traditional Indonesian fishermen in detention. New policy is needed on the fishermen; and tensions over the issue are escalating on both sides. My thinking is strongly affected by Ruth Balint's book and documentary on this topic.[10]
2   Australian film-makers make good documentaries that could increase Indonesians' knowledge of Australia. The rights to them should be purchased; they should be subtitled or dubbed into Indonesian, and they should be given free to Indonesian television channels.
3   More teeth and effort need to be put into the government's response to the 28 recommendations of the 2004 parliamentary inquiry into Australia–Indonesia relations, particularly the recommendations in section 6, 'At the heart of the relationship – people'.[11]
4   The Asian Studies Association of Australia has provided a detailed blueprint on how to maximise Australia's knowledge of Asia (ASAA 2005). The government should act on the innovative measures proposed in its 2005 federal budget submission.

There are many on the Indonesian side who will welcome and support such endeavours. Perceptions can be changed, though not quickly. Some of the deepest prejudices are short-sighted; we should also try to make them more short-lived.

AFTERWORD

In my spoken presentation, I used Australian political cartoons from 1858 to 2005 to suggest continuities in some Australian perceptions of Indonesia and 'Asia'. To give some of the feel of this, a short article by Louise Williams on the political cartoons follows (see box).

NOTES

1 Cynthia Banham, who covers defence and foreign affairs for the *Sydney Morning Herald*, was at talks organised by the Australia–Indonesia Institute and the Habibie Centre in Bandung. There were 30 participants, half Indonesians, half Australians: 'public prosecutors, bankers, florists, doctors, MPs, academics, journalists, police commissioners, bureaucrats and novelists who shared a common interest in the Australian–Indonesian dynamic'.

2 With great thanks to Rinduan Zain and Iskandar P. Nugroho for their research assistance. The translations are my responsibility.

3 The increasing globalisation of news is one of the key themes of the Corby case.

4 Bullets were sent to the Indonesian consulate in Perth, and huge publicity surrounded an apparent attempt to send anthrax to the Indonesian embassy in Canberra. The issue was defused when the powder turned out to be talcum, but this sequence of events was malicious and murderous in tone, if not in effect.

5 Heri, an Indonesian fisherman from Probolinggo, Java, died on his boat in late April 2005 after the boat and crew were apprehended by Australian customs. According to an ABC report on 13 May 2005, the death was from natural causes, but at the time of writing the Darwin coroner, who is investigating the death, had not returned a finding.

6 In May 2005 Hok Doen Heng was said to have been burned by boiling cooking oil, apparently as a result of – or during – an altercation with one of his crewmates, while both were in Australian custody.

7 For some preliminary findings, see Novotny (2005: 19–23).

8 See <www.acicis.murdoch.edu.au>.

9 With thanks to the witty cartoonists whose work I used in my address to the Update conference, especially to Leunig.

10 See Balint (2005) and the video 'Troubled Waters', Resonance Productions, 2001.

11 For the inquiry, see Foreign Affairs Subcommittee (2004). For the government response see DFAT (2005b).

HOW A LITTLE BOY STIRS UP BIG
TROUBLE WITH THE NEIGHBOURS

Louise Williams

Australians have good reason to regard Indonesia with suspicion, and it's not because of Schapelle Corby or even the Bali bombings. The truth is we didn't much like Indonesia anyway.

A survey has found that almost one in three Australians regards Indonesia as a threat. And the antagonism is not new. The Australian Strategic Policy Institute survey notes Australians began to consistently single out Indonesia from the 1970s and that it has since displaced China as the nation Australians most fear.

But Indonesia is merely the latest villain in a long-running play, that familiar Australian tale of a looming threat from the north.

The Foreign Minister, Alexander Downer, this week conceded Australia's marked distrust of Indonesia but said it was born mainly out of 'complete ignorance'.

'They [Australians] need to understand these are not scary places full of bad people, that these are not the badlands', he told a conference in Melbourne this week.

It seems extraordinary that decades into Australia's engagement with Asia, with the White Australia policy long behind us – and with modern Asia emerging as the globe's economic engine – such psychological divisions persist.

Not so, says Associate Professor David Reeve, of the University of NSW, an Indonesia expert. Our unrelentingly negative views of modern Indonesia, he argues, are simply an extension of historic insecurities firmly embedded in the Australian psyche.

Ever since the First Fleet landed in 1788 to claim Aboriginal lands, Australian settlers have looked north with trepidation. First there were rival colonial navies like those of the Dutch and French on the horizon.

Then, from the 1800s, when the first Chinese began arriving on the goldfields, our gaze shifted firmly towards the swarming Asian masses.

Cartoon images of floods or plagues of locusts with Chinese and, later, Japanese faces filled Australian newspapers and magazines. Invasion plots, foiled by brave bush heroes, dominated popular novels.

Around the same time Uncle Sam emerged to personify the United States, Australian cartoonists were creating a character known as the Little Boy from Manly. This cute, vulnerable little boy in a sailor suit was used to represent Australia until the early 1900s. In his cartoon adventures

No innocent ... the Little Boy from Manly, left, drawn by Hop, as he appeared in The Bulletin *in 1895.*

he was threatened with drowning by a menacing Chinaman and standing with his finger in the dyke to hold back the Japanese flood.

'These underlying attitudes are not at all surprising', Professor Reeve says. 'Australian settlers were a small, relatively rich population in a vast land, surrounded by huge Asian powers of teeming multitudes.

'I don't think the Corby case, for example, caused these emotions, but it did provide the opportunity for these long-held and deep-seated feelings to be freely and vociferously expressed.'

After World War II, fresh from the Allied defeat of the Japanese, Australia briefly appeared in cartoons as a towering, patronising figure in the region. But this was a historic anomaly, Professor Reeve says.

Australia's cartoon self-image has again shrunk to a diminutive figure, overshadowed by our gigantic Asian neighbours. And over the past two decades at least 15 Australian authors have published novels dealing with the threat from the north, Professor Reeve notes. John Marsden's successful series of contemporary invasion novels features a group of resourceful Australian teenagers who challenge a generic Asian occupation that has split Australia in half, reminiscent of the imagined wartime 'Brisbane line'.

However, contemporary Australian fears are far more complex than 19th and 20th century stereotypes. Many Australians are comfortable with Asia. And those who aren't seem to reserve most of their racism and anger for Indonesia, which is portrayed variously as a tiger, monkey, crocodile or jackal. China, instead, has been largely rebranded as an economic opportunity.

A string of violent events in Indonesia since the late 1990s, especially the rise of anti-Western terrorism, have directed anxieties towards Indonesia.

But what is missing in Australia's popular imagination is the other side of the modern Indonesian tale: its mainly peaceful democratic transition.

'Just because you understand where the feelings come from, it doesn't mean they're justified or that you shouldn't do something about them', Professor Reeve says.

Mr Downer rightly argues that the answer to fear is knowledge and says he's exasperated that many young Australians don't even know where Java is. But Asian studies in Australian schools and universities are in decline, which means we are definitely not getting to know the neighbours. This is a leadership and policy issue that must first be tackled in Canberra.

Unless the knowledge deficit is challenged the innocent-faced little boy from Manly will just keep stirring up trouble.

First published in the Sydney Morning Herald on 25 June 2005.
Reprinted by permission of Louise Williams.

8 THE INDONESIAN STUDENT MARKET TO AUSTRALIA: TRENDS AND CHALLENGES

Isla Rogers-Winarto*

BACKGROUND

For the past decade, Australia has been the overseas study destination of first choice for Indonesians. Its major competitive advantages are its proximity to Indonesia, the quality of its education and the range of courses available to international students. Indonesians are also attracted to Australia because it is an English-speaking country and has a reasonable cost of living compared with other Western countries.

Australia currently enjoys approximately 37 per cent of the overseas-bound Indonesian student market. The United States attracts another 22 per cent of the market, Singapore 15 per cent and Malaysia 7 per cent. At the end of August 2005, 15,158 Indonesians were enrolled in study programs in Australia. Education was Australia's fourth-largest export commodity in 2003–04, worth A$5.9 billion (DFAT 2005a). The export of education to Indonesia alone yields approximately A$500 million per annum for Australia. This amount is derived predominantly from living costs and tuition fees from on-shore programs.

Australian education and training services, delivered through the Australian Development Scholarship (ADS) scheme, the Australian Partnership Scholarship (APS) scheme, the Indonesia–Australia Specialised Training Project and so on, account for a total of 50 per cent of Australia's aid to Indonesia. Through the ADS and APS schemes, 600 Indonesians are awarded scholarships annually for postgraduate study in Australia.

Indonesia, as a developing nation, is under great pressure in the area of education. With a population of approximately 220 million people, more than 44 million of whom are in the 19–24-year age bracket, Indonesia's ability to provide its citizens with access to all levels of education has become a critical issue.

87

With development emerge aspirations for a good education and equal employment opportunities. Both are crucial to social and political stability.

Unfortunately, Indonesia is still unable to provide its people with the standard of education they need for their nation to progress in the world, nor is it
able to cater adequately for the growing demand for more university placements. Remaining competitive regionally is also proving to be a challenge for
Indonesia owing to its lack of skilled labour. Compared to neighbouring Association of Southeast Asian Nations (ASEAN) countries, Indonesia currently
ranks among the lowest in relation to access to and quality of education and
overall quality of human resources.

Indonesia will need to focus on capacity building in areas that are important
for its development over the next decade. To assist it to reach its human resource
development goals, Australia, through its education exports to Indonesia, will
continue to be a leading player. In addition to the obvious economic advantages
of international education, enhanced educational links such as those existing
between Indonesia and Australia undoubtedly provide innumerable intangible
benefits. These lie mainly in the building of stronger bridges between the two
countries through lifelong personal, cultural and business ties as well as scientific and technological transfers. Perhaps of greatest importance during these
globally challenging times is for each country to gain a better knowledge of the
culture of the other, as a way of promoting racial and religious harmony.

A report prepared by the Foreign Affairs Subcommittee of the Australian
parliament's Joint Standing Committee on Foreign Affairs, Defence and Trade
stresses the role of education in improving the understanding between Indonesia and Australia:

> The quality of our engagement with our neighbour is critically affected by our
> endeavours to understand and communicate. In the Committee's view, the impor-
> tance that we attach to the relationship must be matched by a comparable level of
> effort towards building our capacity for an enhanced relationship. Many of the sug-
> gestions made in submissions regarding how best to do this relate in one way or
> another to education (Foreign Affairs Subcommittee 2004: 144).

Of the 28 major recommendations in this report, 10 relate directly to education. Most of them are with reference to sponsored training for Indonesians, but
the third recommendation of the report focuses on managing the educational
relationship in general. It states:

> The Committee recommends that the Federal Government jointly invite the States to
> examine ways in which the educational relationship with Indonesia can be more
> cohesively managed (Foreign Affairs Subcommittee 2004: xix).

If implemented, this recommendation would in itself assist in providing solutions to several of the problems currently being experienced in the Indonesian
education market to Australia.

Many Indonesians are aware of the benefits to be gained from studying abroad. In a letter to the *Jakarta Post* in April 2005, Nino Manuwoto of Bogor, West Java, describes some of these perceived benefits as follows:

> There are several advantages in obtaining or continuing ... studies abroad. First of all, [it] is the experience of assimilating with an environment that is quite different compared with the one in Indonesia, especially in the developed West, where life is quick and the system more complicated. Another is the difference in systems, such as the education, administration, politics and lifestyle of the community the student is involved in. Assimilating with the foreign community, mainly the academic community, gives the opportunity for one to adapt, compete, transfer or receive new experiences through direct communication, observation and involvement. When returning, they will not only have learned new experiences, but will be affected, maybe intensely, by the culture they were in.

Another postgraduate Indonesian student still studying at a major Australian university makes observations on the humane and forgiving nature of the Australian public, commenting:

> ... we still need greater efforts to help our fellow countrymen truly comprehend and appreciate the character of our southern neighbour. While one cannot make generalisations, it is nevertheless a fact that exposing ourselves to their lives is an invaluable experience and helps us gain a clearer picture of the way in which Australians perceive us as their northern neighbour. I found that education is the best bridge that can facilitate this. Further educational collaboration, such as student exchange programs, will enhance genuine understanding between the people of our two countries. As John Howard once said: We can change our friends but not our neighbour (Amirrachman 2005).

MARKET TRENDS

There has been a distinct shift over the past three years in the Indonesian student market to Australia. Higher education (undergraduate and postgraduate, mainly Master's) programs now have the highest numbers of Indonesian students, with fewer Indonesian students advancing from Australian feeder programs to university. University enrolments may therefore eventually experience lower enrolments from Indonesia. Table 8.1 illustrates the latest trends in Indonesian student enrolments across all sectors.

While most Indonesians studying in Australia are private, full-fee-paying students enrolled in the higher education sector, there are now over 1,000 Indonesians studying in Australia on scholarships awarded by major donor agencies such as the Australian Agency for International Development, the Asian Development Bank and the World Bank. Increasingly, Indonesian students studying in Australia are from provinces other than Jakarta. In contrast to the late 1990s, when 70 per cent of Indonesians studying in Australia came from

Table 8.1 *Indonesian enrolments and commencements in Australian education*[a]

Sector	2002 (no.)	2003 (no.)	02/03 (% change)	2004 (no.)	03/04 (% change)	2005 (no.)	04/05 (% change)
Enrolments							
ELICOS	1,487	1,553	4	1,255	−19	1,089	−13
Higher education	11,242	11,214	0	10,389	−7	9,487	−9
Other (non-award courses, enabling courses)	836	873	4	745	−15	595	−20
Schools	1,309	1,205	−8	1,008	−16	787	−22
VET	4,590	4,186	−9	3,618	−14	3,200	−12
Total	19,464	19,031	−2	17,015	−11	15,158	−11
Commencements							
ELICOS	1,054	1,078	2	825	−23	780	−5
Higher education	4,486	4,027	−10	3,588	−11	3,168	−12
Other (non-award courses, enabling courses)	518	536	3	418	−22	364	−13
Schools	426	415	−3	316	−24	193	−39
VET	1,828	1,801	−1	1,470	−18	1,330	−10
Total	8,312	7,857	−5	6,617	−16	5,835	−12

ELICOS = (government-affiliated) English Language Intensive Courses for Overseas Students; VET = vocational education and training.

a Enrolments refer to the number of courses in which private, full-fee-paying Indonesian students were enrolled during January–August 2002–05. In the case of a student attending two different courses in the same reference period, both enrolments would be counted. Commencements refer to the combined number of new course enrolments by Indonesians during the period in question.

Source: AEI's Provider Registration and International Student Management System (PRISMS) database, September 2005.

Jakarta, 54 per cent of students are now from provinces other than Jakarta. This development points to the fact that information on Australia appears to be successfully penetrating the outerlying regions of Indonesia, through increased institutional linkages, through the promotional activities of Australian organisations such as IDP Education Australia and Australia Education International (AEI),[1] through agents and, increasingly, through the alumni of Australian programs.

Victoria and NSW combined account for about 75 per cent of Indonesian student enrolments in Australia. Western Australia, with about 14 per cent, is the third most popular Australian state, followed by Queensland with around 7 per cent of the market. Enrolments in the remaining states are negligible.

As is evident from Table 8.1, the total number of Indonesian student enrolments and Indonesian student commencements in Australia have both been declining steadily since 2002. This is true across almost all sectors. In 2000 Indonesia, with 17,431 student enrolments, was the main source of international students in Australia, followed by China with 13,939 students and Malaysia with 11,629 students. Despite a record 20,336 student enrolments at the end of 2003, however, Indonesia was only the fourth largest provider of international students to Australia in that year. Ahead of it were China (57,579 students), Hong Kong (23,803 students) and South Korea (22,159 students). By the end of the following year Indonesia, with 18,102 student enrolments in Australia, had dropped to seventh position. The top three providers in 2004 were China with 68,857 student enrolments, South Korea with 23,810 enrolments and Hong Kong with 22,970 enrolments. Indonesia's lower ranking in terms of student numbers has been caused not so much by a decline in its enrolments as by a surge in enrolments from other countries in the region since 2000. Tables 8.2 and 8.3 illustrate Indonesia's market position in 2003 and 2004 in relation to other key players.

Indonesia's contribution to international student numbers in Australia decreased from 12 per cent in 1998 to 9.5 per cent in 2000, 6.7 per cent in 2003 and 5.6 per cent in 2004. A corresponding decline of approximately 40 per cent since 1997 in the number of Indonesians applying for visas to study in Australia is apparent in Figure 8.1. This will mean that as Indonesian students already enrolled in Australia complete their studies, there will no longer be substantial numbers of incoming Indonesian students to replace them.

Based on current trends, it appears that Indonesian student visa applications to Australia are unlikely to increase markedly in the short term – unless, of course, the market is affected by significant factors such as social unrest in Indonesia brought about by economic instability, personal security concerns due to increased acts of terrorism in Indonesia, or disenchantment with in-country local or foreign-linked educational programs.

Table 8.2   Main source countries of international student enrolments in Australia, 2003[a]

Rank/ Source country	Enrolments	
	(no.)	(%)
1 China	57,579	18.9
2 Hong Kong	23,803	7.8
3 South Korea	22,159	7.3
4 Indonesia	20,336	6.7
5 Malaysia	19,779	6.5
6 Japan	18,897	6.3
7 Thailand	17,025	5.6
8 India	14,386	4.7

a   January–December.
Source: AEI.

Table 8.3   Main source countries of international student enrolments in Australia, 2004[a]

Rank/ Source country	Enrolments	
	(no.)	(%)
1 China	68,857	21.3
2 South Korea	23,810	7.4
3 Hong Kong	22,970	7.1
4 India	20,749	6.4
5 Malaysia	19,998	6.2
6 Japan	19,743	6.1
7 Indonesia	18,102	5.6
8 Thailand	16,289	5.0

a   January–December.
Source: AEI.

Figure 8.1   Indonesian student visa applications for study in Australia, 1997–2004 (no.)

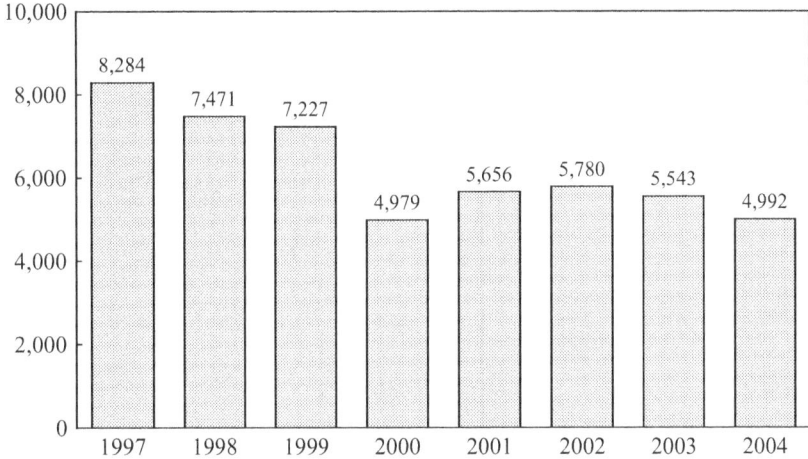

Source: 1997–2000: AEI Jakarta; 2001–04: IDP Indonesia.

On a more positive note, applications to study in Australia could conceivably go up once more should the Australian government introduce policies designed to allow greater flexibility for international students. This may, indeed, commence when the Department of Immigration and Multicultural Affairs introduces its new conditions for international students completing vocational education programs in Australia.[2] Sound decisions such as this can only serve to boost a somewhat deflated student market.

The reasons for the current decline in Indonesian student visas to Australia are varied. It is interesting to note, however, that the peaks and valleys in enrolments mirror, quite distinctly, specific political and social issues affecting Indonesia, and the bilateral relationship more generally (Figure 8.2). Before the Asian economic crisis of 1997, more than 18,000 Indonesian students were enrolled in Australian education programs. Numbers were to drop in 1998 as the economic crisis deepened and fewer Indonesians could afford to study overseas. In 1999, student enrolments increased following the exodus to Australia of young Indonesians, mainly ethnic Chinese, seeking to escape to a safer environment after the May 1998 riots in Indonesia in which the nation's frustrations were taken out on Indonesian Chinese in particular. At the end of 1999 and the beginning of 2000, student numbers to Australia were again negatively affected, this time by serious strains in the bilateral relationship over East Timor.

*Figure 8.2   Political and economic influences on total Indonesian student
           enrolments in Australia, 1996–2004 (thousand)*

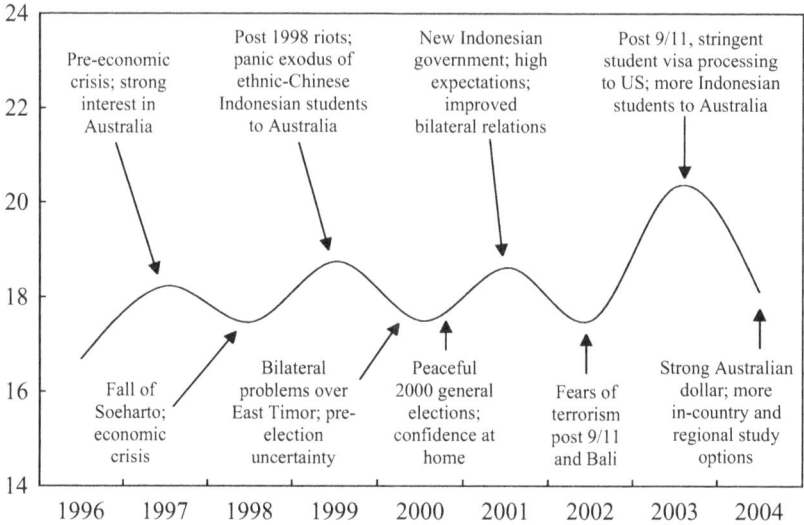

Source: 1996–2000: AEI Jakarta; 2001–04: IDP Indonesia.

Renewed confidence at home in the newly elected government of President Abdurrahman Wahid led to larger numbers of Indonesian students taking up studies in Australia in 2000–01. During this period, bilateral ties were also slowly improving. In 2002, however, after the terrorist attacks in the United States on 11 September 2001, international students globally chose to stay home in the security of their families. In 2003, one year after the United States began imposing more stringent rules on student visas, Australia recorded a peak in Indonesian enrolments, of 20,336 students. This was followed by a downward trend in student numbers in 2004.

FACTORS CONTRIBUTING TO THE DECLINE

Broadly speaking, the major factors causing Indonesian student enrolments in Australia to fall can be summarised as being cost related. The decline in the value of the Indonesian rupiah against the Australian dollar since 1998, and the appreciation of the Australian dollar relative to the US dollar since 2002, have undoubtedly caused Australia to lose its competitive edge in cost-sensitive markets such as Indonesia.

The steady increase in tuition fees, predominantly at Australian universities, has further contributed to Australia losing its competitive edge. Combined with the high cost of living in Melbourne and Sydney, by far the most popular cities with Indonesians, this would seem to be discouraging many prospective students.

In addition to the cost factors, there is also the impact on the market of the warnings against non-essential travel to Indonesia issued by Australia's Department of Foreign Affairs and Trade (DFAT). Such notices have been issued regularly as a result of the tragic terrorist bombings in Bali in 2002 and 2005, the Marriott Hotel bombing in 2003 and the bombing outside the Australian embassy in Jakarta in 2004. Consequently, marketing by representatives of Australian institutions is now rare. Many do not come to Indonesia, fearing for their personal safety in the event of future attacks. Some are prevented from coming by their home institutions, which point to insurance company clauses denying full cover to travellers who knowingly enter a country for which a travel warning has been issued. Without regular marketing, Australian education has lost some of its profile in Indonesia, where competition from other major rivals is alive and well.

A comparatively new issue which has emerged over the past three years is the concern of some prospective Indonesian students that their personal safety may be at risk while in Australia. Muslim students in particular harbour fears of reprisals for the deaths of 92 Australians in the 2002 and 2005 Bali bomb attacks and for the 2004 bombing outside the Australian embassy in Jakarta.

Perhaps indirectly related to the above is the perception among a growing number of Indonesians that there is racism in Australia, predominantly towards Asians. The staff of IDP Education Australia occasionally receive inquiries from prospective Indonesian students worried about whether they will be accepted by the Australian community. For example, an IDP education counsellor in Jakarta received the following email the day after the bombing outside the Australian embassy:

> 10 September 2004
> Mbak Marta:
>
> Based on the situation of the bombing near the Australian embassy, would there be any restriction of Indonesian nationals to travel to and study in Australia? I need assurance that if I go to [name of institution], people like myself wearing a *jilbab*[3] can still be accepted by Australian citizens. Please advise.

A notable development has been the easing of visa restrictions for foreign students seeking entry into the United States, from January 2005 onwards. In spite of the difficulties Indonesians have experienced in entering the United States as students since 11 September 2001, they now appear to be looking forward to the prospect of studying there once more. Parents inquiring about study in Australia for their children often compare the overall costs with those in the

United States. Unless there are strong reasons for choosing Australia, many of them may now opt for the United States.

At the same time, the United Kingdom is actively seeking to attract more Indonesian students. Most Indonesian students in the United Kingdom study at the postgraduate level. It is conceivable that the July 2005 terrorist attacks in London could affect the UK-bound international student market. To date, however, there has been no indication of a downturn in the UK-bound student market from Indonesia, according to the British Council in Jakarta.

Competition from other countries

Major competition from other sources cannot be overlooked as a leading factor in the current decline of Indonesian student visa applications to Australia. Influenced by cost factors and aggressive promotional activity, many Indonesian students are now looking seriously at the education programs offered by neighbouring Malaysia and Singapore. Both countries are positioning themselves as centres of excellence in education in the region. Overall, these regional competitors offer considerably more affordable options than do Australian institutions, with the added advantage that they provide a more familiar environment for Asians.

Malaysia, due to its strong religious, cultural and linguistic similarities with Indonesia, is attracting many younger Muslim Indonesian students. The proliferation of Australian twinning programs in Malaysia serves to provide a greater number of options for such students. For example, after completing one or two years of a diploma program in Malaysia, students may be able to articulate into an Australia-based degree course.

Singapore's proximity to Indonesia and its inexpensive, uncomplicated procedures for issuing student visas make it a natural choice for many Indonesian students, particularly those of high-school age and those studying for diplomas. Like Malaysia, Singapore offers many feeder programs with Australian links. Also attractive to Indonesian students are the scholarships offered by the Singapore government to students from ASEAN countries demonstrating academic excellence, for study at high school to postgraduate level. Being eligible to apply for permanent residence in Singapore upon completion of one's studies is another major drawcard, particularly for ethnic-Chinese male graduates seeking employment opportunities outside Indonesia.

The proposal by the University of New South Wales (UNSW) Asia – Singapore's first international, privately funded university – to launch degree programs in 2007 may cause a further decline in the number of Indonesian students headed for Australia. UNSW Asia will offer up to 70 per cent of its places to international students, with the remainder reserved for Singaporeans. It is predicted that the majority of international students applying to study at UNSW Asia will come from Indonesia, India and China.

Since 2000, international programs have become increasingly prominent throughout Indonesia. While some have not received full recognition or the appropriate licences from the Indonesian government authorities, their appeal to young Indonesian students nevertheless cannot be overlooked. As determined by Indonesian law, such programs are conducted in joint venture or partnership with local institutions. Most are located on impressive, even luxurious, campuses, with nearly all classes taught in English. They are usually less expensive than similar programs conducted overseas by the same international institutions. Most importantly, students remain in Indonesia, thereby saving substantially on living costs.

In-country international education programs, from high-school and diploma level to undergraduate and postgraduate programs, can be found in several major Indonesian cities. Even foreign kindergartens are opening up to cater for Indonesian children of pre-school age whose parents want them schooled in a more progressive educational environment where English is taught from an early age.

The choices available to Indonesian students through the major international programs of higher education include one to two-year foundation or diploma programs which can be commenced in-country and which then allow articulation into programs overseas; joint or twinning programs which can be completed in English or in Indonesian at top local institutions, including the University of Indonesia and Gadjah Mada University; and double degree programs. The fields of study on offer are those that commonly attract Asian and especially Indonesian students, namely business and commerce, information technology and computer science, and engineering.

Most of the international programs currently available in Indonesia are in partnership with international providers. It is worth noting that approximately 30 such programs have Australian links, constituting by far the most significant involvement of any country. Australian universities already represented in Indonesia include the Royal Melbourne Institute of Technology, the University of Melbourne, the University of Queensland, the University of Technology in Sydney and Monash University. A growing number of other Australian universities are conducting similar programs, mainly in Jakarta, or are in the process of signing memoranda of understanding to do so.

International schools, using curricula mostly from Australia, Europe, the United States, the United Kingdom, Singapore, South Korea and Japan, are springing up in major cities across Indonesia. All are now permitted to accept up to 20 per cent Indonesian students as part of their total student body. Australian international schools, established in south and north Jakarta as well as in Bali, have experienced considerable growth in their Indonesian student enrolments since this policy was introduced three years ago.

Other countries are marketing their services widely across Indonesia, predominantly through high-profile education exhibitions. The main players in this area, apart from Australia, are the United Kingdom, the United States, the Netherlands, Canada and Malaysia. Marketing is predominantly through local education agents, some of whom represent several countries.

To date, no major research has been conducted on Indonesians' views of the in-country international programs available. However, in a recent survey of visitors to an Australian postgraduate education exhibition held in five major Indonesian cities, respondents were asked if they were more interested in international programs conducted in Indonesia or in overseas study programs.[4] In each of the five cities, a minimum of 70 per cent indicated they would prefer to study overseas. Reasons given were a distrust of the promises made in relation to the international-affiliated programs, uncertainty about the quality of such programs and an interest in the overall overseas study experience.

SCHOLARSHIPS

Scholarships are undoubtedly a strong drawcard for Indonesians during the present period of economic uncertainty. In addition to international donor agencies, a number of international as well as local corporations and organisations are now providing scholarships to promising Indonesian students. One of the most prominent is the Indonesian cigarette company Sampoerna, which offers scholarships for Indonesians to study abroad in countries such as Australia, France, the United States, the United Kingdom, Japan, Germany and Italy, and even Russia and China now offer scholarships to Indonesians. Most of Sampoerna's scholarships are awarded to students undertaking postgraduate studies in important development-related areas or, in the case of those going to China, Chinese-language studies. Since the tsunami of 26 December 2004, students in Aceh in northern Sumatra have been inundated with offers of scholarships, most of them for overseas study, but a smaller number for study at local universities.

INDONESIAN STUDENTS' PERCEPTIONS OF AUSTRALIA

In July 2004, the Indonesian offices of IDP Education Australia and AEI conducted a survey of 2,250 Indonesians attending educational events and bi-monthly International English Language Testing System (IELTS) sessions, or studying at selected local private and international high schools.[5] The aim of the survey was to gain insights into what motivates Indonesians to study overseas, which countries they favour, and why.

Overall, Australia emerges outright as the study destination of first choice, followed by the United Kingdom, United States, Malaysia and Japan. However, there are distinct regional variations, with countries such as Malaysia, Japan and

Table 8.4   Reasons Indonesians study overseas (% of responses)

Reason	Share
Overseas programs are better	64
To gain a better understanding of Western culture	24
Course not available in home country	12
Intend to migrate to this country	5
Unable to gain access to a local institution	1

Source: IDP and AEI.

the United Kingdom emerging as clear favourites in Medan, Pekanbaru, Lampung, Jakarta, Bandung, Surabaya, Denpasar and Makassar. This could be due to increased marketing in Indonesia by Malaysia and the United Kingdom. The scholarships being offered by other countries such as Japan and Germany could also account for the higher interest in some of the Indonesian regions in question.

The responses to the question 'Which of the following reasons were important in your decision to study overseas?' provide strong confirmation of the well-recognised fact that Indonesian students pursue studies abroad primarily to gain a better-quality education than is available in their own country (Table 8.4). Most Indonesians surveyed appear to have a negative view of their country's quality of education generally. This point is worthy of note. Should it be perceived in the future that the quality of education available in Indonesia has improved relative to education in the potential overseas study destination, the number of Indonesian students studying overseas would presumably decline. Furthermore, if local education were perceived as having improved markedly, it is likely that we would see many more Indonesian students placing greater emphasis on a meaningful experience while studying overseas.

When seeking an overseas education, the Indonesian respondents indicated that they look for high quality, reasonable cost and a meaningful life experience, in that order. It is obvious that Indonesian students are becoming increasingly sophisticated in their choices compared to just a few years ago, and are more savvy about the quality of education available to them. They want value for their money and are keen to seek new cultural experiences to complement the educational experience.

The responses to the survey confirm some commonly held perceptions ('true') and challenge others ('false'), as indicated by the statements below.

Indonesia is now a more price-sensitive market (TRUE)
With the appreciation of the Australian dollar and the depreciation of the local currency, Indonesians are becoming much more cost conscious.

Indonesian education is regarded as inferior to that available overseas (TRUE)
In reliable, annual global human development reports, Indonesia consistently scores poorly for the quality and accessibility of its education, placing it well behind other Asian countries. Indonesians are acutely aware of this.

Many Indonesians still aspire to study in the United States (TRUE)
Despite imposing tighter visa-processing regulations since the 11 September terrorist attacks, the United States still manages to attract thousands of Indonesian students, many of them with close family and business links to the United States.

Some Indonesian students perceive Australians as racist (TRUE)
Among Indonesian students and parents alike, there are mounting concerns regarding perceived racism among Australians, especially towards Asians.

Australia's proximity to Indonesia provides a strong competitive advantage (FALSE)
Indonesians now appear to be prepared to travel much further afield than before to study, if they believe that the study destination offers the conditions they are seeking.

Having friends and relatives in the study destination is paramount (FALSE)
For postgraduate and mature-age students, the most important considerations are the reputation of the institution, the cost of the program and a conducive study environment.

Most Indonesian students want to migrate to Australia (FALSE)
While it is undeniable that some Indonesian students will wish to apply for permanent residence in Australia, most plan to return home upon graduation. Generally speaking, Indonesians have strong family ties. Even among those who have been successful in obtaining Australian permanent residence, it is not unusual to find some returning to Indonesia to live and work, and to be with family. For ethnic-Chinese Indonesians, permanent resident status is often a fallback option in case they should need to leave Indonesia, for whatever reason, in the future.

Table 8.5 provides a summary of the five most important reasons for Indonesians to choose to study in the five most popular study destinations: Australia, the United Kingdom, the United States, Malaysia and Japan. Among the most prominent reasons for Indonesians to choose Australia are the quality of education in Australia, which is perceived to be good, and the fact that Australian

Table 8.5   The five most important factors for Indonesians in choosing the five most popular study destinations

1 Australia	2 United Kingdom	3 United States	4 Malaysia	5 Japan
1 Quality of education	Qualification recognised	Reputation of institution	Safe environment	Quality of education
2 Qualification recognised at home	Quality of education	Quality of education	Quiet & studious environment	Qualification recognised at home
3 Easy to obtain information	Safe environment	Qualification recognised at home	Quality of education	Quiet & studious environment
4 Quiet & studious environment	Quiet & studious environment	Easy to obtain information	Entry qualifications accepted	Reputation of institution
5 Reputation of institution	Reputation of institution	Entry qualifications accepted	Reputation of institution	Easy to obtain information

Source: IDP and AEI.

qualifications are recognised at home. Indonesians also value the ease with which they can obtain information on Australian study opportunities. A quiet and studious environment and institutional reputation are also pertinent.

Third on the list for the United Kingdom is safety, a factor not mentioned for Australia. This may have been a common perception before the July 2005 bombings in London. Institutional reputation rates as the most important factor for the United States but least important for Australia. Safety is the most important factor for Malaysia. In addition, Indonesians believe that their qualifications will be accepted more readily by Malaysian institutions than by those in other countries. Japan attracts Indonesians for most of the reasons cited for choosing Australia. However, the institution's reputation seems to be more relevant for Japan and is placed slightly higher than for Australia.

The countries ranked sixth to tenth by Indonesians in order of preference as a study destination are Singapore, Germany, New Zealand, Canada and the Netherlands. Among the five most important factors for choosing Singapore are its lower course fees and the perception that there is little racial discrimination there. Interestingly enough, the reasons for choosing Malaysia do not include lack of racial discrimination, despite the country's cultural and geographical proximity to Indonesia and its popularity as a tourist destination. For both Canada and the Netherlands, however, a low level of racial discrimination features among the main reasons for choosing to study in those countries. An important reason for Indonesians to choose Germany as a study destination is that their qualifications are accepted for entry into educational programs there. Not captured in this survey is another well-known factor in Indonesians' choice of Germany, namely the free tuition offered to international students.

The reasons for *not* choosing Australia as a study destination are for the most part straightforward. A lack of knowledge about Australia or Australian universities is mentioned as one of the main reasons. Concern that tuition fees in Australia are too high also stands out. Some respondents, especially those from Bandung, West Java, express a fear of racism among Australians. While this does not rate as a major deterrent overall to studying in Australia, this perception is nevertheless somewhat unsettling. Interestingly, some respondents regard Australia as too far from home and for this reason are unlikely to choose to study there. This is true of respondents in Medan and Pekanbaru in Sumatra. Conversely, some respondents in Surabaya, East Java, regard Australia as being *too close* to home.

Of those for whom Australia is not the first choice, a few believe that the quality of Australian education is not good enough. Generally speaking, however, the decision not to study in Australia is based on other factors, such as having a relative in the country of choice, not knowing enough about Australia or even the perception that there are already too many Indonesians in Australia. In the past, the latter factor may have been considered an added attraction in choosing to study in one country over another. These days, however, Indonesians seem less inclined to want to be in a classroom full of fellow Indonesians. Once again this points to the greater importance being placed on gaining a meaningful experience while overseas. The rationale seems to be that if one is in a classroom full of Indonesians, why bother going overseas to study?

IMPLICATIONS FOR AUSTRALIA

Indonesians seeking an overseas education are now more sophisticated, more discerning and more price sensitive. Students are more aware of their options; they are asking more questions. Before making a final decision on where to study, they are evaluating more fully the advantages and disadvantages of each country in order to make the best possible choice.

The challenge for Australia lies in keeping pace with market changes, understanding what is causing such changes, and adopting a new, more sound and integrated approach to attracting international students. To remain competitive as a study destination, Australia needs to analyse the international education environment carefully, and become more responsive to market demand.

Several areas of focus will become important for Australian institutions aiming to increase or even merely to maintain their current Indonesian student numbers. Foremost is the need to adapt marketing strategies to a changing, more dynamic environment. This will involve reviewing the suite of programs available to international students and assessing their content and suitability, particularly to the Asian market. To the extent possible, to satisfy more international students, Australian institutions should consider mixed mode delivery. For example, they could collaborate with leading overseas universities to offer joint degrees, sandwich programs and a combination of online (off-shore) and face-to-face (on-shore) teaching options. In the near future, Australian institutions should embark on a more integrated program of improved, widespread, intensified marketing of Australian education to Indonesians.

Strengthening institution–student relations and adopting best-practice student application systems and processes will also be crucial. Those operating in the area of overseas student recruitment on behalf of Australia frequently complain about the time taken to process student applications, especially at the postgraduate level. Given the growing array of choices available to Indonesians, it would be in Australia's interests to review how it deals with international students generally, to ensure that students from important source countries such as Indonesia continue to favour Australia over other study destinations.

Tuition fees for higher education, where most of the demand from Indonesia lies, need to be contained. A good understanding of the market means being aware that Indonesian students do now have a variety of options at home and in the region. Introducing an effective and fair costing strategy would be beneficial in showing students that Australia cares about their business.

Student services must be upgraded continually to better serve the needs of international students, who expect to pay for such services but who equally expect to receive high-quality services. Rather than reducing funding for international offices when there is a downturn in the international education business, Australian institutions should be budgeting for better student facilities and more staff, preferably with international work experience.

While the current DFAT warning against non-essential travel to Indonesia remains in place, institutions should be developing alternative marketing strategies so that they can continue to market education effectively in Indonesia. This may involve using tele-conferencing or video-conferencing facilities to maintain contact with prospective students and in-country representatives. Institutions could also conduct agent updates or workshops in the region rather than in Indonesia. To manage in-country promotional activities, cooperative joint marketing is another strategy that could be considered.

Nurturing the people-to-people links brought about by international education cannot be emphasised enough. Through such links, lasting personal and business relationships can be forged for the future, to the benefit of all parties. There is therefore a need to revisit the policy of discontinuing Indonesian-language programs in Australian schools and universities. The policy, as it currently stands, sends the wrong signal to young Australian students; by not promoting the study of Indonesia and Indonesian, it signals that Australia no longer regards Indonesia as significant. To persuade more Australian students to take up Indonesian studies, the Australian government may need to become more proactive in providing schools with information on the importance of understanding Indonesia's language, culture, politics and religion. Related to this is the promotion of teacher and student exchange programs. It is encouraging to note that, despite the acts of terrorism in Indonesia and the DFAT notice, a small number of Australians have decided to remain in Indonesia on exchange programs.

Maintaining ties with Indonesian alumni, some of the best ambassadors for Australia, can further enhance the educational and social links between Australia and Indonesia. Currently there are well in excess of 100,000 Indonesian alumni of Australian educational institutions, and yet anecdotal evidence suggests that fewer than 5,000 of them are registered members of in-country alumni chapters. Furthermore, contact between alumni and their alma maters appears to be more the exception than the rule.

Australia would be foolish to regard international students merely as a commercial commodity. There are immeasurable benefits and advantages to having international students in Australia, apart from the financial considerations.

CONCLUSION

Over the past decade, Australia has enjoyed unprecedented popularity as a study destination for students from Southeast Asia, particularly Indonesia. Despite the recent slowdown in market growth from Indonesia, significant potential still exists for further expansion of Australian education services to Indonesians. However, as competition emerges in the region, Australia will need to adopt new strategies to keep pace with the changes that are taking place in the market, and seek constantly to improve its global competitiveness.

As the quality of education slowly improves in Indonesia, largely through international programs provided locally by a number of countries, including Australia, more choices will become available domestically. Indonesians will continue to become better informed about the options available to them to study at home and abroad.

How welcome Indonesians feel in Australia will be important when they make the choice about where to study. If quality, cost, and course content and variety are more or less equal, it will be the promise of a different but enjoyable overall experience that will ultimately help Indonesians decide whether or not to choose Australia. A good impression of Australians' attitude towards international students will undoubtedly count.

Australia must face the current challenges in the Indonesian market with a positive outlook and determination to stand by Indonesia, for the long haul. As Indonesia's closest neighbour, Australia can continue to play a key role in offering promising young Indonesians a top-quality education and providing them with valuable experiences. This will not only assist them to reach their personal goals in life but also have far-reaching benefits for both Indonesia and Australia over the long term.

NOTES

* Copyright of AEI-created material contained in this publication is owned by the Commonwealth of Australia. Enquiries for use should be directed to: Chief Executive Officer, Australian Education International (AEI), GPO Box 9880, Canberra City, ACT, 2601. Ph. (02) 6240 8111. Email: aeiweb@dest.gov.au <mailto:aeiweb@ dest.gov.au>.

1 The former is a non-profit organisation; the latter is a peak body funded by the Australian government.

2 From 1 November 2005, on completion of their studies in Australia, overseas students will be able to apply for an occupational trainee visa to undertake up to 12 months of supervised on-the-job training in their area of expertise. Employers will also be able to offer overseas students with an occupational trainee visa practical employment experience where this leads to registration in their chosen profession in Australia.

3 A *jilbab* is the headscarf worn by many Muslim women.

4 IDP Education Australia's Post Graduate Exhibition was conducted in Jakarta, Bandung, Semarang, Surabaya and Yogyakarta in September 2005. At each of IDP's four education exhibitions conducted annually in Indonesia, visitors are surveyed on their reasons for attending the event, where they want to study, how they perceive Australian education, what they plan to study while overseas and other key issues.

5 The results were analysed by IDP Education Australia's Research Unit, Sydney, in August 2004. It should be noted that visitors attending IDP Education Australia's in-country education exhibitions were not surveyed, to avoid any possible Australia bias.

9 THE CENTRALITY OF THE PERIPHERY: AUSTRALIA, INDONESIA AND PAPUA

*Richard Chauvel**

In the roller-coaster ride that has been the history of the bilateral relationship between Australia and Indonesia, regions of the eastern archipelago, particularly East Timor and Papua, have been issues of particular sensitivity and have at times even dominated the relationship. Strategic interest in the regions closest to Australian territory and perceptions about the eastern archipelago's cultural diversity and governance have been among Australian concerns, while suspicions about Australia's interests and intentions in the archipelago, especially after the international intervention in East Timor in 1999, remain at the forefront of Indonesia's concerns. There are elements of Australian government thinking of the 1950s and early 1960s, and some sections of current public opinion, that question the legitimacy of the Indonesian state in the culturally diverse parts of the eastern archipelago. Sir Wilfred Kent Hughes, one-time minister in the Menzies government, provided an ill-informed but influential example of this attitude when he wrote in the *Melbourne Herald* in 1950:

> The inhabitants of New Guinea are foreigners as far as the Indonesians are concerned. They belong almost entirely to the frizzy-haired families of mankind. Indonesians are straight-haired (Kent Hughes 1950).

Sir Wilfred asserted that neither historically nor racially had New Guinea ever been part of Indonesia.

Informed in part by attitudes not too dissimilar to those of Kent Hughes, Australia supported a continued Netherlands administration in Papua until 1962. In January of that year, when diplomatic tensions between Indonesia and the Netherlands seemed likely to spill over into military conflict, the minister for external affairs, Sir Garfield Barwick, persuaded the Menzies government that Australia's interests would be best served by a close and cooperative relationship with a united Indonesia.[1] Barwick argued that it was not in Australia's interest to support an independent Papua, as foreshadowed by the Dutch. He said that such a state would be small, unviable, indefensible and the focus of Indonesian antagonism. The Australian government may have been embarrassed and uncomfortable with the manner in which Indonesia conducted the 1969 'Act of Free Choice',[2] but the outcome – Papua's incorporation into Indonesia – was consistent with the strategic decision it made in 1962. The logic of the policy pursued by Australian governments since 1962 is that Australia has an interest in Indonesia successfully accommodating Papua and convincing Papuans that their preferred future should be as part of Indonesia.

Papua was the focus of a protracted but ultimately successful Indonesian campaign to assert its sovereignty over territory the Dutch had attempted to separate from Indonesia. President Sukarno used the West Irian campaign as an issue to unify Indonesia as a political community. West Irian was one issue on which nearly all Indonesian political leaders and parties could agree. The Indonesian defeat of the Dutch in 1962 was a nationalist triumph. In the campaign against the Dutch, Papuans were not participants in the campaign but rather the object of it. Paradoxically, Papua's importance in the nationalist enterprise has made Papua's accommodation into Indonesia more difficult. The process of incorporation has been impeded by Papua's cultural distinctiveness and the existence in 1962 of an alternative national identity and ideal, together with limited Papuan participation in Indonesia's national struggles.

The history of Papua under Indonesian rule has been one of rapid socioeconomic change and massive demographic transformation. The exploitation of Papua's resources, the systemic abuse of human rights and the harsh application of the 'security approach' have fuelled the growth of Papuan nationalism. The post-Soeharto transformation of Papuan resistance from the armed struggle of the Free Papua Organisation (OPM) to non-violent strategies has posed complex policy challenges for governments in Jakarta. How much political openness could be tolerated if it was used to mobilise popular support for independence? Would the implementation of Law 21/2001 on Special Autonomy in Papua Province (referred to hereafter as the Special Autonomy Law) facilitate successful accommodation of Papua into Indonesia, or would it be used as a vehicle to promote separation? Which leaders and groups within the Papuan elite could be trusted to support Papua's incorporation into Indonesia? How could Jakarta's authority be maintained without resort to the very methods that, in the longer term, serve only to fuel Papuan resistance to and alienation from Indonesia? Reflecting these dilemmas, Jakarta's Papua policies have vacillated between accommodation and repression. The separation of East Timor, the revival of Papua as an international issue and the August 2005 agreement on Aceh have made Papua an issue of the greatest sensitivity. President Susilo Bambang Yudhoyono has made a commitment to a political resolution in Papua, but has done little to resolve the policy confusion and contradictions his administration inherited from former President Megawati Sukarnoputri.

Papua is an issue that goes to the heart of Indonesia as a nation and as such has been a salient international and governance issue since before Indonesia was proclaimed as an independent state. Given that Papua has been part of Indonesia since 1963, the question now is whether Indonesia can accommodate Papua in the face of the development of a Papuan national identity based on a sharp distinction between Papuans and Indonesians.

Papua impinges on Australia's relations with Indonesia for reasons of geographic proximity, because of the history of Australia's role in the Netherlands–Indonesia dispute and in the intervention in East Timor, and because of its potential to replace East Timor as the 'pebble in the shoe'. Papua is not likely to become a less conspicuous international issue until there is some discernible movement in governance reform. This chapter will explore the history of this conflict and examine how the cultural distinctiveness of Papua, human rights issues and governance make it a matter of particular sensitivity, one in which the governments of both Indonesia and Australia share an interest in finding a political resolution through which Papuans come to see Indonesia as their preferred future.

PAPUA AS AN INTERNATIONAL ISSUE

Papua was the focus of an international dispute between Indonesia and the Netherlands until the issue was resolved in 1962. The United Nations recognised Indonesia's sovereignty in Papua in 1969 after the Act of Free Choice. Yet Papuan nationalists have successfully revived it as an international issue since the fall of Soeharto. There are several examples of how Papuan interpretations of Papua's incorporation into Indonesia and of an alternate Papuan nationalism have found currency in the international community, despite the United Nations' longstanding acceptance of Indonesian sovereignty. One was the draft bill for the Foreign Relations Authorization Act, Fiscal Years 2006 and 2007 (H.R. 2601), which came before the US Congress in 2005. Others were Papuan diplomacy in the Pacific Islands Forum and the Dutch parliament's research on the 1969 Act of Free Choice (see Drooglever 2005). It is notable that the renewed resonance of Papua as an international issue has so far found few echoes in Australia, Indonesia's neighbour with the most at stake from a settlement in Papua, yet the issue impacts on Australia's relations with Indonesia.

The most significant reminder that Papua remains both an international issue and an intractable domestic policy conundrum has come from the US Congress. In July 2005 the US House of Representatives passed H.R. 2601 by a vote of 351 to 78. The bill included specific references to Indonesia and Papua. If it is passed by the Senate, the State Department will be required to report to Congress on the implementation of the Special Autonomy Law, including the allocation of resources and decision-making power to Papua; access to Papua by the international press and NGOs; the deployment and conduct of Indonesian security forces; and US efforts to promote human rights. Further, the State Department will be obliged to report on the conduct of the 1969 Act of Free Choice. As important as these specific reporting requirements was the way the bill constructed the nature of the conflict in Papua, and Papua's incorporation into Indonesia. The bill identifies indigenous Papuans as Melanesians rather than Indonesians. It asserts that:

> indigenous Papuans have suffered extensive human rights abuses, natural resource exploitation, environmental degradation, and commercial dominance by immigrant communities, and some individuals and groups estimate that more than 100,000 Papuans have been killed during Indonesian rule, primarily during the Sukarno and Soeharto administrations (H.R. 2601, section 1115, 'Developments in and policy toward Indonesia').

According to the bill, the 1962 New York Agreement provided that Papuans would participate in an act of self-determination conducted in accordance with international practice. However, the bill states that the 1969 Act of Free Choice was subject to both overt and covert forms of manipulation. It adds that:

> while the United States supports the territorial integrity of Indonesia, Indonesia's historical reliance on force for the maintenance of control [in Papua] has been counterproductive, and ... abuses by security forces have galvanized independence sentiments among many Papuans (H.R. 2601, section 1115, 'Developments in and policy toward Indonesia').

The bill followed a letter sent by members of the Congressional Black Caucus to Secretary of State Condoleezza Rice in March 2005.[3] The letter opposed the renewal of the International Military Education and Training (IMET) program for the Indonesian military and raised the related issue of the FBI investigations into the murder of two American citizens near the Freeport mine in August 2002. The members of the Black Caucus reminded Rice of the role the United States had played in mediating the 1962 agreement between Indonesia and the Netherlands. They asserted that in the 1960s it had been US national policy to sacrifice the lives and future of Papuans in the hope that Sukarno and Soeharto would become America's friends. The members referred to President George W. Bush's pledge in his 2005 State of the Union speech that America would stand with the allies of freedom to support democratic movements and build a community of free and independent nations, with governments that answer to their citizens and reflect their own culture. They argued that the president's 'mantra' should include Papua.

In the letter, the members of the Black Caucus referred to Papuans as 'our brothers and sisters'. In identifying with Papuans as Melanesians 'believed to be of African descent', they may not have been aware of the role that African Americans played at another stage in the evolution of Papuan identity. E.J. Bonay, a Papuan nationalist and the first governor of West Irian, argued that General MacArthur's forces, which liberated Papua from the Japanese in early 1944, breathed life into Papuan nationalism. Bonay recalled that Papuans admired the African Americans, both men and women, in the Allied Forces:

> They [the African Americans] worked and fought shoulder to shoulder with their white comrades. [They] flew fighter planes, commanded warships, fired artillery, and drove vehicles and so forth. Many [African American] women were in the Women Auxiliary Corps along with white women. Seeing this, Papuans asked themselves why can the [African Americans] do these things and the Papuans not? Is not our skin color and hair the same? (Bonay 1984: 44–5).

The congressional bill reflects some of the complexity of Papua as an international issue and an intractable policy challenge for Indonesia. It highlights cultural difference, human rights abuses and economic exploitation as well as the process by which Papua became part of Indonesia. The issue of Papua's cultural distinctiveness has been a factor for as long as Indonesia has been independent. Human rights and economic exploitation, however, have only become prominent since 1963. In an international environment that, post Yugoslavia and Rwanda, has become unsympathetic to ethnic nationalism, especially one as crudely expressed as the Papuan one, it is remarkable how it features in the congressional bill. It is as if Papua's ethnic nationalism has become legitimate *because* of human rights abuses and economic exploitation.

The Indonesian authorities are also aware of the relationship between human rights abuses and international attention. A police operation in Papua in 2002 targeted:

> individuals and social organisations who oppose the policy of the government by using violations of human rights as a cover and who engage in other activities that can undermine the authority of the government and the state.[4]

Similarly, it is unlikely that Papuan arguments about the conduct of the Act of Free Choice and the legitimacy of Indonesia's incorporation of Papua would have attracted much international interest but for the nature of Indonesian governance since 1963.

The US Congress's draft bill has provoked a strong response in Indonesia. In a speech in New York on 15 September 2005, President Yudhoyono appealed to his audience not to:

> underestimate the political and psychological impact of this draft bill among Indonesians, who want to do their best to sort out our internal problems but who are very sensitive about things which are reflected in that draft bill (Yudhoyono 2005b).

In contrast, Papuans were reported to have welcomed the news of Congress's interest (Poulgrain 2005). Reverend Socratez Yoman, the head of the Baptist Church in Papua, argued that international involvement in Papua was inevitable if the Indonesian government did not take the issue seriously (Hartadi 2005). It is not the purpose of this article to examine the effect the bill might have on US–Indonesia relations if pressure from the Bush administration and lobbying from Indonesia fail to have it amended in the Senate. Rather the objective of this discussion is to argue that the bill identifies the importance of Papua in defining both the borders and the rationale of Indonesia, and explains the persistence of Papua as an international issue. It is in these two respects that Papua has helped shape relations between Indonesia and Australia.

WHY PAPUA IS PART OF INDONESIA

The discussion within Indonesia about Papua – whether or not it should be included in an independent Indonesia – commenced in the debates in the Indonesian Independence Investigatory Body (BPKI) that preceded the proclamation of independence. Considering the peripheral nature of Papua in the pre-war Netherlands Indies and the limited experience nationalist leaders had of Papua, it is remarkable that there was so much discussion. It is a testimony to the manner in which Papua has helped determine the borders and the rationale of Indonesia.

Mohammad Hatta was the only major contributor to the debate who had been exiled to Boven Digul in Dutch New Guinea,[5] and thus had some experience of Papuan society. Like the US members of Congress over half a century later, Hatta recognised that the Papuan people were Melanesian, and questioned the wisdom of including Papua in Indonesia. In a speech on 11 July 1945, he said:

> We must not forget that to the east our people are greatly intermixed with Melanesians, just as Indonesians in the centre and west are intermixed with the Arabs, Chinese and Hindus. This is the fate of peoples who live in the middle of international thoroughfares to associate with other peoples. So don't let us place Papua in the same situation we find in the eastern archipelago, where Indonesians have intermixed with Melanesians. … I only want to say that we should not be worried about Papua; it can be given to the Papuans themselves. I acknowledge that the Papuans also have the right to become an independent people, but Indonesians for the time being, for a few decades, will not have the capacity or sufficient resources to teach the Papuans until they become an independent people (quoted in Yamin 1959: 203).

Hatta's views did not prevail. Sukarno and his ally Mohammed Yamin[6] were more persuasive and more ambitious. In a speech on 1 June 1945, Sukarno argued that God had divided the world into national units and that even a child could see that the Indonesian archipelago was one such unit. He said:

> So where is this entity we call our fatherland? Geo-politically, Indonesia our fatherland, the complete Indonesia, not just Java, not just Sumatra, or only Borneo or Celebes or merely Ambon or Maluku, but all the islands which have been designated

by God to become the unit, between two continents and two oceans, that is our fatherland! (quoted in Yamin 1959: 70–1).

Yamin advocated that the state should coincide with the 'Indonesian fatherland', the scope of which had been determined by the fourteenth-century state of Majapahit, stretching from peninsular Malaya to 'Papua'. According to Yamin 'Papua' was a special case. Since ancient times, he argued, 'Papua' and the surrounding islands had been occupied by the Papuan people and had been a place of migration for Indonesians. Also, part of it had been in the territory of 'Tidore-Halmahera'. He asserted:

> Papua was Austronesian territory, which was the centre of our fatherland. During a thousand years of history Papua has been united with the Moluccas, and became unified with Indonesia (Republic of Indonesia 1995: 4).[7]

Yamin and Sukarno recognised cultural differences, but did not consider them to be an important factor in determining the basis of the state. It was as if, in order to minimise the archipelago's ethnic and cultural diversity, the concept of Indonesia was expanded to encompass Melanesia and Polynesia as well as the Malay world.

In 1954 Indonesia took the Papua issue to the United Nations. In so doing Indonesia had to justify its claim to the territory. One of the arguments advanced at the United Nations was that Indonesia was a political concept rather than a cultural or ethnic one. Indonesia stated that the Papuans were merely one of 17 ethnic groups that made up Indonesia. It argued that Papuans were different from other Indonesians, but that the differences were no greater than those between, say, Eskimos or Indians and other Canadians.

Indonesian representatives at the United Nations were fond of quoting J.H. van Roijen, the senior Dutch negotiator during the 1945–49 Indonesian revolution and later ambassador to Washington. For example, in a speech to the United Nations in 1954, L.N. Palar quoted van Roijen as follows:

> [T]he population of Indonesia consists of about seventeen main ethnic and linguistic groups which, in turn, contain a still greater number of subgroups. The unity of Indonesia, which has gradually grown, is a product of common Netherlands sovereignty ... Common existence under the Netherlands Crown has created a sense of Indonesian nationality and the will toward an Indonesian state ...[8]

Yamin argued that it was not the case that Papuans or the people of the island of Nias (off west Sumatra) were not 'Indonesians' in an anthropological sense. Some groups that were part of the nation-forming process could in no ethnographic sense be considered 'Indonesian', he said, for example the Eurasians. According to Yamin, it was the common experience and common struggle rather than ethnicity that were important in the nation-forming process. He noted that the peoples of eastern New Guinea, north Borneo and east Timor had been separated from ethnically similar groups by colonial boundaries for several centuries and did not participate in the Indonesian struggle for independence. He suggested that they had lost, or may never have had, a feeling of togetherness with Indonesia, and therefore could not be considered part of Indonesia (Netherlands–Indonesian Union 1950: 42). In a broader context, Yamin argued that the history of state and nation-forming processes demonstrates that uniformity in linguistic and ethnographic character is not a decisive factor in determining whether a particular region becomes part of a state (Netherlands–Indonesian Union 1950: 101). He pointed out that the United States, Russia and many other nations contain regions of diverse ethnographic character.

Papua's distinctiveness was recognised in another way. Indonesia's representatives at the United Nations argued that Indonesian freedom fighters, like their counterparts elsewhere in the world, naturally acted on behalf of the hundreds and thousands of Papuans still living in the 'Stone Age' and unaware that their leaders were fighting for their freedom.[9] This echoed Sukarno's response to Hatta's arguments in 1945, that Papuans did not know what they wanted and did not understand politics. Papua's future would have to be determined by others, as it had been historically by the inclusion of Papua in the territory of the fourteenth-century Hindu Javanese kingdom of Majapahit.[10]

The nationalists did recognise something of Papua's ethnic distinctiveness. However, this only made it more important that Papua be included in Indonesia, to demonstrate that Indonesia was a political concept rather than a nation based on an assertion of ethnic or cultural unity.

AUSTRALIAN ATTITUDES

Although Australia was a strong supporter of Indonesia during its struggle for independence, the Chifley government supported the Dutch policy to exclude Papua from the transfer of sovereignty to Indonesia in December 1949. In the early months of 1950 the attitude of the newly elected Menzies government became one of outright rejection of Indonesia's claim to Papua as part of Indonesian territory.

The Australian policy had two elements. First, it was asserted that Australia had a vital strategic interest in Papua, which was part of New Guinea and 'the island areas immediately adjacent to Australia'. Percy Spender, Menzies' first external affairs minister, claimed that these islands were 'the last ring of defence against aggression', that 'Australia must be vitally concerned with whatever fundamental changes take place in any of these areas' and that the 'Australian people are deeply interested in what happens anywhere in New Guinea'.[11] Second, Spender argued that west Papua did not naturally form part of Indonesia but rather had more in common with the Australian territories of New Guinea and Papua. He said:

> It [Papua] is part of the one mainland, divided merely by a line drawn on a map. It is inhabited almost wholly by people of the same ethnic origin and having the same social and economic problems as those of the people of Papua and Australian New Guinea.[12]

As Australian policy developed in the 1950s, the strategic and ethnographic arguments became fused. At the end of 1950, Spender proclaimed that Australia had 'no other motive or aspiration than the interests of the people of New Guinea'. He claimed that the interests of 'the inarticulate mass of the native people of Dutch New Guinea' had become fused with the vital strategic interests of Australia. Australia's strategic interests were Papuan interests, and vice versa.[13]

Although the strategic and ethnic arguments had become fused in Spender's mind, it has been suggested that Australia's 'selfless' advancement of Papuan interests served to provide an ethical legitimation for Australia's perceived strategic interests. When Indonesia took the issue to the United Nations in 1954, Australian arguments emphasised Papuan interests, cultural differences and the Papuans' right of self-determination.[14] Australia's argument about the unity of New Guinea was given concrete expression in the 1957 agreement on cooperation between the Australian and Dutch colonial administrations.

The ethnographic argument disappeared from Australian official public discourse with the reversal of Australian policy in 1962. The change of policy was argued in strategic terms: that Australia had a strategic interest in friendly and cooperative relations with a strong and united Indonesia; that it was not in Australia's interests that a small, unviable and indefensible state be created in Papua; and that Australia recognised and accepted the Indonesian nationalist conception of the Indonesian nation state (that Papua might be culturally different, but was nevertheless part of Indonesia).[15]

PAPUAN VOICES

In 1962 Indonesia won the diplomatic and military struggle with the Dutch. Its success marked the failure of a 12-year-old Australian policy. By default, Indonesia had also won the ethnic argument that Papua has a proper place in an inclusive, secular, multi-ethnic, multi-faith Indonesia. The Indonesian case was persuasive in international forums and among some Papuans. It reflected the most admirable civic, secular and inclusive pluralist values in Indonesian nationalism.

The Indonesian victory of 1962 has been brought into question by the post-Soeharto revival of Papuan nationalism. There is much in Papuan nationalism, with its strong primordial tenor, that questions whether the admirable values of Indonesian nationalism have been realised in the governance of Papua since 1963.

Percy Spender purported to represent the interests of 'the inarticulate mass of the native people of Dutch New Guinea'. Papuans do not need the advocacy of an Australian minister, but Spender would readily recognise the way in which Papuans have articulated their identity in terms of a stark ethnic and cultural contrast to Indonesians. In August 1998 an Indonesian parliamentary delegation was sent to Papua to investigate why people wanted 'a free Papua'. Mrs Agu Iwanggin, deputy synod secretary of the Papuan Protestant Church, gave a particularly confronting version of how Papuans distinguish themselves from Indonesians. As she explained to the delegation:

> God created people to be different. Papuans are different to Javanese, and different to other people too. God gave Papua to Papuans as a home, so they could eat sago and sweet potatoes there. God gave them a penis gourd (*koteka*) and loincloth (*cawat*) for clothes. God gave them curly hair and black skin. Papuans are Papuans. They can never be turned into Javanese or Sumatrans, or vice versa. The Javanese were given Java. *Tahu* (soya bean curd) and *tempe* (soya bean cake) is their food. Their skin is light and their hair straight (Rev. Mrs Agu Iwanggin, cited in Giay 2001).

There is a paradox in how Papuan identity has been constructed: sharp distinctions are made between Papuans and Indonesians, but within Papuan society there is a mosaic of over 300 ethno-linguistic groups. The distinctions Papuan nationalists make between Papuans and Indonesians are part of a process of creating a pan-Papuan identity. Papuans recognise that they are not the only distinctive ethnic group in Indonesia, but this is not reflected in Papuan nationalist rhetoric (Chauvel 2005). Closely related to the assertions of ethnic difference have been arguments like those advanced by Benny Giay: that Jakarta-centric policies on development (*pembangunan*) have served to incapacitate and marginalise Papuans, that there has been no proper place for the dignity and status of the Papuan people, and that, in Indonesian eyes, Papuans have no worth. In Giay's opinion, the Indonesian government values the resources of Papua more highly than it does the Papuan people (Giay 2000: 30, 35, 55). He quotes a delegate from Nabire at the Papuan Mass Consultation in February 2000 as saying:

> Indonesians have never given Papuans a proper place. Because indeed they are Indonesians and we are Papuans. We are murdered, enslaved and colonized by Indonesians. In another 10 years time Papuans will be finished, murdered by the Indonesian military. Because of that it is better that we just become independent (Giay 2000: 15).

Percy Spender and his Dutch counterparts might recognise and identify with the sentiments expressed by Papuan nationalists in the *reformasi* era, but these constructions are not reformulations of the Dutch and Australian arguments of the 1950s and early 1960s. Rather, they reflect Papuan experience of Indonesian rule since 1963 and interpret Papua's integration into Indonesia.[16] Indeed, the arguments about cultural distinctiveness and whether Papua should or should not be part of Indonesia resonate in Papua, and in Papuans' international lobbying, precisely because of the experience of human rights abuses and the economic exploitation of Papua's resources by international corporations and 'Jakarta' since 1963. Just as Giay has argued that Papuans were marginalised by the economic development policies of the Soeharto government, he has also associated the suffering of the Papuan people since integration with Indonesia with killings and human rights abuses. In Giay's construction of Papuan nationalism and experience of Indonesian rule, human rights abuses have served to consolidate Papuan identity and define it in distinct primordial terms.[17] It is worth noting that the construction of Papuan nationalism in the post-Soeharto *reformasi* period is much more primordial than in the formulations of the early 1960s.

The sharp distinctions Papuans make between themselves and Indonesians are closely related to the massive demographic transformations Papua has experienced since 1963. In 1960 the 'Asian' population, mainly eastern Indonesians, Javanese and Chinese, numbered just 18,600, or 2.5 per cent of an estimated population of 736,700 (Netherlands Government 1960: 6–7). The 2000 census indicated that the number of non-Papuans resident in the province was 772,684, or 35 per cent of the total population. In the capital, Jayapura, the settler communities constitute about 68 per cent of the population, as they do in Sorong and Fakfak.[18] Migration from elsewhere in Indonesia has taken two forms: official migration through government transmigration programs, and 'spontaneous' migration. As shown in the quotation from Herman Wayoi below, in terms of the impact on their society Papuans often do not distinguish between official and voluntary migration and consider that the government encourages, even if it does not organise, the latter.

Wayoi, one of the 1960s generation of nationalists, experienced the influx of Indonesians into Papua and wrote in a report to President Habibie:

> It was as if the Indonesian Government sought only to 'dominate' (*menguasai*) the territory, then planned to exterminate the ethnic Melanesians and replace them with ethnic Malays from Indonesia. Transmigration 'proved' this impression; transporting thousands from outside to settle in the fertile valleys of the land of Papua (Wayoi 2002: 64).

The ethnic dimension of nationalism was expressed across the Papuan political spectrum, including by leaders willing to cooperate with the Indonesian authorities. In April 2001 the governor of Papua, Jaap Solossa, presented his administration's proposal for the Special Autonomy Law. It reflected Papuan political and cultural values and ideals combined with a substantial devolution of decision-making authority and distribution of resources from the centre to the province. While the proposal did not contain a demand for independence, it was nevertheless a strong statement of Papuan nationalism. The proposal established Papua as a region of self-government within Indonesia. It made a distinction between indigenous Papuans and other residents of the province, by requiring the governor and deputy governor to be Papuans. It ensured Papuan dominance of the legislature through the creation of two houses of parliament, with a Papuan upper house consisting of customary (*adat*), religious and women representatives.[19]

Foreshadowing the Indonesian government's memorandum of understanding with the Free Aceh Movement (GAM) in August 2005, the governor's proposal for special autonomy provided that local as well as national political parties could contest the elections for the lower house of parliament. Under the proposal, the province would be called Papua and would have its own flag, anthem and coat of arms, in addition to the Indonesian national ones. There would be no transmigration. Priority would be given to the employment of Papuans in all sectors of the economy. The provincial government would be required to protect and develop Papuan culture. There would be provision for the protection and representation of traditional institutions, for the advancement of human rights and for ecologically sustainable economic development.[20]

Although the Special Autonomy Law did determine that the governor and deputy governor should be Papuans, the adequacy of indigenous Papuan representation has remained an issue. During the election of local government leaders (*pilkada*) in 2005, Papuan activists were concerned about the tendency of political parties to nominate a Papuan as the candidate for district head (*bupati* or *walikota*) and an immigrant as the deputy. Nominations of Papuan–settler 'tickets' made good electoral politics in the areas of Papua with substantial settler populations and also reflected the extent of settler control of the political parties' organisations. Activists wanted the provincial parliament to secure Papuan representation at the district level in the same way the Special Autonomy Law had done at the provincial level.[21]

The post-Soeharto, *reformasi*-era revival of Papuan nationalism has been organised around the straightforward demand for *merdeka* (independence), as stated by the Team of 100 elite Papuans who met President Habibie in February 1999, and as formalised in the resolutions of the second Papua Congress in mid-2000. Like Indonesian nationalists before them, Papuans use the term *Papua merdeka* (free Papua) to imply a great deal more than liberation from Indonesian rule (McVey 2003: 17). *Merdeka* means freedom from poverty, backwardness, poor education, corruption and state violence, and includes the provision of economic opportunities. It is possible that Papua could become independent and yet these ideals not be realised. Alternatively, they could be achieved within the Indonesian state. Indeed, during the campaign for special autonomy Bas Suebu, the former governor of Papua, acknowledged that Papuans supported independence and rejected autonomy, but argued that special autonomy was nearly the same as independence, although still within the Indonesian state. He argued that independence and special autonomy should not be seen as alternatives; he thought that both would head Papua in the same direction.[22]

Papua is a diverse and plural society. In Dutch colonial times there was a distinct regional dimension to political orientation. The island of Biak had a strong pro-Dutch elite, then a strong pro-independence elite. The neighbouring island of Japen was home to the most substantial and longest-lasting pro-Indonesia organisation, the Indonesian Independence Party Irian (PKII). In the early 1960s it provided much of the leadership for Parna, Papua's first nationalist party. Most sections of the Jayapura-based Papuan elite opposed Megawati's 2003 decision to divide Papua into three provinces, yet partition found supporters in some regions, including some – like Manokwari, Biak and the highlands – known for their support of the *merdeka* movement. The killings at Wamena in October 2000 and the election of the governor and deputy governor in the same year revealed considerable tensions between highlanders and coastal Papuans, yet Indonesian officials identify highlanders as the hard core of the independence movement. There is a complex set of relationships between political orientation – *merdeka*, autonomy, or complete incorporation within the unitary state of Indonesia – and region. Control over resources and government positions seems as important a factor as region (Chauvel 2003).

THE NATIONAL INTEGRITY OF AUSTRALIA AND INDONESIA: EAST TIMOR AND PAPUA

In the years following the fall of Soeharto, the coincidence of the revival of Papuan nationalism and the separation of East Timor from Indonesia once again made Papua a factor in the bilateral relationship. Australia's role in the international intervention in East Timor and the reversal of its longstanding policy in support of Indonesian sovereignty in the former Portuguese territory meant that Indonesia's concerns about further territorial disintegration directly affected relations with its southern neighbour. The enquiry of the Joint Standing Committee on Foreign Affairs, Defence and Trade into Australia's relations with Indonesia noted 'a deep mistrust of Australia's intentions with regard to Papua' during meetings in Jakarta in February 2004 (Foreign Affairs Subcommittee 2004: 128). The committee reported that its members took every opportunity to reiterate Australia's unequivocal support for Indonesia's territorial integrity, with members stating that 'an independent Papua was not in any way in Australia's national interest' (Foreign Affairs Subcommittee 2004: 128). The credibility of Australia's protestations of support for Indonesia's territorial integrity, in the eyes of many inside and outside the government in Jakarta, was in inverse relationship to their frequency.

The Timor precedent evokes the Indonesian response that, while support for Indonesian sovereignty had been Australia's longstanding position, this support evaporated when it mattered most to Jakarta. Contrary to Australia's objectives in 1999, as expressed in a letter from Prime Minister Howard to President Habibie in December 1998 concerning the future of East Timor,[23] the Howard government's later celebration of its 'liberation' of East Timor convinced many Indonesians that East Timor's independence was the desired outcome for Australia. This impression has fuelled suspicions about Australia's intentions in Papua. It also raises the question of whether the intervention represents a departure from the 'Barwick doctrine', which saw the emergence of small states in the eastern archipelago as not being in Australia's interest (see Chapter 5, this volume).

Indonesia's concerns following the international intervention in East Timor were not simply focused on the bilateral relationship with Australia. Writing in 2000, former Foreign Minister Ali Alatas raised concerns about the new global doctrine of 'humanitarian intervention'. Ali Alatas did not dispute the legitimacy of intervention to stop massive and systematic violations of human rights. However, he said, intervention must always be based on the principles of legitimacy, universal applicability and non-discrimination and must be applied justly and consistently, irrespective of which country or region is affected. He noted that those undertaking humanitarian interventions were inevitably advanced countries, and those subject to interventions the developing countries of the South. He said that this gave rise to a potential for neo-colonialism, and that there was concern about the degree to which the principle of state sovereignty could be circumscribed by 'humanitarian intervention' (Alatas 2000).

Ali Alatas's concerns would have been strengthened when, at the 2005 World Summit, the United Nations adopted the principle of 'responsibility to protect'. This principle means that in cases of gross human rights violations, genocide and ethnic cleansing, the primary responsibility rests with the sovereign state, but if the responsible state is unwilling or unable to intervene, the responsibility transfers to the international community.[24] Underlying Indonesia's anxieties about Papua's re-emergence as an international issue is an assessment that foreign governments are unlikely to question Indonesian sovereignty but that even friendly governments might come under pressure from public opinion in their own countries. Many Indonesians believe that this is the lesson of East Timor. The international network of solidarity groups that support Papuan independence may be much less strong than was the case with East Timor; nevertheless recent research reports from Yale University and the University of Sydney have made allegations of gross human rights abuses and genocide in Papua (Allard K. Lowenstein International Human Rights Clinic 2004; Wing and King 2005).

Wing and King (2005) focus on the human rights abuses associated with the Indonesian military's operations in the highlands of Papua since August 2004. Based principally on information supplied by the Baptist Church of Papua, the report alleges that the military operations have left large numbers of people homeless and have led to the deaths of scores of people, including the Baptist minister Elisa Tabuni. The church alleges that on 17 September 2004 Tabuni was killed by Special Forces (Kopassus) troops, and his son Weties shot and wounded. According to the church's reports, during the operations in Puncak Jaya, Kopassus troops burnt down 371 homes of indigenous inhabitants; by the end of 2004 some 6,393 people had fled into the jungle. The Baptist Church also asserts that special autonomy funds were used to support these military operations (Wing and King 2005: 18–19). The military operations described by the Baptist Church conform to a pattern: Papuan attacks on security forces followed by indiscriminate reprisals. According to Amnesty International, the operations in Puncak Jaya in 2004, as well as those in Abepura, Sarmi, Wasior and Wamena in 2000 and 2001:

> were all conducted in response to attacks by armed groups. In all cases, the civilians who became the victims of retaliatory raids reportedly had no involvement with the initial attacks.[25]

WHY IS PAPUA POLICY SO DIFFICULT AND SENSITIVE?

In a speech to the United States–Indonesia Society in September 2005, President Yudhoyono simultaneously warned and reassured his audience of American business people and diplomats (Yudhoyono 2005b). He reassured them that Indonesians wanted to solve their own domestic problems; he warned them that Indonesians were very sensitive about the issues raised in the draft bill before Congress.

This chapter has argued that the issues of cultural distinctiveness and appropriate governance that pre-date the proclamation of Indonesian independence were at the core of the Indonesian dispute with the Netherlands and have over-shadowed Indonesian rule since 1963. The difficulties surrounding Papuan policy are no better illustrated than in the policy confusion and contradictions Yudhoyono inherited from Megawati. Through her decision in 2003 to divide Papua into three provinces, Megawati undermined the Special Autonomy Law that had been negotiated with considerable Papuan participation during 2001, and that had seemed to offer some prospect of accommodating Papuan ideals and aspirations within the Indonesian state (ICG 2003a).

Yudhoyono's task of developing a coherent policy was further complicated by the Constitutional Court's November 2004 decision that the 1999 law that was the basis of Megawati's decision to divide Papua into three provinces was unconstitutional, but that the province of West Irian Jaya, because it already existed, should be allowed to continue to exist, even if its basis in law was invalid.[26] In a number of meetings with Papuan leaders, the president reassured them that special autonomy would be the basis of his policy.[27] Yet, in his Independence Day speech, he did nothing to resolve the policy contradictions and confusion. Both the division of Papua and the implementation of special autonomy would remain government policy.[28]

Papua confronts Yudhoyono's government with a complex set of intractable political and policy issues. His predecessor, Megawati, captured something of the importance of Papua in the Indonesian national enterprise when she recalled a childhood conversation with her father. She asked why he had visited Papua when it was so far away. Sukarno replied: 'Without Irian Jaya, Indonesia is not complete to become the national territory of the Unitary Republic of Indonesia'.[29]

The 'return' of West Irian (Papua) to the fatherland in 1962 marked a great diplomatic victory over the old colonial foe, one that was celebrated by most Indonesians. The fact that, in the dominant Papuan interpretation of history, the 'return' was a matter to be 'rectified' rather than celebrated has made the ideological accommodation of Papua difficult. The Papuan assertion of cultural distinctiveness has also made accommodation a policy challenge. Papuans' ethnic nationalism is an affront to the inclusive multi-ethnic and pluralist values of Indonesian nationalism. A group of distinguished Indonesians implicitly recognised these policy dilemmas and the imperative for Indonesia to find an accommodation with Papua when it established a Papua Forum in September 2005. The forum's deputy chair, Marzuki Darusman, explained its objective in the following terms:

> People feel they have been excluded by the government from the efforts to settle the Aceh problem. Now that the President has announced the government's intention of addressing the Papua issue, we hope that this forum will be capable of ensuring greater public participation (Saraswati 2005).

Papuan leaders tend to welcome initiatives of this nature by sympathetic Indonesians. Some of the forum members are well known and respected in Papua. In the last analysis, Papuans want to be participants in the process of resolving the differences between them and the Indonesian government.

Megawati's partly implemented policy of partition generated much tension and some violence in Papua as well as contributing to a decline in the provision of public services and an increase in corruption. If Megawati's purpose was to fragment the independence movement, she has been partially successful. The continuing policy uncertainties in Jakarta under Yudhoyono, together with violence generated by the operations of the Indonesian National Army (TNI) in the highlands since August 2004, and by newspaper reports of further troop deployments to Papua, have created an unstable and deteriorating situation in Papua.[30] The symbolic return of the Special Autonomy Law in August suggests that, in Papuan eyes, the credibility of this law as a policy framework to resolve the Papua issue, leaving Papua within the Indonesian state, has diminished if not disappeared.[31] Special autonomy was the policy the Indonesian government had

successfully sold to friendly governments, including Australia, as the framework for resolution.

IS A RESOLUTION POSSIBLE?

I do not want to suggest that there is no prospect of a peaceful resolution of the
conflict. Papuan leaders have shown themselves to be remarkably adaptable
when they participate in the political process and when they see some possibility of change in the government's approach. Broad elite support for special
autonomy in 2000–02 was a demonstration of this flexibility. The government's
negotiation of the Aceh memorandum of understanding in 2005 was a positive
sign of its capacity to deal with a regional dispute, one as intractable as Papua
if for somewhat different reasons.

There are at least three imaginable scenarios with respect to Indonesian policy and developments in Papua. First, Yudhoyono could move to implement his
commitment to a political resolution in Papua, building on the momentum generated by the agreement on Aceh. It is unclear whether the Special Autonomy
Law retains sufficient support and credibility among key groups within the
Papuan elite to be used as the policy framework for such a settlement. Whether
or not the law can be revived, the key factor suggesting that special autonomy
does offer hope for a resolution is that Papuans participated in its formulation.
In any imaginable successful accommodation of Papua in Indonesia, broad
Papuan participation is a prerequisite. The Papuan dialogue with the Habibie
and Wahid governments until December 2000 and the subsequent negotiations
on the Special Autonomy Law suggest that Papuans can be flexible when they
perceive that the government is also being flexible.

Resolution would probably involve the disestablishment of the province of
West Irian Jaya and a commitment by the central government to let Papuans
themselves determine the structures of administration and the distribution of
government revenues and decision-making authority. There are elements in the
Aceh agreement that would be a necessary part of any resolution in Papua. The
participation of local parties in the electoral process and the withdrawal of 'non-
organic' troops from Papua are examples. None of these policy changes would
be easy for the president, nor would they be without political cost. However, resolution does offer the prospect of removing Papua from the international
agenda, diminishing a longstanding threat to Indonesia's territorial integrity and
overcoming an obstacle to Indonesia's further democratisation.

The second scenario is a continuation of the status quo. It is characterised by
policy confusion and indecision in Jakarta and by growing tensions and sporadic
violence in Papua. Policy indecision and the lack of commitment to implement
special autonomy have further undermined support from those sections of

Papuan society that had previously supported the Special Autonomy Law. The corruption and decline in the provision of government services by the Papua provincial government and the even more obvious incapacities of the provincial government in West Irian Jaya do nothing to address the challenges of development in Papua and compound the alienation of Papuans. It is a political environment where Papuans naively place their hope in the US Congress or the Netherlands parliament to rescue them from Indonesian rule.

The second scenario has within it the seeds of a third and much more dangerous one. During the 2005 Indonesia Update conference, *The Australian*'s editor-at-large, Paul Kelly, expressed his concern about the effect an outbreak of violence in Papua might have on Australia's relations with Indonesia. Kelly anticipated that the media and groups on the left and right of Australian politics would unite in support of Papuan independence. The sharply anti-Indonesian sentiments in the populist response to the Schapelle Corby case in some parts of the Australian media suggest that an effective network of solidarity groups might not be needed to mobilise support for Papua.

It is difficult to anticipate what the catalyst for an outbreak of more spectacular or larger-scale violence in Papua might be. The risk is two-fold. It is inherent in the methods Jakarta has used in the past to assert its authority in Papua. There is risk also in the likelihood of credible international reporting of human rights abuses, as happened when the 1991 Dili massacre was caught on video, greatly harming Indonesia's international standing. An outbreak of violence would have greater potency if it coincided with international attention on Papua. So far, both the security forces and Papuan political leaders have refrained from inciting tensions between indigenous Papuans and Indonesian settlers. However, the killings in Wamena in October 2000 show the potential for such violence. The sectarian violence in neighbouring Maluku has also cast a shadow on what might be possible in Papua.

History does not repeat itself exactly, but it is all too easy to imagine an Australian government being confronted with a 'Timor in 1999'-type situation, where it is forced to make decisions other than those determined by its long-term assessment of strategic interests. Given Indonesian suspicions about Australia's interests and intentions in Papua, even supportive gestures in favour of an autonomy-type arrangement might provoke a negative reaction from Jakarta. However, if Australia does nothing to encourage Indonesia to reach a peaceful and political resolution in Papua, reduce its dependence on force and thereby lessen the possibilities of an outbreak of violence, the consequences could be far worse.

NOTES

*   The author would like to thank the anonymous reviewers and Jamie Mackie for their insightful and constructive comments on an earlier version of this paper.
1   Memorandum by Sir Garfield Barwick, Minister for External Affairs, on Cabinet Submission No. 10, 11 January 1962. Prime Minister's file C508, Part 3, CRS A4940, National Archives of Australia.
2   Under the terms of the 1962 New York Agreement, the Act of Free Choice was supervised by the United Nations. Many Papuans assert that the process through which 1,025 selected Papuans voted unanimously to join Indonesia did not comply with the letter or the spirit of the New York Agreement (see Drooglever 2005).
3   The letter was sent by 37 members of the Congressional Black Caucus, including Congressmen Eni Faleomavaega and Donald Payne, on 14 March 2005. The Black Caucus also sent a letter to UN Secretary-General Kofi Annan asking that the United Nations review its conduct towards West Papua in the 1960s.
4   'Sadar Matoa', Instruction No. 3/VII/2002, Inspector General Drs Made M. Pastika, 17 July 2002, para. 3b.
5   Hatta was imprisoned in Boven Digul during 1935. His experiences are related in Hatta (1979).
6   Yamin was a minister, historian and ideologue whose work, including the work cited in this chapter, contributed much to Indonesian nationalist historiography.
7   This volume includes the debates that took place in the BPKI prior to the proclamation of independence.
8   J.H. van Roijen, quoted in a speech by L.N. Palar to the United Nations in 1954, Arsip Nasional RI, Jakarta, inv. 115.
9   L.N. Palar, Memorandum on West Irian, October 1961: 'West Irian and Indonesian Nationalism, 1961'. Personal Collection of L.N. Palar, Arsip Nasional Jakarta, inv. 159, 163.
10   Sukarno outlined these views in a speech on 11 July 1945 (see Yamin 1959: 206).
11   Commonwealth of Australia Parliamentary Debates, House of Representatives, 9 March 1950, pp. 632–3.
12   See 'Message to be conveyed through the Australian Ambassador to the United States of Indonesia to the Government of the United States of Indonesia' [formulated by Spender and approved by cabinet], 21 April 1950. DEA File 3036/6/1, Part 1, CRS A1836, National Archives of Australia.
13   See 'Statement by the Australian Minister for External Affairs, Mr. P.C. Spender, The Hague, 28 August 1950'. DEA File 5/3/3, CRS A8108, National Archives of Australia.
14   Cablegram 672 from P.C. Spender [then ambassador to the United States of America] to R.G. Casey [then Minister for External Affairs], 26 October 1954. DEA File 3036/6/1 Part 12, CRS A1838. National Archives of Australia.
15   Memorandum by Sir Garfield Barwick, Minister for External Affairs, on Cabinet Submission No. 10, 11 January 1962. Prime Minister's File C508 Part 3, CRS A4940, National Archives of Australia.
16   For a discussion of Papuan nationalism and Papuan constructions of the territory's integration into Indonesia, see Chauvel (2005).

17 See Giay (2000: 6–7). The human rights abuses Giay cites took place during 1970–99, in Biak, Sarmi, Tiom and Wamena. He argues (p. 7) that the experience was very traumatic and still resonates in the collective memory of the Papuan people.

18 *Tifa Papua*, Jayapura, third week of May 2002, p. 5.

19 Rancangan Undang-undang Republik Indonesia Nomor: .... Tahun 2001 tentang Otonomi Khusus Bagi Propinsi Papua dalam Bentuk Wilayah Berpemerintahan Sendiri [Bill of the Republic of Indonesia Number: .... of 2001 on Special Autonomy for Papua Province in the Form of a Self-governing Territory: Initiative Proposal of the House of Representatives of the Republic of Indonesia], Jayapura, 2001.

20 Although the Special Autonomy Law did not incorporate all aspects of the Papuan proposal, many of its ethnic nationalist aspirations were accepted. The central government's implementation of the law has become the subject of political contestation.

21 Information from the author's interview with Johannis Bonay, Jakarta, 18 June 2005. It is worth noting that only one of Papua's representatives in the national parliament (DPR), elected in 2004, is a Papuan (Simon Morin).

22 'Peserta Seminar Otonomi minta Irja merdeka' [Participants of the Autonomy Seminar request independence for Irian Jaya], *Republika*, 29 March 2001. This line of argument may have had appeal for a Papuan audience, but could have been unsettling for some in Jakarta who feared that special autonomy could be used as a platform to promote independence.

23 In the letter, Howard suggested that the 'long term prospects for a peaceful resolution of the East Timor issue would be best served by an act of self-determination by the East Timorese at some future time, following a substantial period of autonomy'. Howard also made clear the Australian government's preference for East Timor to remain part of Indonesia. See Foreign Affairs Subcommittee (2004: 44–5).

24 United Nations General Assembly Resolution 60/1, '2005 World Summit Outcome', 15 September 2005, New York, A/60/L.1.

25 Amnesty International, Public Statement, 6 December 2004, AI Index: ASA 21/052/2004 (Public).

26 'Central Irian Jaya province annulled', *Laksamana.net*, 12 November 2004, <http://www.kabar-irian.com/pipermail/kabar-irian/2004-November/000584.html>; see also Saraswati (2004).

27 'Presiden-para tokoh Papua bahas otonomi khusus' [President–Papuan leaders analyse special autonomy], *Media Indonesia*, Rabu, 10 August 2005.

28 'Pidato kenegaraan Presiden Republik Indonesia serta keterangan pemerintah' [State speech of the President of the Republic of Indonesia together with a government statement], Jakarta, 16 August 2005; see <http://www.antara.co.id/seenws/index.php?id=16079>.

29 *Tifa Irian*, Jayapura, 20–31 December 1999, p. 8.

30 'Seruan bersama, Gereja Kemah Injil (Kingmi) Papua, Gereja Injili di Indonesia (GIDI), persekutuan Gereja Gereja Baptis Papua' [Joint appeal of the Kingmi, GIDI and Baptist Churches in Papua], Elsham News Service, 23 November 2004.

31 'DAP merasa tak dihargai' [Customary Law Council of Papua (DAP) feels that it is not valued], *Cendrawasih Pos*, 16 September 2005, <http://www.cenderawasihpos.com/Utama/h.6.html>.

PART IV

The Economic Partnership: Aid, Economics and Business

10   THE AUSTRALIA–INDONESIA PARTNERSHIP FOR RECONSTRUCTION AND DEVELOPMENT

Scott Dawson

The massive earthquakes and tsunami that hit countries on the Indian Ocean rim on 26 December 2004 produced a natural disaster on a scale seldom seen. In Indonesia alone, three-quarters of a million people were direct victims: more than 150,000 people died or are still missing, over 500,000 people lost their homes and 150,000 children lost their schools (World Bank 2005b). The Australian government's response was quick and comprehensive, with the immediate commitment of seven emergency medical teams, major Australian Defence Force assets, civilian disaster experts, and $60 million in humanitarian assistance funding and material support for the emergency relief effort across the region.

Within a few days it was clear from the initial damage reports that Indonesia should be the focus of Australia's relief and reconstruction efforts. It was also clear that the task of reconstruction would be enormous, and would add significantly to the challenges facing the new administration of President Susilo Bambang Yudhoyono in restoring international confidence in Indonesia's economy and improving the quality of life of more than 220 million Indonesians.

This thinking underpinned the design of the Australia–Indonesia Partnership for Reconstruction and Development (AIPRD). From initial discussions of the concept among Australian officials to its public announcement by Australian Prime Minister John Howard and Indonesian President Yudhoyono on 5 January 2005 the entire process took less than a week, a remarkably fast timeframe for a $1 billion package that constituted Australia's largest ever foreign aid commitment.

The Australian prime minister referred to the new partnership as 'an historic step' in the relations between Australia and Indonesia and 'a strategic commitment' to raise living standards in Indonesia. He noted that this would be 'significantly different in scale and approach from any previous aid effort' and that it would 'serve to bring our countries and peoples closer together' (Howard 2005a, 2005b). He also emphasised a number of other characteristics of the package, in particular that it was a bilateral undertaking to be implemented jointly, that the funding would be additional to Australia's existing aid commitments to Indonesia and that, while there would be a clear focus on tsunami-affected areas, all areas of Indonesia would be eligible for assistance under the partnership.

The announcement of the AIPRD should also be seen in the context of a steadily increasing engagement on aid and development issues by the Howard government. The $1 billion AIPRD commitment followed major aid initiatives in the Solomon Islands[1] and Papua New Guinea (PNG),[2] and preceded the prime minister's announcement of the government's intention to double Australia's overseas aid allocation to about $4 billion per year by 2010 (Howard 2005e). Australia was not alone in making a generous commitment to Indonesia after the tsunami, but the speed and scale of its commitment stood out.[3]

OBJECTIVES, PRINCIPLES AND GOVERNANCE

The details of the package are straightforward: $1 billion, half as grant aid and half as highly concessional loans, all to be delivered over five years. The stated objective of the program is largely unremarkable; it is:

> to support Indonesia's reconstruction and development efforts, both in and beyond tsunami-affected areas, through sustained cooperation focused on the Indonesian Government's programs of reform, with an emphasis on economic and social development (Downer 2005a).[4]

The governance arrangements for the AIPRD are, however, innovative and reflect the significance of the partnership for both governments. At the government-to-government level, instead of being managed through the existing working relationship between Australia's official development assistance agency, the Australian Agency for International Development (AusAID), and Indonesia's national planning agency, Bappenas,[5] a ministerial-level Joint Commission has been established as the peak decision-making body (Downer 2005a). The principal mandate of the Joint Commission is to set strategic directions for the partnership and identify priorities for the allocation of funding from the $1 billion package. The Joint Commission comprises the Australian and Indonesian foreign ministers, as well as the economics ministers of both countries.[6] Its work is 'overseen by the heads of government' of the two countries, an unusually high level of political involvement for a bilateral development cooperation program. On the Australian side, the partnership is being managed as a 'whole-of-government' undertaking, with a core of very senior officials from a range of Australian government agencies closely involved in advising Australian ministers.[7]

The guiding principles of the AIPRD were articulated by the first Joint Commission meeting on 17 March 2005 (Downer 2005a). They emphasise the two governments' 'shared interest in a strong, stable and prosperous Indonesian economy and society' and the Indonesian government's responsibility for setting Indonesia's development and reform priorities. As is now expected in Australia's foreign aid program, human resource development and good governance are particularly emphasised, as are principles of transparency and accountability.[8] Unusually for an official development cooperation program, there is also a 'special emphasis' on the development of linkages between Australian government agencies and institutions and their Indonesian counterparts, as well as on strengthening people-to-people links. The guiding principles call for a 'partnership approach' in implementing the package, through joint decision making at all stages.

FUNDING PRIORITIES

In the 11 months to December 2005, almost 95 per cent of the $1 billion had been committed to a range of priority reconstruction and development programs. Major commitments have been made to rehabilitation and reconstruction work in Aceh,[9] but other large allocations of funding have also been made to a range of longer-term development programs with an Indonesia-wide focus. These include support for national road improvement and basic education; doubling the number of aid-funded Australian postgraduate scholarships available to Indonesians; a program of partnerships between Australian and Indonesian government agencies directed at improving economic and financial management as well as public sector management; and other commitments to develop agribusiness and improve Indonesia's systems of emergency preparedness and response.[10]

The Joint Commission has approved a 'Partnership Framework' (in effect a program strategy) setting out the overall priorities for funding under the AIPRD. Besides emergency preparedness and response, the Partnership Framework has a strong emphasis on securing broad-based economic growth through education and training, improved governance, infrastructure development, rural productivity and private sector development (Downer 2005c).

Such a focus aligns strongly with Indonesia's main national development needs and challenges,[11] in particular:

- the very large numbers of people with incomes just above the formal poverty line who are vulnerable to being pushed into poverty if their economic or personal circumstances change;
- high unemployment rates and large numbers of young people joining the labour force each year, requiring broad-based growth at rates of 6–7 per cent just to absorb new entrants into the labour market;

- continuing weak levels of investment, with lack of investment in infrastructure a major impediment to higher growth rates;
- severe underfunding of basic services such as health and education;
- the poor quality of Indonesia's education outcomes by regional standards, affecting the supply of skilled workers to meet the needs of a growing economy;
- the need for major improvements in governance to improve the enabling environment for private sector growth, through legal and judicial reform, improvements in economic and financial management, better public administration and business regulation, and efforts to tackle corruption;
- continuing weakness in the implementation of decentralisation, with implications for basic service delivery and budgetary planning and management; and
- the need to boost productivity in the agricultural and rural economy, to improve the living standards of the 135 million Indonesians living in rural areas, including the bulk of Indonesia's poor.

AUSTRALIA'S AID VOLUME

The AIPRD constitutes the largest boost to Australia's official development assistance to neighbouring countries in recent years. It comes on top of steady growth in the value of Australian development cooperation with Indonesia, from $122 million in 2001–02 to $158 million in 2003–04 and, after including substantial humanitarian assistance in the wake of the Asian tsunami disaster, to $270 million in 2004–05 (AusAID 2005a: xiv). Given that the $1 billion package will be additional to Australia's existing bilateral development cooperation program with Indonesia, Australian aid flows to Indonesia over the five years of the AIPRD are expected to total $2 billion.

By any reckoning this is a very substantial commitment of resources for development. While Australia is accustomed to the role of major donor in PNG, the South Pacific and East Timor, the AIPRD marks the first occasion on which Australia will play such a significant donor role in a large developing country. The annual quantum of Australia's aid to Indonesia is now likely to exceed that of Germany and the United States, ranking second among bilateral donors behind only Japan (AusAID 2005b: 20).[12] There will inevitably be management and administrative challenges in programming such a large quantum of funds in such a short space of time. This will require that particular attention be paid to choosing high-impact programs that can be implemented quickly on a large scale, and that Australia work in close collaboration with other significant development partners – such as the international development banks – that have more extensive experience in managing high volumes of aid.

But size also brings opportunity. In particular, the major increase in aid to Indonesia under the AIPRD will allow Australia to achieve things that were not previously possible, for example by funding a critical mass of 1,200 new post-graduate study awards. The new $500 million concessional loan program provides the opportunity for the first time in a decade to support infrastructure development in Indonesia, a very timely change given Indonesia's urgent need to attract new financing for infrastructure.[13] Similarly, while Australia's aid program has begun to play a significant role in improving both access to and the quality of basic education in both the state and Islamic education systems in Indonesia, the substantial new funding available under the AIPRD will enable far better results to be achieved, by improving teacher training and school management, for example, and by financing better school materials and new school infrastructure.[14]

A 'WHOLE-OF-GOVERNMENT' APPROACH

The adoption of whole-of-government or 'joined-up' government approaches to public policy and administration issues has become more widespread in a number of Western countries in recent years.[15] The Australian government has enthusiastically followed this innovation, including in the growth of its official aid program, so it is not surprising that the AIPRD is characterised by a similar whole-of-government approach.[16]

The two main whole-of-government characteristics of the AIPRD are the wide range of Australian government agencies directly involved in the implementation of the scheme and the way in which advice to ministers on key policy or program issues is coordinated centrally by a core group of key agencies. Accountability for expenditure and outcomes rests formally with AusAID, ensuring a strong focus on development and critical related issues, such as the long-term sustainability of assistance programs. In a practical sense AusAID manages the AIPRD alongside the pre-existing bilateral development cooperation program. However, the involvement of economic and other central agencies in the governance of the AIPRD on the Australian side brings a variety of important perspectives to the management of what is now a central element in the bilateral relationship between Australia and Indonesia (Howard 2005c; Costello 2005b).

A wide range of Indonesian government agencies are now regularly involved in helping determine the directions of the partnership. As the focus of the AIPRD moves progressively from agreement on 'big picture' policy issues such as principles and objectives to more detailed decisions about the choice and implementation of specific programs and projects, so there is a need for more day-to-day consultations between Australian and Indonesian officials at working level. Regular 'partnership coordination meetings' have been instituted in Jakarta between Australian representatives and senior representatives of the relevant Indonesian government agencies, including Bappenas, the Ministry of Finance, the Ministry of Foreign Affairs, the State Secretariat, and the agency overseeing the reconstruction of tsunami-devastated areas, the Rehabilitation and Reconstruction Agency (BRR).

Australian government agencies other than AusAID have been involved in the delivery of technical assistance programs in regional developing countries for many years. For the most part, until recently, their involvement has been relatively minor, including in Indonesia. However, with the growing emphasis on improved governance in Australia's aid program, there is greater reason to look to public sector agencies rather than private sector contractors to provide the required technical skills and expertise. This is because many specific and up-to-date technical skills (in central bank operations or financial sector regulation, for example) will be found more readily in specialist public sector bodies. It is also clear that Indonesian partner agencies facing the task of designing and implementing complex policy and management reform programs will often prefer to deal directly with experienced public sector practitioners rather than private sector experts. This approach is not without its challenges; many public sector agencies do not have extensive experience in undertaking technical assistance work in a developing country context and most are not resourced to play such a role on a longer-term basis.

Will such new government-to-government partnerships result in sustained improvements in governance? Technical assistance and capacity-building interventions, whether undertaken by public or private sector personnel, do not in themselves automatically translate into improved government performance. Failures of governance are usually due not to technical weaknesses, but to the political culture and the structure of incentives that determine public sector performance. However, where the political culture is supportive of reform efforts, well-executed technical assistance can have a significant, positive effect.

In a significant innovation in aid delivery under the AIPRD, a $50 million Government Partnerships Fund is being developed that will support Australian government agencies to build long-term programs of technical cooperation with Indonesian counterpart agencies. This new fund will draw on the technical expertise of specialist economic, financial and public sector management agencies and link this with AusAID's expertise in the development and implementation of long-term programs of capacity building and institution strengthening. A very broad range of Australian government agencies will potentially be involved, including the Departments of Treasury, Finance and Administration, and Prime Minister and Cabinet, the Reserve Bank of Australia, the Productivity Commission, the Australian Bureau of Statistics, the Australian Public Service Commission, the Australian Government Ombudsman, the Australian

National Audit Office and a range of Treasury portfolio agencies. Technical assistance from such bodies will play an important role as the Yudhoyono administration clarifies and pushes ahead with the implementation of its own plans for economic and public sector reform.

The success of such public sector-led technical assistance efforts will also depend on how they are managed. Successful capacity-building interventions are likely to require significant commitments of time from senior personnel on both sides and the allocation of a large number of experienced technical-level staff to work collaboratively on designated priority issues.[17]

In the longer term, the development of strong institutional and 'peer-to-peer' relationships involving a wide range of Australian and Indonesian government agencies can also be expected to bring an important new dimension to the bilateral relationship overall, including through the development of new people-to-people links.[18]

RECONSTRUCTING ACEH

Without doubt, the most difficult immediate challenge for the AIPRD is to make a timely and effective contribution to the international reconstruction effort in Aceh. In confronting this challenge two issues regularly arise: the amount of funding for Aceh and the pace of reconstruction work.

Despite very clear statements from Australian ministers that the AIPRD will support reconstruction and development both in tsunami-affected areas and in other areas of Indonesia, media and other commentators still appear to be surprised that the entire $1 billion package is not being devoted to Aceh's reconstruction. This would make little sense given that the reconstruction effort in Aceh is already extraordinarily well resourced from a wide range of official and private sources.[19] Equity is also an important consideration: there remain both a very high incidence of poverty[20] and vast areas of need (for example in terms of funding requirements for economic and social infrastructure) in other regions of Indonesia.

The key challenge in the reconstruction of Aceh is not the availability of funds, but how to use pledged funds most effectively. Concern about the slow pace of reconstruction work is understandable; no one wishes to see large numbers of Acehnese remain in temporary or emergency accommodation for an extended period. But expectations about the pace of reconstruction may also be unrealistic. In any large-scale post-disaster reconstruction effort, whether in a developing or a developed economy, a significant period is required for planning and preparation, and the physical reconstruction process itself can take five or more years. Australians experienced this first-hand in the reconstruction of Darwin after Cyclone Tracy in 1972.[21]

The BRR for Aceh and Nias has had its critics – see Aguswandi (2005), for example – but, after a troubled start, the agency is now able to point to a number of indicators of progress. The BRR began its operations on 30 April 2005 but was initially hamstrung by slow access to budgetary resources, even to support its own operations. Its immediate focus has been on the reconstruction of community infrastructure, particularly housing, on local government capacity building and on strengthening accountability regimes. More recent indicators of progress include \$3.6 billion in approved projects; over 10,000 housing units built and nearly 14,000 more under construction; over 4,000 boats distributed; and 3,640 micro-finance loans made (BRR 2005a).

Nevertheless, several significant challenges lie ahead, including improving coordination among donors, overcoming bureaucratic delays, and managing logistics and supply chains to ensure supplies of materials and transport are available to meet the demands of reconstruction.

The practical difficulties of reconstruction in Aceh are well demonstrated in the housing sector. It is estimated that 80–90,000 replacement dwellings will need to be constructed and significant repairs undertaken to a further 80,000 houses. The BRR is confident that pledges of funding for housing already made by donor agencies are adequate to meet these needs. However, immense practical challenges are involved in converting a funding pledge into new housing units. Aceh's existing land records were destroyed in the tsunami. Many people did not in any case hold formal title to their land, or were long-term tenants. On the ground, much physical evidence of land boundaries has been obliterated. Large areas of land have subsided, have been inundated or are at risk of inundation and may be unsuitable for rebuilding. Essential infrastructure such as roads and water supplies has been destroyed. Local administrative offices, responsible for issuing documents of ownership and inheritance necessary for rebuilding, have been destroyed, along with the communities they served. In such circumstances there is no practical alternative to undertaking a painstaking process of community consultation to establish land rights and map the boundaries of every individual land parcel prior to rebuilding. Obviously this takes time, but without such a process there is a very high risk that people will be approved to build on land that is not theirs, institutionalising community disputes in a society trying to recover from both the trauma of the tsunami and a pre-existing armed conflict.

What is especially required in these circumstances is patience, to permit careful preparation for rebuilding. Most people displaced by the tsunami want to return to their own land and build permanent accommodation there. They do not see any significant advantage in temporary accommodation,[22] and provided they can see a clear process in train that will deliver them a house on their own land within a reasonable timeframe they will be prepared to wait for that process to be worked through. A similar patient process of proper planning needs to be followed for all Aceh's reconstruction tasks, to ensure that the resources pledged by the international community and the government of Indonesia are used effectively and accountably.

In circumstances where there appears to be adequate funding available for the overall reconstruction effort in Aceh, Australia has tried to ensure that its contributions, both under the AIPRD and through its earlier emergency program, are strategic and facilitative. For example, to facilitate housing reconstruction, Australia is supporting a community-based land-mapping program to produce maps of thousands of individual land parcels that will provide the basis for housing construction funded by other aid organisations. To help strengthen the overall planning of the reconstruction effort, Australia has provided start-up assistance and expert technical support to the BRR. While much of Australia's reconstruction funding will go towards the physical reconstruction of schools, health facilities and community infrastructure, there is also a particular focus on rebuilding Aceh's human resource base, for example through health worker training and support for tertiary education and research.

AID COORDINATION

In reconstructing Aceh, as in efforts to promote broad-based economic growth or improve standards of health care and education elsewhere in Indonesia, no aid agency can hope to have a lasting effect on its own. Collaboration and close coordination between government agencies, bilateral donors, multilateral agencies and other development partners is essential. Although the AIPRD was established as a bilateral partnership, the need to 'coordinate with the activities and planning of other international development partners' was acknowledged from the start (Downer 2005a).

The bilateral nature of the partnership does not exclude direct collaboration with other donors, either bilateral or multilateral. Thus Australia and Germany are sharing the task of rehabilitating Banda Aceh's main hospital. Australia is working with the World Bank to prepare a major collaborative program of support for national road betterment and improvement (Costello 2005a). Australia will also continue to work with a range of international development partners to achieve a coordinated, sector-wide approach to the improvement of outcomes in the education sector. However, where Australia has the capacity to deliver effective assistance programs directly on a bilateral basis, it will coordinate with, but not always channel aid through, multilateral or pooled funding mechanisms.[23]

Internal coordination will also be important. Common objectives and a joint management structure will ensure consistency of approach between the pre-existing bilateral development cooperation program and the AIPRD, especially in sectors such as education and governance where funding will come from two sources.

CONCESSIONAL LOANS

Australia has never managed a development loan program,[24] but good progress is being made in establishing a suitable legal and administrative framework and accountability controls for loans under the AIPRD. Since the lead times for preparation of loan-financed projects are typically lengthy and the timeframe for the implementation of the AIPRD is short, it will be important to conclude loan arrangements and commence loan project implementation quickly. To achieve this there has been an early focus on the design of large loan activities.[25]

Perhaps as a result of the international debate about debt sustainability, some commentators on development issues favour grants over loans. However, concessional loans remain a widely accepted form of development financing, especially for infrastructure. Indonesia has vast experience in the use of concessional loans. It has also been very successful in reducing public debt to GDP ratios in recent years,[26] and there should be no concern about taking out relatively small concessional loans, for example to carry out urgent upgrading of economic and social infrastructure.[27]

In considering alternative sources of financing, cost matters. The Joint Commission has agreed that AIPRD loans will be highly concessional, based on zero interest, with a repayment period of 40 years and no repayment of principal required for 10 years (Downer 2005a). This finance is among the cheapest available and compares favourably with the loan funding available from the multilateral development banks. At this price AIPRD loan funding should be very attractive, with the potential to make a very useful contribution to Indonesia's priority development needs.

There are also likely to be collateral benefits from the establishment of a new AIPRD concessional loan program. Unlike the grants program, where procurement, contracting and funds disbursal are typically a donor responsibility (albeit with significant Indonesian involvement under the AIPRD), a loan program is likely to draw more heavily on Indonesian implementation systems. This is good development practice, so long as issues of transparency, accountability and risk management are managed carefully. The Joint Commission has determined that the AIPRD loan program should be 'undertaken consistent ... with international best practice' (Downer 2005a). The program provides an opportunity for the transfer of best-practice Australian approaches to transparency and accountability in government procurement and contracting.

CONCLUSIONS AND CHALLENGES

The AIPRD is an ambitious initiative involving a range of significant challenges. Its timeframe is relatively short, given the nature of many of the development outcomes it is seeking to achieve. The volume of development funds now to be managed by Australia in Indonesia is unprecedented. Some of the delivery mechanisms to be used, for example concessional loans, are new, at least for Australia. Some areas of proposed assistance, such as scholarships and support for basic education, are ones where Australia has recognised skills and experience as a development partner in Indonesia and regionally; others, such as public sector management and private sector development for rural productivity, are relatively new for Australia's aid program and challenging for most donors in Indonesia.

The AIPRD will make a major contribution to Indonesia's reform and development efforts over the next several years. In areas such as infrastructure and human resource development, and the reconstruction of Aceh, there will be widespread and tangible results from Australia's $1 billion commitment. Ultimately, however, the real significance of the AIPRD may derive less from the specific projects and programs that are to be funded and implemented, and more from the way in which this initiative is able to encourage different types of dialogue, partnership and collaborative work. While economic issues have grown in prominence in the bilateral relationship in recent years, the AIPRD has taken dialogue on Indonesia's development challenges to a new level. A wider group of senior ministers and senior officials from both countries is now involved in this dialogue. The basis is being laid for collaborative work between a much broader range of Indonesian and Australian institutions, both within and outside government. The longer-term outcomes of these new partnerships will be worth watching.

NOTES

1   The Regional Assistance Mission to Solomon Islands (RAMSI) was deployed on 24 July 2003. RAMSI has achieved significant success in stabilising law and order and government finances in the Solomons. Early gains have been consolidated by helping the Solomon Islands conduct High Court trials for serious crimes and corruption; taking forward a comprehensive long-term reform agenda to strengthen the economy and rebuild the machinery of government; and supporting broad-based growth and provincial development.

2   Australia and PNG agreed in December 2003 to an Enhanced Cooperation Program to help address PNG's development challenges in the areas of law and order, justice, economic management, public sector reform, border control, and transport security and safety.

3   Among bilateral donors, the United States, Japan, the Netherlands and Germany all made large pledges, and significant funding has also been channelled through the European Commission, the World Bank and the Asian Development Bank (ADB). Accurate comparative data on donor pledges is difficult to find, and what compar-

isons are available routinely fail to distinguish between immediate emergency and humanitarian relief, longer-term reconstruction assistance and broader development cooperation funding.

4   The explicit reference to programs of reform in the objective for a bilateral develop-ment cooperation program is notable, but not unique, in Australia's contemporary aid relations. For example, the objective of Australia's Indonesia Country Program Strategy from 2003 strongly emphasises support for economic and legal reform.

5   AusAID and Bappenas are the designated coordinating authorities as defined under article III of the General Agreement on Development Cooperation between the Gov-ernment of Australia and the Government of the Republic of Indonesia. This article defines the role of the coordinating authorities as establishing priorities under the program; choosing activities for implementation under the program; monitoring, reviewing and reporting on progress to the two governments; and recommending to the two governments any appropriate changes to the program, including budget and future development.

6   The Joint Commission comprises, on the Australian side, the minister for foreign affairs and the treasurer, and, on the Indonesian side, the ministers for foreign affairs and finance and the state minister of national development planning.

7   Advice to Australian ministers concerning the AIPRD comes from a committee comprising the secretaries of the Department of Foreign Affairs and Trade, the Department of the Prime Minister and Cabinet, the Treasury and the Department of Finance and Administration, as well as the director-general of AusAID.

8   At the first Joint Commission meeting both Australian and Indonesian ministers went out of their way to stress the high levels of of accountability and transparency that would be required in implementing the $1 billion package, to meet public expectations and to guard against the risks of corruption. See, for example, com-ments at a joint press conference on 17 March by Indonesian Foreign Minister Wira-juda and Australian Treasurer Costello (Downer 2005b). In 2005–06 governance will account for 36 per cent of total Australian overseas development assistance (AusAID 2005a: 9).

9   Commitments to Aceh totalled over $150 million as of 7 December 2005 and included support for the restoration of hospital, health, education and local govern-ment services, the reconstruction of community and economic infrastructure, assis-tance to re-establish livelihoods and ensure food security and support for tertiary education research and training (Downer 2005c).

10 The following commitments have been made: national road improvement, $328 million; junior secondary education, $300 million; government partnerships for improved governance, $50 million; emergency preparedness and response, $10 mil-lion; other disasters, $5 million; Australian Partnership Scholarships, $78 million; smallholder agribusiness, $25 million (Downer 2005c).

11 The economic and social development priorities for the term of the Yudhoyono administration are set out in Indonesia's medium-term development strategy for 2004–09, and have been analysed extensively by both bilateral and multilateral development cooperation partners (see, for example, AusAID 2005b; World Bank 2005a).

12   The major multilaterals, the World Bank and the ADB, also provide substantially more assistance to Indonesia than Australia does.

13   Between 1982 and 1996, under the Development Import Finance Facility (DIFF), close to $400 million in grant aid was combined with official export credits to finance infrastructure projects in Indonesia valued at over $1.1 billion. The DIFF program had a heavy focus on transport infrastructure, especially road and rail transport. For example, DIFF grants have helped finance approximately 50,000 metres of steel bridging, largely in eastern Indonesia.

14   Education programs will account for 47 per cent of Australian aid expenditure in Indonesia in 2005–06. They include a major initiative in Islamic education. The Learning Assistance Program for Islamic Schools (LAPIS) aims to improve the quality of education in Islamic schools, which play a significant role in educating students from poor families, including girls. Asyumadi Azra, rector of the State Islamic University of Jakarta, recently commended Australia's involvement in LAPIS:

> Some may suspect Australia has a 'secularisation' interest. I can assure you this is not so. They work in genuine partnership with Islamic education and civil society organizations such as us, and genuinely heed our advice and respond to real needs' (*Republika*, 3 June 2005).

15   The Australian Public Service Commission has defined 'whole of government' in the Australian Public Service as follows:

> Whole of government denotes public service agencies working across portfolio boundaries to achieve a shared goal and an integrated government response to particular issues. Approaches can be formal and informal. They can focus on policy development, program management and service delivery (APSC 2005).

See also Shergold (2005).

16   More Australian government agencies have become involved in aid program delivery in recent years, in particular through interventions in the Solomon Islands, Nauru and PNG and through cooperation to counter transnational crime.

17   The collaboration between the Australian Federal Police and the Indonesian National Police after the first Bali bombings in 2002 is widely cited as a successful model of technical cooperation.

18   Improved people-to-people links between Indonesia and Australia can also be expected to emerge from academic and other exchanges, increasing numbers of volunteer placements and work with Indonesian civil society organisations.

19   Basic reconstruction needs in Aceh and Nias are estimated by the BRR, the World Bank and others to total around $5.8 billion. This figure includes inflation estimates arising from high demand for reconstruction-related goods. One year after the tsunami, $4.4 billion had already been allocated for specific projects. As of December 2005, total pledges for reconstruction and development in Aceh and Nias amounted to about $9 billion, providing an opportunity to 'build back better' if all partners involved in the reconstruction effort honour their funding commitments. The government of Indonesia, donors and NGOs are each expected to contribute $2.5–3.5 billion (BRR 2005b: 12–13).

20 In 2002, the national human development index for Indonesia as a whole was 65.8; the index for the province of Aceh was slightly higher at 66.0. Of 30 provinces in Indonesia Aceh ranked fifteenth, with provinces in eastern Indonesia such as East Java, West Nusa Tenggara and East Nusa Tenggara ranking amongst the lowest (BPS, Bappenas and UNDP 2004).

21 By September 1975, more than nine months after Cyclone Tracy, not one new house had been completed in Darwin (http://www.ntlib.nt.gov.au/tracy/advanced/Post.html). In comparison, the BRR advised that nine months after the tsunami, more than 6,000 permanent new dwellings had been constructed in Aceh.

22 Some displaced people are reportedly concerned that, by moving from emergency shelter to better temporary accommodation, they will disqualify themselves from assistance with permanent rebuilding; there is also a clear local preference, believed to derive from Dutch colonial land laws, for the use of permanent construction materials such as bricks and concrete rather than timber.

23 Australia has elected not to contribute directly to a multidonor trust fund for Aceh's reconstruction managed by the World Bank but is continuing to support the fund with technical assistance and by coordinating closely with all donor members on policies relating to Aceh's reconstruction.

24 Australia has previously offered budget support financing on concessional terms and until 1996 operated a mixed credit scheme, the DIFF (see footnote 13). With no requirement for competitive tendering, the DIFF scheme suffered from being heavily supplier driven. It was phased out in parallel with tighter international disciplines on the use of officially supported export credits.

25 See the AIPRD advertisement seeking a project preparation consultant to identify and design a three-year rehabilitation program for over 2,000 kilometres of national roads and bridges in eastern Indonesia (*The Australian*, 24 September 2005).

26 Indonesia's public debt to GDP ratio fell from 81 per cent in 2001 to an estimated, and much more sustainable, 56 per cent in 2004. The government revealed at the January 2005 meeting of the Consultative Group on Indonesia that it intends to reduce the ratio to 48 per cent in 2005 and stop foreign borrowing to finance budget deficits by 2009. While this responds to popular concerns about external debt, it may not be desirable or realistic in light of Indonesia's large requirements for infrastructure and other necessities, and the costs of alternative forms of budget financing. Bappenas is preparing a medium-term borrowing strategy to clarify the government's position on future financing requirements and sources, including official loans and grants.

27 The $500 million AIPRD concessional loan funding available over five years is relatively small compared to World Bank projections of gross financing needs ($11–12 billion per annum through to 2009), of which an average of $4 billion per annum is projected to come from external financing.

11 THE SBY PROMISE TO THE BUSINESS WORLD

Noke Kiroyan

President Susilo Bambang Yudhoyono (SBY) swept into office on 20 October 2004 on the back of popular support not seen in Indonesia since the early days of the republic, that is, if we discount the 'landslide election victories' during the Soeharto era.

Optimism flooded the nation as Indonesians of most political persuasions – SBY had won more than 60 per cent of the vote – ushered him into the job that was waiting for him. People were reminded of the secret hope for a 'white knight' (*satrya piningit*) who would rescue the country from the clutches of an evil regime that seemed to have been in power forever. In the mid-1990s, as President Soeharto's stifling stranglehold appeared unshakeable and as Indonesians watched with resignation as the president's eldest daughter appeared to be getting ready to accept the sceptre from the ageing autocrat, anxious whispers, not restricted to believers in Javanese mysticism, began to make the rounds that a *satrya piningit* was waiting in the wings to come to the rescue of the nation at the right moment. After President Soeharto's 'abdication', the presidents that ruled in quick succession, respectively the diminutive non-Javanese (B.J Habibie), the blind cleric (Abdurrahman Wahid or 'Gus Dur') and the daughter of the first president (Megawati Sukarnoputri), did not exactly live up to the image of a Javanese knight, so when the scholarly general with his 'presidential' demeanour and matching physique was duly elected, people recollected the dreams and there were knowing nods all round that this might be the knight the nation had been longing for. So, with some delay, the prophecy proved to be accurate after all.

The depth and breadth of goodwill and support was such that right after the results of the presidential election in September 2004 became inescapably clear, political analysts issued dire warnings that the almost desperate longing for a superhuman to turn things round might turn into disillusionment if the president failed to deliver within a relatively short period of time. Until the end of the first semester nothing much had changed in terms of support for the president. Borrowing a chapter from the Reagan presidency, newspapers began describing SBY as the 'teflon president', as he always seemed to emerge unscathed from skirmishes with parliament and mean-spirited politicians. Despite the fact that no new legislation had been promulgated to jumpstart the economy as promised, and issues giving rise to a perception of lack of legal certainty had not been resolved, the good news kept pouring in. Economic growth of 6 per cent was projected to be reached ahead of schedule, investors began to come in, the Jakarta stock index rose in leaps and bounds reflecting the confidence and bullishness of stock market players, the automotive sector revised its earlier projection of new cars to be sold in 2005 from 550,000 to close to 600,000 – that is, far above pre-crisis levels – and the rupiah/$ exchange rate, albeit a little on the high side, appeared stable enough and in no particular danger of tumbling down any time soon.

The president's inauguration speech on 21 October 2004 set out the objectives he intended to achieve in the short term. Concentrating on domestic problems and constituting his promise to the Indonesian people, they comprised the following items:

1 Stimulate the economy to achieve higher growth as a means to create employment and alleviate poverty.
2 Adopt and implement open economic policies to integrate the Indonesian economy with regional and international economies.
3 Encourage investment in infrastructure.
4 Actively conduct an anti-corruption program that the president himself will personally lead.
5 Pay special attention to the handling of the conflicts in Aceh and Papua.
6 Place priority on education and health.
7 Intensify constructive dialogue with the business community, which is expected to be the engine of the economy.
8 Establish clean and good governance.

In January 2005 the government held a hastily organised infrastructure summit at which it issued a strong public invitation for private sector investment in Indonesian infrastructure projects, apparently in realisation of item 3 in the president's inauguration speech. In total 91 projects were offered to the international business community, covering basic infrastructure needs such as railways, toll roads, airports, power supply, gas pipelines and telecommunications. The total value of the projects offered was $22.5 billion, about 83 per cent of which was expected to come from private investors, domestic and international alike. However, half a year down the track, apart from the tendering of a few toll road projects, not much progress had been made. This indicated that the government had grossly underestimated the bureaucratic and legal hurdles to be overcome to get major infrastructure projects moving again after a standstill since the crisis of 1997. Rizal Ramli, the former minister of finance under Gus Dur, summed up the reasons for the failure in the title of an article he wrote for the *Jakarta Post* on 8 July 2005: 'Unrealistic targets and inadequate preparations for infrastructure'. He called the summit 'no more than a promotion of policies'. In the meantime the government announced plans to hold a second infrastructure summit in November 2005 (later rescheduled for February 2006, and then again for mid-2006). It would offer $53 billion worth of projects, double the value of projects included in the first summit. Given the results achieved at the first summit, and with its credibility at stake, it seemed hazardous for the government to proceed without taking stock of the reasons for the failure of the first summit.

Nevertheless, the general bullishness continued unabated. In June 2005, one of Indonesia's bright young economists in the private sector, Fauzi Ichsan, vice-president of Standard Chartered Bank in Jakarta, concluded a presentation to the British Chamber of Commerce in Indonesia with the following summary of the situation in Indonesia:

- Indonesia has survived its worst political and economic crises.
- SBY's election marks a new era of stability and growth.
- Investment is rising, albeit from a low base.
- The tsunami disaster has resulted in large-scale international assistance.
- To accelerate foreign direct investment, Indonesia must tackle structural issues, including widespread corruption.
- With post-election stability and extra-constitutional powers, SBY is in a good position to tackle these issues.

This rosy outlook was based on the fact that until May, a little over six months into the first year of the administration, the economy showed a lot of promise: GDP in US dollars had recovered to pre-crisis levels; the World Bank, the Asian Development Bank and the IMF had concurred with the Indonesian government in raising GDP growth forecasts for 2005; rating agencies were upgrading Indonesia's sovereign risk ratings; and investor and consumer surveys indicated rising optimism. Apart from the miscalculation about the infrastructure program, Indonesia seemed on track to deliver on the promises made to the nation in SBY's inauguration speech.

THE ENERGY CRISIS: THE END OF THE DREAM?

Then the energy crisis struck. It appeared to catch the government totally off guard. The president, who had been scheduled to visit China and Thailand in early July, postponed his visit by a few weeks and then confined it to China.

From the government's early reactions it appears that the rising trend of fuel prices was initially regarded as a temporary phenomenon or mere spike. The government seems to have expected that prices would 'normalise' more or less at previous levels, a view reflected in its adjusted budget for 2005, which fixed the oil price at $45. Even as the international oil price continued its relentless march upwards, the government submitted a budget proposal for 2006 in which the oil price assumption, at $40 per barrel, was even lower than that in the adjusted budget for 2005. This prompted *Tempo* magazine to ask sarcastically in its 28 August edition: 'Optimistic or naive?' The parliament, although generally aligned with the government after Vice-President Jusuf Kalla took over the chairmanship of Golkar from Akbar Tanjung, also promptly made its scepticism over the budget known. The mainstream media uniformly adopted the same stance as *Tempo* in condemning the government's unrealistic budget assumptions.

Oil is a commodity that has traditionally been subsidised since the Soeharto era; the immediate effect of decreasing subsidies would be an automatic increase in fuel prices followed by inflation. Successive government policies since the early days of nationhood have created the popular sentiment that Indonesians are entitled to low fuel prices in all circumstances; as a result, the expectation of fuel subsidies has permeated the entire fabric of Indonesian society. The seemingly simple act of reducing subsidies is believed, directly or indirectly, to have led to the downfall of a number of Indonesian presidents in the republic's history. No matter how ridiculous artificially low fuel prices appear to cold and calculating business people and economists, Indonesian heads of government approach the subject with extreme caution, thereby helping to further entrench the myth of entitlement in people's minds. More than in any other country, fuel prices are not merely an economic issue, but a major factor combining equally important political and economic elements. At a world oil price of $50 per barrel, fuel subsidies would amount to a staggering $12–13 billion, or about one-quarter of the government budget. This is money that would not be available for education, health infrastructure and other measures that could help the country achieve its targeted growth rate of close to 7 per cent over the current term of office of the president.

The market's reaction to the government's unrealistic budget assumptions precipitated a fall in the value of the rupiah in the last 10 days of August 2005. On 20 August the rupiah was at the psychologically important threshold of Rp 10,000/$. This level was breached two days later and by the end of the month the rupiah seemed utterly defenceless. It crashed easily through the Rp 11,000/$ mark, sending jitters through the country, which has yet to overcome the trauma of a freefall in the currency in late 1998. After the barrage of criticism from all segments of society, the government finally decided to revise the 2006 budget, based on an assumed oil price of $57.

The impression one gets from the steps taken by the government is that its decisions were based on assumptions that held true at the time, without considering forward-looking, 'what-if' scenarios including varying degrees of deterioration in the individual components of those assumptions. Such an approach would have enabled the government to take quicker action when its initial assumptions proved to be incorrect. Instead, the situation was left unresolved, allowing it to expand into a financial crisis with increasingly political dimensions. The government appeared at a loss when its decisions were overtaken by events, as its vacillation over fuel price assumptions demonstrates.

The energy crisis brought the smooth coasting of the administration over all obstacles to an abrupt halt. It is too early to tell whether the energy crisis is a precursor to a larger crisis, but at the end of August 2005 an atmosphere of doom and gloom prevailed, particularly because Indonesia had now joined the league of oil importers. Unlike previous oil crises, which were a boon for Indonesia because oil exports made up a significant part of the country's foreign exchange earnings, this crisis occurred at a time when oil production was falling and the state oil company, Pertamina, was paying $1.6 billion per month for oil imports.

The oil crunch came at a time when the country had barely enough power-generating capacity to meet current needs. With rising demand for electrical power as the economy began to stir, this precarious situation manifested itself in a number of blackouts. These have been ascribed to several factors. First, there is no reserve capacity left, so when there are peaks in demand the system is unable to cope. This problem is exacerbated by breakdowns in the country's ageing power plants, and the postponement of long-overdue maintenance. Second, there are problems with transmission lines. The Jakarta transmission line, for instance, has no backup because the alternative southern transmission line on Java has yet to be completed.

The shortage in power-generating capacity is thus compounded by less than secure transmission capacity. This raises questions about the capacity of the country's power stations to provide the additional energy needed for economic growth. It is clear that the existing infrastructure is stretched to breaking point, but adding capacity would involve building new power plants that will take years to complete. The higher economic growth rates projected by the government will require increased supplies of electrical power, but the recent problems highlight the fact that energy constraints may frustrate the achievement of these targets.

The lack of electrical power capacity and the dwindling of oil production can be traced to the same root cause: lack of legal certainty and inconsistent policy directions in the *reformasi* era. No new oil exploration has been undertaken since *reformasi* in 1998, and the one certain large-scale oil deposit that is ready to be developed, the Cepu oilfield in Central Java, is mired in controversy. Successive Pertamina chief executives have been allowed to pursue their own personal whims, seemingly without regard to the prevailing government policy direction. This has further delayed a final resolution of the contractual issues between Pertamina and ExxonMobil over the Cepu oilfield, which could have brought Indonesia closer to increasing its oil production. Similarly, no significant infrastructure development has taken place for years, including in power-generating capacity. With the government grappling with the pressing issue of coping with persistently high fuel prices, the capacity of SBY to handle the serious challenges facing the country was put to the test for the first time during his presidency. A *Kompas* poll held in late August 2005 showed that the president remained popular. However, almost 40 per cent of the population thought that the economic situation had deteriorated, versus only 24 per cent who believed that it had not.

BACK TO REALITY

At the end of SBY's first year in office, it appeared that of the eight items mentioned in his inauguration speech, those concerned with the political arena had fared best. This is ironic considering that the president himself places higher priority on the economy. Although the first three items on his agenda concern economic development, the first substantial success achieved by his administration was the peace accord with the Free Aceh Movement (GAM). The accord enjoys widespread popular support despite strong pockets of resistance among the political elite, including various factions in parliament. On the economic front, real progress has been achieved only in the area of improving communication with the business community (item 7), something SBY embarked on even before he became president. The infrastructure summit held in January 2005 and the sizeable number of business people SBY always includes in his entourage during overseas trips are further evidence of the sincerity of his commitment.

On 2 August 2004, the two presidential candidates, SBY and Megawati, faced the business community at an event organised by the Indonesian Chamber of Commerce and Industry (Kadin). SBY dazzled the audience with his communication skills and rational presentation. He immediately struck a chord with the assembled business elite by saying that economic problems required economic solutions, while peppering his presentation with the graphs that business people are so fond of. He listed six points that would constitute the government's part of the bargain in developing the economy if he should be elected. These were:

- appropriate economic policies;
- development of a healthy business climate;
- establishing the rule of law and rules of the game;
- providing opportunities to the business world;

- developing infrastructure to boost the economy; and
- establishing good governance.

SBY's delivery was typically smooth and convincing. Also, unlike his presidential rival, he engaged in a direct question-and-answer session afterwards. It was obvious that SBY had a very firm grasp of the issues he was speaking about. All the above items in one form or another were incorporated into the eight items mentioned in the president's inauguration speech, so it must be admitted that SBY has been very consistent in delivering his message. He also stated that if he was elected president, he would conduct a regular dialogue with the business community through Kadin, in order to receive direct input from those actively engaged in making the wheels of the economy turn.

On 30 August 2005 SBY again faced the business community, this time at a Foreign Investors Forum organised by the International Business Chamber, which comprises most of the bilateral business chambers in Jakarta. Again he reiterated his pro-business mantra. Perhaps in response to critics who did not share his pro-business attitude, of whom there is no shortage in Indonesia, he said:

> I believe that being pro-business goes hand in hand with being pro-growth, pro-jobs, and pro-poor. Look around in China, in India, in Malaysia, in Thailand, and you will find that there is no contradiction between being pro-business and pro-poor.

The president is unwaveringly following the route of dialogue with the business community as a means of motivating it to do its part in developing the economy. He has certainly made good on his promise to listen to the business world, but still has a long way to go to boost the confidence of investors. The crisis sparked by the rising price of oil with its domestic ramifications will for the foreseeable future be foremost in the collective mind of cabinet; realistically, the development of business-friendly policies will have to take a back seat. Combined with the energy constraints described earlier, this casts serious doubts on the achievability of SBY's stated economic growth target of 7.8 per cent.

GOOD GOVERNANCE AND BUREAUCRATIC REFORM TO RESTORE BUSINESS CONFIDENCE

A constantly recurring theme in the president's speeches is the need for good public and corporate governance. One manifestation of this was the establishment on 30 November 2004 – relatively early in his term of office – of a National Committee on Governance Policy. It consists of two subcommittees, one on public governance and the other on corporate governance. Like its predecessors, the National Committee on Governance Policy was placed under the auspices of the coordinating minister for economic affairs, the difference being that the new organisation has been expanded to include the public sector. The fact that public governance is included in the revamped national committee reflects SBY's belief that public and corporate governance go hand in hand, that you cannot have one without the other. The committee's brief is as follows:

1   Compile guidelines and codes of conduct on good governance for the public and private sectors.
2   Conduct studies and provide recommendations for regulatory improvements on the basis of good governance principles.
3   Conduct activities to improve appreciation and implementation of good governance principles.
4   Monitor and assess implementation of corporate governance in various business sectors, including state-owned enterprises (SOEs) and small and medium-sized enterprises (SMEs).
5   Undertake advocacy of good governance principles.
6   Provide input on assessment procedures for commissioners and directors on the basis of corporate governance principles.

The Indonesian Institute for Directors and Commissioners (LKDI), an operational arm of the national committee, has been tasked with training commissioners and directors of SOEs in principles of good corporate governance, starting with a pilot project involving 100 SOEs from various sectors. To provide guidance in achieving its objectives, the National Committee on Governance Policy has set up the performance indicators outlined in Table 11.1.

Some state institutions have not been empowered by the head of government to fulfil their brief to strengthen good governance, despite having been in existence for at least two years. The Committee for the Eradication of Corruption (KPK), for example, has been practically silent since its inception by President Megawati in 2003. Lately, however, it has begun to take action against corrupt state officials, beginning with the much celebrated incarceration of the chairman of the General Election Committee, some of his staff, and a committee member who was apprehended while attempting to bribe an official of the State Audit Agency (BPK). Notwithstanding the indictment of the governor of Aceh, a prominent member of Golkar, for misappropriation of the provincial budget, some critics contend that the KPK is targeting academics with no political backing and corrupt members of regional parliaments, while lacking the courage to pursue cases against the politically powerful. Whether or not this is true, at least the KPK has been credited with making government officials much more cautious in the conduct of their daily business.

The president himself and a number of senior officials have stated the need for bureaucratic reform to increase the efficiency of government, but so far no concrete measures have been taken. This is particularly disturbing for the business world, which suffers from excessive bureaucracy in every aspect of con-

Table 11.1 Performance indicators for the National Committee on Governance Policy

Corporate subcommittee	Public subcommittee
Corporation Law to be improved by including principles of good governance	A more rational remuneration system to be instituted for civil servants, allowing them to achieve a reasonable living standard on their salaries
All SOEs, financial service companies and public companies to take part in assessment and rating programs for the application of good governance	A national system for open recruitment of echelon I and II officials to be established
Privately held companies and SMEs to be managed on the basis of principles of good corporate governance	Supervisory bodies to function effectively, institutions to be robust and competently staffed, and their findings to be used as a reference for policy making and remedial action
All commissioners of SOEs, banks and public companies to be certified graduates from accredited directorship courses	There is to be minimal misappropriation of funds, on both the revenue and expenditure sides
Corporate institutions (annual general meetings, commissioners, directors) as well as governance apparatuses (corporate committees, independent commissioners, corporate secretaries) of all SOEs, financial services companies and public companies to be capable of functioning effectively	E-procurement and e-reporting procedures to be introduced in all government agencies and for large-scale projects

Source: National Committee on Governance Policy.

ducting a business. As the president has pointed out several times, the time it takes to establish a new venture – 151 days according to a World Bank survey – must be brought down to more competitive levels if the Indonesian economy is to grow. The scope of the task is enormous. The job of reforming the bureaucracy will take more than one presidential term to complete; after all, it took President Soeharto many terms to mould it into its current bloated shape. Dismantling this ingrained system will require careful planning. It can only be done when the economy is stable and flourishing, to prevent a massive backlash from the country's millions of government employees, who may perceive the reforms as being detrimental to their interest. As well, in Indonesian politics there is always a group of disgruntled former officials and politicians constantly on the ready to pounce on the incumbent the moment he exhibits signs of weakness or if an opportunity to strike presents itself. This could be the case if civil servants turned restive *en masse*.

WHAT THE FUTURE HOLDS UNDER SBY

The setbacks to SBY's plans, including the energy crisis, raise the question of what the future holds for the business world, particularly Australian companies doing business in or with Indonesia. Gallows humour emerges in grave situations, and there is a popular joke, particularly among foreign business people in Indonesia, that 'in the long term we are all optimistic; it is just the short term that kills us'. Although some exaggeration is invariably involved in anything said in jest, there is a great deal of truth to this. The size of the Indonesian market, the riches yet to be exploited and the industriousness of the population all hold promise for the future, but unresolved issues affecting the business world are conniving with macroeconomic factors to dampen the enthusiasm of the international business community for doing business in Indonesia.[1] Pledges of support for SBY abound, but the flow of cash has yet to materialise.

In general it can be said that those companies that are already in the country are motivated to hang on and take advantage of their local market savvy to expand their businesses, while those who are still on the outside looking in remain wary about initiating operations in Indonesia. In the course of preparing this article, I conducted intensive discussions with Australia's senior trade commissioner in Jakarta, the top management in Indonesia of Leighton Contractors and Bluescope Steel, and the proprietor of the insurance brokerage firm dMAC. These companies by no means represent a scientific sample of Australian companies operating in Indonesia, let alone the entire spectrum, but I would classify them as 'durable' given that they all successfully weathered the lean years during and immediately following the financial crisis in 1997–98. They all possess specialist knowledge of the Indonesian market and people, and are positive about the outlook for their businesses. It is therefore reasonable to expect that they will do even better once SBY's economic programs take hold. These companies provide products and services essential to a growing economy, and they are reasonably comfortable doing business in a tough environment that they know like their own backyard. Familiarity with the region and its people born of the geographical proximity of the two countries gives Australian business people a comparative advantage over their counterparts from other Western economies – an intangible factor that should not be underestimated in doing business in Indonesia.

The Australian managers I spoke to expressed confidence in the outlook for their businesses. Bluescope, for example, predicted that the next five years would be better than the last five years, and Leighton Contractors was one of the few foreign companies to tender for projects touted at the first infrastructure summit. The company says that it intends to participate in future tenders and remains optimistic about the future growth of its business in Indonesia. It has reservations, however, about the capacity of the government to implement some of its intentions. dMAC has experienced the ups and downs of the Indonesian economy over the last few years and will not easily be intimidated by the latest upheavals. In all likelihood it will continue to thrive in Indonesia. The insurance broker's office was previously located next to the Australian embassy and suffered severe damage from the bomb blast on 9 September 2004, fortunately without injury to any of its staff. It has now moved to another office building further away from the embassy but still in the same general area.

Based on statistics available to his office, the Australian senior trade commissioner believes that business will continue to grow for Australian companies operating in Indonesia. Indonesia is already the second-largest market for new exporters from Australia offering a product range as diverse as the Australian economy. The commissioner remarked that the size of Indonesia's middle class is much larger than that of Singapore. This makes Indonesia an attractive destination for a wide range of products and services, especially for Australian companies that can put their knowledge of Indonesia to good use. Another positive development has been the increase in the number of board meetings of Australian companies being held in Indonesia. The commissioner also noted an increase in the number of Australian companies contacting the Australian Trade Commission to enquire about doing business in Indonesia, an indicator of heightened interest in the country.

Another perspective on business prospects in Indonesia is provided by Table 11.2. Borrowed from Fauzi Ichsan's presentation to the British Chamber of Commerce mentioned earlier, it is very useful in showing the potential risks of doing business on the one hand, and the potential benefits to be derived on the other, irrespective of the current speculation surrounding fuel prices.

Table 11.2 Business prospects in Indonesia

Prospects	Sector characteristics	Sector
High growth, low risk	Servicing retail consumers directly and indirectly	Automotive, cigarettes, cement, telecommunications, leasing, pharmaceuticals, packaging
High growth, high risk	Heavily regulated, strong role for parliament, need for government guarantees	Infrastructure: toll roads, electricity, ports, tap water
High potential, low risk	Exported commodities	Palm oil, rubber, cocoa
High potential, high risk	Heavily regulated, legal uncertainty, regional autonomy issues	Oil and gas, mining
Low growth, low risk	Steady 'annuity' business	Trade, insurance
Low growth, high risk	Labour-intensive, competing with China, India and Vietnam	Textiles, shoes, toys, low-end electronics

Source: Fauzi Ichsan.

A few of the industries mentioned in the table need to be highlighted because of their prominence in the past, in stark contrast to their current loss of importance in the Indonesian economy. It comes as no surprise to find that oil and gas and the mining industry are among the sectors bearing the brunt of Indonesia's stifling bureaucracy. The steadily declining production figures for oil are clear enough for anyone to see, although the situation in the mining industry is not so readily apparent. A cursory glance at the figures might lead one to conclude that everything is fine in the mining sector because production of the various commodities keeps growing. However, the increase is coming from an ever smaller number of mines, as no major greenfield development has taken place since 1998. If this trend continues, Indonesia will disappear from the map of major mining countries as existing mines mature and then decline with the depletion of resources. Newmont's Batu Hijau mine, which began production in 2001, is the only large-scale mine to come on stream in recent years. In the meantime two sizeable goldmines, Kelian Equatorial Mining and Newmont Minahasa

Raya, have closed down according to plan as they have run out of resources, with no new mines to replace them.

The challenges facing the SBY administration, some inherited from previous administrations, are immense. One important source of support for his policies is the business world, with Kadin throwing its support behind the president virtually since he announced his candidacy. Business remains supportive of SBY, but in the longer term he will need to fulfil his part of the covenant. The program that he proclaimed to the world at his inauguration needs to become reality soon if Indonesian business is to unfurl its full potential and do its part in achieving the economic growth objectives set by the president for his administration.

NOTE

1 Examples include the ongoing dispute between the Indonesian government and the Mexican cement company Cemex over the latter's attempt to take a controlling stake in Indonesia's largest cement group; the court proceedings against Newmont for its alleged involvement in the contamination of Buyat Bay; and the contractual issues between Pertamina and ExxonMobil that are hindering development of the Cepu oilfield.

12 AUSTRALIA AND INDONESIA IN THE WIDER CONTEXT OF REGIONAL ECONOMIC RELATIONS

Stephen Grenville

This chapter notes the progress that is being made in regional economic cooperation, places Indonesia in this context, and examines how the relationship between Indonesia and Australia might develop to enhance both regional cooperation and, at the same time, the relationship between Australia and Indonesia.

REGIONAL RELATIONSHIPS AND GROUPINGS

Slowly but surely, more economic content ('ballast') is being put into regional arrangements. This process was given impetus by the Asian crisis of 1997. The original economic focus of the Association of Southeast Asian Nations (ASEAN) was largely on trade, but the crisis led to an emphasis on exchange rates and arrangements to share foreign exchange reserves through substantial currency swap arrangements. It also heightened the recognition that the multilateral international financial institutions – notably the IMF – may not always promote the interests of East Asia effectively. While the idea of a unified currency arrangement along European lines seems a very long way off, there are opportunities for integrating financial markets and achieving greater uniformity of rules and regulations. Financial markets, by their nature, are governed by complex and pervasive rules and understandings, and if capital is to move easily between these countries, there has to be greater uniformity, not only of the rules, but also of their implementation (including dispute resolution through the domestic courts). Worth noting is the launch of the two Asian Bond Funds. The first is a relatively simple fund involving the packaging of dollar-denominated debt of the participating countries (basically, all the East Asian countries that have substantive financial markets), to be held largely by central banks. The second fund is more ambitious, combining debt obligations in local currencies. While the marketability of this is still to be properly tested, one test of success has already been registered – many institutions are claiming 'fatherhood' of the bond fund idea: 'success has many fathers'.

Overshadowing this, however, has been the rise and rise of China. China is still receiving overwhelmingly the main part (two-thirds) of foreign investment flows into the region. Part of this must be natural – either it is domestic investment taking a round-trip through Hong Kong to qualify for some advantage, or it is Taiwan money. The investment that drove the manufacturing growth in Southeast Asia in the 1970s, 1980s and early 1990s represented the restructuring of Japanese industry as it shifted its labour-intensive manufacturing offshore. This transfer may be largely complete or, to the extent that it is not, China may be the favoured destination. This same sort of shift of low-labour-cost industry is taking place from South Korea and from Taiwan, and it is natural for the shift in production to go to China rather than elsewhere in Asia. Of course, there will still be substantial investment in resources in countries like Indonesia, but this sort of investment carries with it the connotation of the recipients being 'hewers of wood and drawers of water', and is also unattractive because of its modest employment-generating potential. Such is the diversity of resources and availability of cheap rural labour in China that it is hard to know in what industry sectors a country like Thailand or Indonesia could be confident of retaining its international competitiveness vis-à-vis China. Even a quite substantial appreciation of the yuan probably would not change this situation much.

This shifting centre of gravity in Asia manifests itself in another way: in tussles over regional leadership. The game has not yet by any means fully played itself out, but there seems little doubt that China has great potential for regional leadership, while Japan has not found the formula for translating its economic strength into an active leadership role.

Where does this leave the countries of Southeast Asia, which might broadly be termed the ASEAN group? The sheer size of China presents a formidable challenge. Measured in terms of purchasing power GDP, China is nearly 10 times as large as Indonesia and has well over three times the combined GDP of the ASEAN countries. None of these countries could, by itself, aspire to lead Asia, but together they might provide a useful counterweight to China. Such a counterweight might ensure that issues in dispute were discussed between the parties, rather than acted on unilaterally, to provide an opportunity for the Churchill maxim of 'jaw-jaw rather than war-war' to operate. In economic terms, it might also mean that when countries cooperate, the fruits of that cooperation can be shared equitably.

The need is to counter the idea that the countries of Southeast Asia will become, over time, more dependent on China, and effectively part of the wider Chinese sphere of influence, not through political means, but through the soft power of economic relationships. To counter this, the ASEAN group has to do more than widen its geographic spread (as it has done); it also needs to 'bulk up' its economic clout and dynamism, and achieve a uniformity of voice and bargaining position in its dealings with China, and, for that matter, the other powerful countries of North Asia.

Indonesia is a key element in this – it comprises one-third (by purchasing power income weight) of ASEAN. Without a strongly growing, confident and outward-looking Indonesia, ASEAN may remain without a clear sense of direction. With India, Australia and New Zealand attached through the East Asia Summit, it is possible to envisage a network with some ability to develop co-operative arrangements with China, and where sensitive issues such as sea-bed rights could be discussed, without being overwhelmed by China's sheer bulk. It may be useful to envisage this as a set of layered meetings. The core ASEAN countries, with their long-established relationships, would meet among themselves to hammer out positions. These agreed positions would then be taken to a broader meeting such as ASEAN+3 (ASEAN plus China, Japan and South Korea). That said, while a grouping around the existing ASEAN relationships has the potential to act as some kind of balance to China, this will require a much stronger unity of purpose, capacity to identify issues of mutual self-interest and willingness to act in concert than exists at present.

The operational problem for all these groupings is the same issue that the TV channels face, that of finding enough interesting 'content' to give the meeting a dynamic which can be translated into policy action. Two suggestions are made here. The first is to use the regional arrangements to mesh with worldwide forums. This would allow ASEAN members to raise issues such as the current international payments imbalances: the US current account deficit (equal to 6 per cent of GDP) and its counterpart surpluses elsewhere in the world. The current large imbalances are usually described as unsustainable, and particular pressure was brought on China to revalue and float the yuan. China's response so far has been trivial in economic terms, but it has satisfied the critics for the moment. China may well find it in its own interest to do more, but there is something of a prisoner's dilemma involved here: none of the Asian countries want to lose competitiveness, but they might use the opportunity of a more substantial Chinese revaluation to carry out some currency realignments of their own, and this could help in a small way to resolve the overall imbalances. This is one serious economic topic for discussion in the region that may help strengthen regional arrangements.

Having sorted out its own position within the more intimate grouping, ASEAN may be able to make a clearer contribution to debate in multilateral forums by pointing out, for example, that the big current account surpluses are to be found in Germany and Japan rather than in China or the rest of Asia. What better way to carry these issues onto the world stage than to get them on the agenda for the next G20 meeting (where East Asia is much better represented than at IMF discussions) and to emphasise an important point – that the G8 is not the proper forum for sorting out the world's economic issues because it does not include China, let alone the other emerging Asian economies. So, while continuing to work on regional arrangements, ASEAN countries should keep one eye on how they will interact with the overall international architecture.

A second area of potentially fruitful regional interaction would be to try to inject some system and sense into the proliferation of bilateral trade agreements. There is a real danger that these diverse deals will impede trade and distort the international division of labour, especially through the hugely different rules of origin that go with each of these agreements. One difficult but worthwhile task would be for ASEAN to develop a standard template for such agreements, particularly on rules of origin. It may not be possible to undo the damage that has already been done to the multilateral framework, but even here there must be some possibilities of greater uniformity of rules over time.

INDONESIA

Where does Indonesia fit into the regional story? It is the largest of the ASEAN countries, and if ASEAN is to provide a counterweight to the growing position of China, a strong and confident Indonesia must be a key element. The historic shift to democracy has occurred more smoothly and effectively than many expected, adding weight to Indonesia's international status. But there was a significant period of several years when this transition was taking attention away from the economy. Indonesia's weight within the region fell, as other countries were quicker to recover from the crisis. There is now a clearer view (or a revival of an earlier understanding) that if Indonesia is not growing at 6–7 per cent per year, it will slip backwards economically.

But this pace of growth is harder to achieve now. Part of the democratisation process has involved decentralisation, which makes economic policy making more cumbersome. Indonesia's stronger labour laws may have been needed, but they seem to be affecting Indonesia's competitiveness as perceived by foreign investors. China is sucking in the sorts of industries that Indonesia needs if it is to absorb the growing labour force. There may also be a loss of momentum in modernisation. The financial sector is back on an even keel, and stronger than in 1997, but not by much. Partial privatisations of the major state-owned banks are not likely to spur the root-and-branch reforms that are needed. State-owned enterprises are still seen as milch-cows for the staff, management and local authorities, and every effort to sell them off is resisted by the vested interests that benefit from the status quo. At the same time, their uneconomic structure makes them unattractive to foreigners, who would find the task of reform truly formidable. Nor is the local business community in a strong position to take over the state-owned enterprises, as it still carries the scars of 1997, and unsatisfactory resolution of earlier debts means that this stigma will not disappear soon. The bureaucracy, for the main part, seems largely unchanged, mired in conservatism and the protection of position.

The surprise, in some ways, is that Indonesia has emerged from the crisis so little changed, having paid a huge price, whether measured by the fiscal transfers associated with bank restructuring or the opportunity cost of below-potential growth in 1998–2004. Disciples of Mancur Olson may have expected the disruption of 1997–98 to have, as its silver lining, a sweeping away of some of the old institutions and vested interests, allowing fresh faces and more dynamic forces to take centre stage (Olson 1965). Perhaps this theory works best if the crisis is not too big – if it sweeps away some institutions and groups but leaves others intact to take their place. In Indonesia, there was hardly a major business group left unscathed, so it is hard to find a core of substantial businesses to do the 'heavy lifting' of the recovery, especially as the state-owned sector is, at the same time, preoccupied in defending its patch against pressures for privatisation.

Whatever the reason, it is surprising how resilient the old institutions have turned out to be, and how little has changed in many areas. More of the privately owned banks are now in foreign hands, and this has to be an improvement. But the major state-owned banks, with all their intrinsic problems of governance and the likelihood that they will be used to provide 'directed' lending or worse, are still as important as they were before the crisis. The government experimented with privatisation before the crisis – the second-largest state bank, BNI, was 25 per cent privatised in 1996, with no discernible effect on its governance – but the most that can be expected is more partial privatisations. Perhaps the banks are run by better people now, but it has taken eight years to remove the CEO of Mandiri, the largest of the state banks. Has bank prudential supervision improved? Probably, but it is worth noting that the aforesaid removal was implemented not by Bank Indonesia (the supervisor) or the owner (the Ministry of State Owned Enterprises), but by the Auditor General. This is not to deny that reform is under way; just to make the point that the opportunity for radical restructuring (say, of the kind that occurred in the Malaysian financial sector immediately after the crisis) has been lost, and the difficult task of piecemeal reform will yield its results only slowly.

'Good governance' is the buzz-word that purports to answer all these problems. It would help if the generalisations about good governance were replaced by a more explicit recognition that markets are a powerful way of making economic decisions. However, for markets to work, they require a set of 'rules of the game' – what Douglass North has called 'institutions'. Much of North's writing resonates with the Indonesian situation. Here are a few samples from his recent book, *Understanding the Process of Economic Change* (North 2004).

The structure we impose on our lives to reduce uncertainty is an accumulation of pre-scriptions and proscriptions. ... The result is a complex mix of formal and informal constraints. If our focus is narrowly on economics, then our concern is with scarcity and hence competition for resources. The structure of constraints we impose to order that competition shapes the way the game is played. ... [T]he consequence of the structure we impose will be to determine whether the competitive structure induces increasing efficiency or stagnation (North 2004: 1).

Economists of the libertarian persuasion have for some time laboured under the delu-sion that there is something called laissez faire and that once there are in place 'effi-cient' property rights and the rule of law the economy will perform well without fur-ther adjustment (North 2004: 122).

A step towards a more comprehensive understanding of [path dependency] is to recognise that the institutions that have accumulated give rise to organisations whose survival depends on the perpetuation of those institutions and hence will devote resources to preventing any alteration that threatens their survival (North 2004: 51).

These three quotes capture much of what was deficient in the otherwise suc-cessful economic policies of the Soeharto era – the failure to build satisfactory institutions (in the North sense of rules). They give insights into the difficulty of doing so now – because the beneficiaries of the old institutions can be expected to try hard to retain the status quo.

AUSTRALIA AND INDONESIA

Where does Australia fit into this picture? Even though it is hugely in Australia's interests for Indonesia to play a larger and more constructive role in regional affairs, Australia's capacity to influence this is small. The economic ties be-tween the two countries are relatively modest, with neither trade nor investment important for either country. Australia's trade with Indonesia represents only around 3 per cent of its total merchandise trade, and Australia's importance to Indonesian trade is of the same order of magnitude (DFAT 2004). The invest-ment relationship is smaller still, with Australia investing more than four times as much in both Singapore and Hong Kong as it does in Indonesia. There are over 15,000 Indonesian students in Australia, but this number seems destined to diminish over time as competing study destinations become more available (see Chapter 8, this volume). In any case it is not clear how these Australian alumni have helped the relationship in the past, although many have made notable con-tributions in Indonesia.

Given the small size of the material economic relationships between the two countries, is there more that can be done? The possibilities lie in two lines of approach: first, through vigorous participation in regional economic arrange-ments; and second, through well-targeted and effective assistance to help Indonesia get back to the sorts of growth rates achieved during the Soeharto era, but hopefully with a greater degree of economic stability and resilience.

As a starting point, at least Australia now has a seat at the East Asia Summit. If it is to have a positive influence, Australia must find the right 'voice' at the meetings. As a 'new chum', it will have to exercise special sensitivity. Things that sound good to an Australian electorate may not help around the regional table, so restraint by the country's politicians is needed. One issue that needs sorting out is Australia's priority between the two groupings, ASEAN and Asia-Pacific Economic Cooperation (APEC). APEC has been a great achievement and Australia should be proud of its part in its development. Along with other members, Australia benefits greatly from the annual meetings of APEC political leaders; as host in 2007, it will certainly want to keep finding substantive tasks for APEC ('the search for content'). But it has to be recognised, at the same time, that most of the action on technical economic issues – that is, the issues that will put content into the relationships – has moved to the ASEAN-based arrangements, notably the Chiang Mai Initiative and ASEAN+3. Whatever sentimental attachment Australia has to APEC (and practical attachment, as host in 2007), the regional economic focus is elsewhere (Gyngell and Cook 2005).

A fruitful line of approach may be to recall that economics teaches us that the greatest gains from trade come when countries have substantial *differences*. Australia can (and should) say that its differences from the countries of the region are not, as some would suggest, a disqualification for effective participation, but are instead *strengths*. So Australia's strong card is to point out that it can bring a different point of view to regional forums, without being so large that it diverts the group from its proper focus on Asian issues, or prevents it from having 'Asian values' (whatever one thinks these are).

Australia may also be able to make a unique contribution in regional debate by interpreting the American position in the Asia forums. The United States is clearly watching the rise of China with some disquiet, and is nervous about any regional arrangements of which it is not a member – such as the East Asia Summit. As America's good and loyal friend, Australia could work to allay its fears, pointing out that it risks being the 'elephant in the canoe' in East Asia groupings – just too big and too dominant, at least for this level of discussions. Just as we don't have all our friends around for dinner at one time, international relationships can be carried forward in successive rounds of discussions, at different levels or layers, with different participants. Such a recognition would help Australia in its relations with Asia: it could go ahead, with clear conscience, in strengthening its place in purely regional arrangements, without feeling the critical stare of the United States over its shoulder.

Offering perhaps the most fruitful avenue for relationship augmentation is the $1 billion tsunami fund, which has triggered a requirement for senior levels of the Australian bureaucracy to find useful ways of cooperating with Indonesia (see Chapter 10, this volume). Before this initiative – and also coming out of a tragedy – the cooperation between the Australian and Indonesian police in investigating the Bali bombings of October 2002 looked, to the outside observer, to be a stunning success. The task now is to reproduce this productive relationship across a wide range of institutions. Clearly not all of them will be as successful at building cooperative relationships as the Australian Federal Police (AFP). The success of the police effort seems to have rested heavily on the attitude and skill of a few key players in each country, and such players are scarce, on both sides. But the pressure is on for the Australian side at least to identify opportunities for cooperation. Not only are the budget funds available for this, but this objective will appear in the work programs of most Commonwealth departments.

This emphasis on agency-to-agency programs has the other major advantage of ensuring that effort is directed where the need is greatest – towards strengthening the Indonesian bureaucracy. Of course 'governance' has been a priority at the Australian Agency for International Development (AusAID) for some time, but this has often been a catch-all term, and governance projects were often put out to tender. Agency-to-agency 'twinning' has more potential than isolated projects given to the lowest tenderer, because it commandeers the services of practising bureaucrats who can bring the full resources of their own institutions to bear to support them.

Moving from the general to the specific, the next few paragraphs explore an area of specific relevance to the creation of institutions: infrastructure. This passage might be read with the North quotes in mind: is this the sort of help and fillip that might make a real contribution to the hard slog of reforming Indonesia's institutions?

The World Bank notes that Indonesia has gone from having better infrastructure than Thailand, China and Taiwan before the 1997 crisis, to being behind these countries now (World Bank 2004). Spending has fallen from 7 per cent of GDP to 3 per cent, and needs to be doubled, to 5–6 per cent, to provide even a minimal level of service. Forty-three per cent of the population is not connected to the electricity grid. Only 4 per cent of people have access to a land-line telephone. Private investment in infrastructure has fallen by 90 per cent since the crisis; serious contractual disputes with some foreign private infrastructure providers have put a dampener on this activity. The infrastructure summit held in Jakarta in January 2005 identified more than 90 projects for tender to the private sector, valued at over $22 billion. The exact figures and specifications may be disputed, but it is not necessary to do a major survey to appreciate the general and widespread deficiencies in infrastructure. The inefficiency that this causes for everyday life is just as obvious. Less obvious is the disincentive it gives to investment, raising the required hurdle rate of return on just about every project. If a company has to deal with inadequate and unreliable water, ports, telecommunications and electricity, it cannot offer an adequate return to investors.

Such is the size of the task that it cannot all be funded by the government, or even by domestic private investors. Foreign funds are needed and public –private partnerships (PPPs) are a relevant model. Infrastructure is, in many ways, a 'natural fit' for foreign private investors: these projects are steady cash earners, offer a physical asset as security, and often have a fixed and predictable market. So why are they not attractive? One major Australian private-sector player in this sector – a world leader in the funding of infrastructure – has indicated that it is not interested, at this stage, in Indonesia because the legal structure is not strong enough. A recent study initiated by the European Commission warns potential investors of the difficulties of projects that are heavily controlled by state-owned enterprises, such as toll roads, terminals, ports and water supply projects, calling these 'high-risk investments' (*Jakarta Post*, 14 July 2005). The Indonesian government has acknowledged the issues – hence the Jakarta infrastructure summit in 2005 – and Bappenas is giving this high priority. The Indonesian government has formed a ministerial committee to coordinate its approach to infrastructure-related issues. Australia, for its part, is providing an advisor to offer specialist advice to Indonesia.

This seems to provide a specific opportunity for Australia to demonstrate its relevance in finding solutions to Indonesia's problems. Infrastructure is a difficult area in which to get the institutions right. The sums of money are huge and the pay-back period long, so long-term certainty about the enforceability of repayment is needed. Although there are physical assets to back up the projects, the detailed property rights to the physical assets are always going to be disputed. If a water supply system or a gas pipeline has been privatised, the customers will constantly bring pressure to bear to prevent price increases – even legitimate ones. Infrastructure projects often provide a 'community service', which adds to the pricing-setting difficulties.

Many of these projects are, in an important sense, monopolies, so it is legitimate to protect users against price gouging. But what is the right balance to strike between the owner and the users? Should the owner of a facility such as a telephone line or gas pipeline be forced to give competitors access to the facility, allowing them to provide a rival supply, and if so, on what terms? Many such projects form part of a wider network of infrastructure, often owned by the government; toll roads, for example, are fed by the untolled road system. What should the owner of a toll road pay for this benefit? Also, many projects impinge on community property rights, requiring the special power of the government to push through enabling measures such as land rights. What should the owner pay in exchange for this special advantage? Above all, what is the best way of sharing the risks between government and investor in a way that maximises incentives to do the right thing?

This is just a fraction of the complex issues that need to be sorted out if privately funded infrastructure is to work well – that is, fairly and efficiently – for all parties (the 'stakeholders' in the favoured governance parlance). Again, Douglass North gives us the framework: markets only work if they are embedded in appropriate institutions, that is, sets of rules. In Australia, these institutions have been developed to a high degree, often evolving the hard way by making mistakes and ending up with unworkable projects or projects that give an unconscionably high return to the owners. Australia has learned, too, of the dangers of 'privatising the profits and socialising the losses'. It also has considerable experience in resolving federal–state jurisdictional disputes. These may not be exactly the same as the turf disputes between Jakarta and the regions, but they do have the same flavour.

Is there an opportunity, now, to use some of the funds available from Canberra to add weight to the current infrastructure initiatives in Indonesia, especially given that the Indonesian government plans to hold a second infrastructure summit in 2006? A central objective might be to develop what may come to be called the 'Jakarta Rules'. Like the 'Paris Club' (covering official debt relief) and the 'London Rules' (covering private sector debt relief), the Jakarta Rules would be a prescriptive and proscriptive set of codes and understandings to govern foreign infrastructure investment. They would set out the broad parameters of finance, the regulatory framework (including price regulation for monopolies), dispute resolution processes, governance arrangements for tendering, and operational issues (such as contract transparency). The Jakarta Rules could be endorsed by the various governments participating, and by the World Bank with its long experience with PPPs, giving them a legitimacy that would ensure they are implemented and enforced, while keeping all the foreign parties on an equal footing.

What is in this for Indonesia? Reducing investor uncertainty means two things: more investment and cheaper funding costs. It would involve, importantly, the creation of an 'oil spot' of superior bureaucratic governance, which might over time spread to other areas of the bureaucracy.

And what is in it for Australia? Other than putting in place new commercial and bureaucratic relationships as ballast for the overall relationship, these sorts of rules remove the disadvantage Australian businesses face when operating in an environment where unethical behaviour is common. Australians want institutions that put a premium on ethical behaviour, because they can operate at their best in such an environment. Of course some of this is already in hand. The issue is whether it can be lifted to a more effective and comprehensive level by coordinating the current efforts and giving them more substance through greater government-to-government involvement. And, last but certainly not least, it is not enough for Australia to want to do it; Indonesia must want to do it too.

In guiding this expanded phase of the assistance program, two sources of real world experience are available. The first of these is the experience of the AFP, and Police Commissioner Mick Keelty might find a way to tell others how it is done. Second, Australia might draw on what may have been the last of the considerable number of contributions Geoff Forrester made to Australia–Indonesia relations over his lifetime: the paper he wrote for the Lowy Institute, published shortly before his untimely death (Forrester 2005). In looking at a number of case studies of AusAID projects in Indonesia in recent years, most of which he knew at first hand, he focused on the need for governance reform, and on the deficiencies in past efforts. The suggestion made above, that greater emphasis be placed on agency-to-agency relationships, resonates with Forrester's findings.

Not everyone will agree with Forrester's analysis, and the aid program is asked to achieve a number of goals that are sometimes incompatible. But the tsunami money clearly presents a huge opportunity. The positive opportunity offered by the combination of funding and high-level commitment has its mirror obverse in the negative possibility that this money may be misspent. No doubt some of it will be wasted, and a program that aims to improve governance and enhance administrative capacity cannot treat administrative deficiencies lightly or carelessly. But it would be just as serious if the tsunami money were *underspent*, through unrealistic processes, lack of imagination and failure of leadership. So there is a lot at stake here.

CONCLUSION

A year ago there was much to be depressed about in the Indonesia–Australia relationship. The previous few years had seen the Australian public reveal its underlying suspicion of Indonesia, and this was reciprocated in Indonesia. At government level, the prime minister was indifferent and the foreign minister was playing 'hard to get' in joining any exclusively East Asian grouping. Indonesia had experienced a sequence of presidents who had other things on their minds. The Indonesia economy was experiencing near-stagnation and investment was weak. At the official bureaucratic level on both sides, being too much in favour of the other country seemed to be a career-damaging attitude. On both sides, an earlier generation of bureaucrats, comprising many who had an intellectual and emotional commitment to the other country, had given way to a generation whose professionalism required them to show how objective, detached, dispassionate and 'un-engaged' they were.

Even before the tsunami, it was clear that Prime Minister John Howard, having successfully distanced himself from predecessor Paul Keating's engagement with the region, had shifted Indonesia to a higher priority. The tsunami saw a dramatic shift in the Australian public's attitude, and this was reflected in the prime minister's offer of a $1 billion assistance package. Meanwhile, in Indonesia, the next stage of the transition to democracy went remarkably smoothly. After some false starts, Indonesia now has a president with the right mix of qualities to fit him for the task ahead. Helped by strong commodity prices, the Indonesian economy is growing at 5 per cent. The investment drought may have broken, with approvals in the first six months of 2005 running 70 per cent higher than a year before.

There still seem to be ample opportunities for things to go wrong between the two countries. The drug trials of young Australians in Bali are but one example of the great potential for strongly held and loudly voiced opposing views, which may revive the underlying antipathies demonstrated in the second half of the 1990s. If economic matters are to contribute ballast to the relationship, it seems unlikely that they will be in the simplest form of trade and investment, although these will play their part. This chapter suggests that there may be two ways in which Australia might add to this rather frail relationship. The first is to participate, with vigour but with sensitivity, in the growing regional economic relationships. The second is to work hard to ensure that the new, increased assistance package is spent in full, and in ways that make a real contribution to a more dynamic Indonesian economy.

PART V

Conclusion

13 REFLECTIONS ON THE BILATERAL RELATIONSHIP – AND BEYOND

Jamie Mackie

In a year when relations between Australia and Indonesia have taken a more encouraging turn for the better than we have seen in nearly a decade, it is worth highlighting a notable feature of the 2005 Update conference, on which this book is based. It has been one of the most well-informed and penetrating discussions of the relationship I have heard during the 60 years since our two countries first had to start thinking about how to become good neighbours as well as independent members of our post-colonial region. All of the papers have provided frank, realistic assessments of the many problems that might obstruct such admirable intentions, instead of the bland platitudes we so often hear about the importance of friendship and cooperation between us, which no one of good sense would want to dispute. While all of the speakers share the hope that cordial relations between our two countries can be maintained and strengthened, they are well aware that this may prove very difficult. It will require better-targeted efforts on both sides to keep the bilateral relationship in good shape than we have seen hitherto. That is a problem I will return to in due course.

Australia's unprecedentedly generous and prompt response to the tsunami disaster in Aceh at the end of 2004 could turn out to be a major step forward in the development of a stronger bilateral relationship, especially as it has been reinforced by the cordial personal relations developed by Prime Minister John Howard and Indonesia's new president, Susilo Bambang Yudhoyono (SBY), since October 2004. Conversely, the support Indonesia gave Australia to help ease its entry into the all-important East Asia Summit in December 2005 is a good omen for the future, for the latter could turn out to be one of the most significant landmarks in our 60-year saga of trying to find an appropriate basis for Australia's acceptance into and participation in the political councils of the region. Any reservations by Jakarta could have wrecked Australia's chances of gaining acceptance there.

Yet the various problems that could still arise between Indonesia and Australia will have to be addressed far more openly and constructively on both sides than previously, if they are to be better understood and resolved in Canberra, Jakarta and well beyond than they have been so far. Mere wishful thinking and pious hopes will not make these problems go away. How to bring about the kinds of better understanding that will be needed to prevent things going wrong is a question with wide ramifications that was not much discussed at the Update and cannot be adequately addressed here. But the urgent need for closer cooperation between us, and for what former Prime Minister Paul Keating called closer Australian 'engagement' with Indonesia, was widely endorsed.

Closer engagement with Indonesia was described by Paul Kelly, editor-at-large for *The Australian*, as a never-ending national priority for Australia (see Chapter 4, this volume). But he also noted that frictions and serious disputes over a wide range of issues could easily escalate to levels that might frustrate any real progress towards such engagement. These issues include our divergent attitudes towards the 'war on terror', the Iraq war and Muslim extremisms (plural, not singular) of the al-Qaeda and Jemaah Islamiyah (JI) type; the seemingly intractable Papua (West New Guinea) problem; our divergent attitudes towards Aceh's demands for greater autonomy; the eternal East Timor 'pebble in the shoe', which has left a legacy of bitterness among some Indonesians over Australia's role in 1999; defence and security strategies more generally; and ideas on both sides about the 'threat' we may or may not pose to each other, as well as an unsavoury tangle of judicial and moral value issues that disturb many Australians.

There are also doubts in Indonesia about the credibility and sustainability of Australian statements of commitment to Indonesia's territorial integrity and sovereignty, profound disagreements about human rights and related issues (such as justice and the judicial system, 'corruption', transparency and governance problems) and increasingly difficult problems over fisheries in the waters between us – not to mention the contemptuous triviality of the Australian media's frenzied treatment of the Corby case. Much broader and deeper communication and mutual comprehension between us on all these matters is going to be essential, especially at the non-governmental level, if closer engagement is ever to achieve real momentum, along with better appreciation of how each country is seen on the other side of the Arafura Sea. These are not just issues to be sorted out between diplomats and governments; they reach down far more deeply into the thinking, feeling, attitudes and stereotypes prevalent in both societies. In fact governments have only a limited part to play in much of that.

Important as all these specific aspects of the bilateral relationship are, it is worth remembering that what matters at least as much in the long run is the extent to which the broader foreign policy objectives and strategies of our two countries at any particular time are pulling us in essentially convergent, not divergent, directions. I will say more about that later, for a comparison of the Sukarno and Soeharto eras is very revealing about how differences in basic policy on broader regional and international issues have impinged on the more specifically bilateral aspects of the relationship. But let us turn first to some of the major points emerging from the papers presented in this book.

TERRORISM, THREATS AND FEARS

Of the six 'markers' mentioned by Richard Woolcott in his opening address (see pages xvii–xxii), the most important to my mind is his observation that if the Indonesian government mishandles the JI problem, or Islamic extremism more generally, it will risk alienating parts of the moderate Muslim community. No government in a democratising Indonesia can afford to incur that risk. Hence it is utterly short-sighted for the Australian government – or our media, churches, NGOs or war-on-terror evangelists – to keep calling for tougher action in Jakarta against JI or its leaders, especially Abu Bakar Ba'asyir. His trouble-making capacities are in any case now severely constrained, so our calls to punish him further out of revenge for the 2002 Bali bombings are likely to carry little weight in Jakarta. If any sort of 'victory' over extremist groups like al-Qaeda and JI is ever to be achieved, it will have to be won by Muslim moderates in Indonesia, not as a result of pressure from non-Muslim outsiders, especially 'crusaders' (as we and our US allies are called by some of them) engaged in a war in the Muslim heartland. So one of Australia's top priorities should surely be to assist the moderates as best we can, not make life harder for them.

The same logic applies more generally to the worldwide problem of Islamic terrorism. The answers to it must come from within the Muslim community of believers (the *ummat*) itself – and that will certainly be a long-term process, not a quick fix as American neo-cons seem to imagine. The fact that Indonesia is the country with the largest number of Muslims in the world, and in some respects the most progressive of the Islamic countries, makes its Muslim leaders uniquely important players in that process, a point we in Australia should seek to benefit from, not obstruct or fear. Not as much was said at the Update about the 'war on terror' as its importance may have warranted, yet it is surely a subject that currently has a central bearing on the politics of our bilateral relationship. It will continue to do so for many years, for it is not a war in which any quick victory can even be imagined.

Another important point raised by Woolcott was the extent to which many Australians still think of Indonesia as some sort of threat to our national security. The Lowy Institute opinion survey on that subject brought up some very depressing figures about the extent of Australian hostility towards Indonesia (Cook 2005). Much of that sense of potential threat stems from the fear of invasion by the Japanese in 1941–42 and even earlier notions of the 'Yellow Peril' emanating from Asia, later focused more specifically on Communist China, and then Indonesia. One might have hoped that all those fantasies would have evaporated by now, since Indonesia is patently not likely to pose any serious military threat to Australia within the foreseeable future. And since much of that inchoate apprehension stems from mistaken notions that 'overpopulation' and resultant poverty must eventually drive Indonesia to seize more land from its neighbours, it is worth stressing the little-known fact that Indonesia's population is now within sight of stabilising at zero population growth by about the middle of this century, at roughly 300 million people, not an especially alarming number in today's circumstances. That was due largely to the family planning program introduced by the much maligned President Soeharto, one of his most beneficial achievements for his country and our entire region.

The other side of the coin is the fact that Australia is now regarded in some circles in Indonesia – rather more credibly, perhaps – as a potential threat to Indonesian sovereignty, due to the foolish rhetoric of the Howard government about Australia's 'deputy sheriff' role in the region, its assertion that Australia has the right to make pre-emptive strikes against terrorists in other countries, and Australia's defence force procurement plans. The implications of all of these arc discussed well by Hugh White (Chapter 5).

The relationship between our two countries is currently at an unusually high tide, observed Paul Kelly, as in the optimistic days of the early 1970s and in the 1990s phase of very cordial relations between Keating and Soeharto (Chapter 4). Yet both those phases ended badly because of our divergent attitudes to the East Timor issue – despite the efforts of both governments to avoid such an outcome. There is no particular reason to fear the same kind of misfortune at the present juncture, although the situation in Papua could slide out of control at any time if it is handled clumsily by either government, as Richard Chauvel makes clear (Chapter 9). Relations between the two countries are always likely to fluctuate, because the cultural gap between us is deep and enduring. Yet our shared interests with regard to broader regional issues should be seen as far outweighing any local or cultural differences that divide us. We have similar interests in the Association of Southeast Asian Nations (ASEAN) region, of course, but also well beyond, especially with regard to the rise of China and how best to handle its increasing economic and possibly political power throughout Southeast Asia in the decades ahead. (Consider only the fact that the fastest-growing economies in ASEAN today, Thailand, Malaysia and Singapore, will almost certainly be inclined to seek accommodation with China rather than try to resist it.) It is not yet clear whether the need to accommodate China will draw Australia and Indonesia closer together in working out our respective policies towards China or create longer-term conflicts of interest between us. My own belief is that we have similar interests of immense importance in inducing China to cooperate with the ASEAN countries in building a rules-based international order there rather than a power-based one. But the test of that will not emerge until it comes fully onto the agenda.

Indonesia's recent shift towards a more open, democratic political system is something that Australians have warmly applauded; but it can also make it harder to constrain the inclination of parliamentarians in Jakarta to express highly critical comments about Australia, and to blame Australia for things that go wrong in their own country. That does not help either government give higher priority to strengthening the bilateral relationship, any more than similar types of comments by Australian politicians do. The Australia–Indonesia Institute, set up by Foreign Ministers Gareth Evans and Ali Alatas in 1989, was established to tackle just this kind of problem, but only to limited effect thus far.

Wiryono Sastrowardoyo, the former Indonesian ambassador to Canberra, notes that:

> in both countries there will always be aggressive statements by members of parliament, and provocative opinion pieces in the mass media that militate against closer ties, no matter how closely the two governments may be working together on issues of common concern … (this volume, Chapter 2: p. 16).

He concludes therefore that 'a judicious practice of public diplomacy' will always be needed. And, he might well have added, acceptance of some kind of self-denying ordinance in the key opinion-forming circles of both countries, as well as both governments, to avoid or minimise the counterproductive practice of 'playing to the gallery' of domestic public prejudices with ill-chosen remarks about the other country simply for the sake of local political point scoring.

White's very informative survey of the security relationship between Indonesia and Australia is illuminating on the intensity of feelings in some parts of Indonesia's elite that some aspects of Australia's defence and foreign policies pose a potentially serious threat to Indonesia's sovereignty (Chapter 5). Such views appear to be widespread in both the officer corps of the Indonesian National Army (TNI) and the Indonesian parliament's Foreign Affairs Committee, places where we can least afford to be subject to such suspicions. Many Indonesians still harbour an acute sense of grievance over Australia's part in the events in 1999 that led to East Timor's achievement of independence, not only because of Prime Minister Howard's letter to President Habibie, which precipitated the latter's decision to hold a referendum there, but also because of the key role of Australian troops in the Interfet force after the referendum, in which Australians took great pride. Some Indonesians even believe that Australia deliberately took advantage of Indonesia's economic and political weakness in 1998–99, after the financial crisis of 1997 and the fall of Soeharto in 1998, to bring about the 'liberation' of East Timor, a phrase some Australian ministers have since rejoiced in. These are fantasies, of course, but it is not surprising that even well-informed Indonesians are inclined to believe them.

White suggests that in order to counter such misunderstandings about Australian motives and security policies, the Australian government should put more effort into explaining them more fully in Indonesia and should restore the defence relationship with the TNI to its pre-1999 level with the aim of making its senior officers more aware of our aims, military capabilities (and limitations) and strategies. The latter is likely to prove a controversial move in some parts of Australian society, but it is a matter that needs to be discussed more fully in both countries on the basis of much better knowledge of the issues than we have had hitherto. In view of the importance of both police cooperation over terrorism and military cooperation, the defence and security side of the bilateral relationship has become far more central than it had earlier seemed to be.

SOME REGIONAL AND OTHER ISSUES

Both Wiryono and K. Kesavapany, a former senior Singaporean diplomat who now heads the influential Institute of Southeast Asian Studies, have provided us with first-hand views from outside Australia of the all-important regional context within which the bilateral relationship must be developed, particularly with regard to ASEAN and the wider set of relations between China, Japan, the rest of Northeast Asia and also the United States, which, significantly, was not involved in the first East Asia Summit (see Chapters 2 and 3). The issues at stake here are likely to be as crucial to Australia's security – and even more so to Indonesia's – as any of the more narrowly bilateral issues that arise between us. An important point made by both Wiryono and Kesavapany is that the political framework provided by the ASEAN+3 arrangement and the East Asia Summit has created the possibility of a useful meeting place for the Northeast Asian powers. Because of old enmities, they would otherwise have had great difficulty in creating such a meeting place among themselves.

I commend to readers the very important papers by Scott Dawson on how Australia's large, post-tsunami aid contribution is being disbursed (Chapter 10), by Rizal Sukma on regional reactions to terrorism (Chapter 6), by Richard Chauvel on the Papua situation (Chapter 9), and by Noke Kiroyan and Stephen Grenville on financial and commercial relations between Indonesia and Australia (Chapters 11 and 12). I would also like to make a few brief remarks on the contributions of Isla Rogers-Winarto (Chapter 8) and David Reeve (Chapter 7), both of whom refer to the ways in which potential students (and others) from Indonesia expect and even fear racial prejudice against them in Australia, severely disadvantaging Australia in the stiffening international competition to attract overseas students to our schools and universities. Rogers-Winarto makes the ominous point that whereas Australia had some degree of comparative advantage in terms of cost and proximity in the 1990s, this is now diminishing and the number of students coming to Australia is showing a declining trend (Chapter 8). To offset that, she suggests a shift in focus from quantity to quality, particularly by seeking to attract graduate students at the top end of the market – but it tends not to be Australia's best tertiary institutions that are most active in Indonesia.

What can be done to counter Australia's reputation for racial prejudice in Indonesia is a far more difficult question – but also a profoundly important one. Australians are in many ways a great deal less racist in their attitudes towards Asians now than they were in the days of the White Australia policy 40 years ago, although the types of racist attitudes manifested these days have no doubt changed for the worse in some respects as well as for the better in others. I doubt that Australians generally are much more guilty of racial prejudice than most Asians. Anti-Chinese prejudice in Indonesia stems in part from many of the same sorts of stereotypes about racial difference that used to underlie the White Australia policy; and it may that both countries could teach the other a thing or two about how they might be countered. We would all benefit from a lot more open and frank discussion of the forms that racism and racial prejudice take in different times and places.

Reeve points to the disjunctions in Australia between popular and elite views of Indonesia and their relevance to the state of relations between our two countries (Chapter 7). He reminds us of the irony that the warm feelings between Indonesians and Australians, and the official relations between us, have never again been as cordial as they were in 1945–49, when almost nothing was known in either country about the other! His illuminating and often hilarious use of caricatures and cartoons to illustrate some of the ideas prevalent in each country about the other led me to think that more frequent exchanges between some of the excellent cartoonists in each country might do more to promote better understanding than just the written word. The outcry in March–April 2006 over controversial portrayals of the political leaders of each country made second thoughts on that score necessary. However, the episode also strengthens the argument that both Indonesians and Australians, including our cartoonists, need to gain a better comprehension of the sensitive edges of public opinion on the other side of the Arafura Sea.

FUTURE DIRECTIONS: CONVERGENCE OR DIVERGENCE?

What can we foretell about the future course of the relationship between our two countries over the next few years? It is not easy to guess, for there are currently too many imponderables to be taken into account. These include divergent government policies and public attitudes on the 'war on terror', our respective assessments of how to react to China's increasing power in East Asia – and the

Japanese and US responses to this – the sustainability of Indonesia's economic recovery from the 1997–98 financial crisis, and the always sensitive issue of (West) Papua's future. It would be impossible to deal adequately here with any of these, but I want to touch briefly on several aspects which may help us put them in a broader historical perspective.

First, I will briefly review how the patterns of convergence or divergence in our respective foreign policy trajectories have fluctuated since 1945. Ideally one would take an even longer historical perspective and think also about the broad sweep of contacts and comparative patterns of socioeconomic development between the Indonesian archipelago and Australia since white settlement began here in 1788 – or go back even further to the many thousands of years of human occupation and occasional contact between the two regions prior to that, a story that has attracted little attention in either country until recently, but may come to be seen as having more significance in the years ahead. Second, the question of how Australia should assess and prioritise the various objectives it must keep in mind in its dealings with Indonesia also needs to be considered more carefully than hitherto. Finally, the meaning to be attached to 'closer engagement' with Indonesia and the rest of Southeast and East Asia warrants deeper thought.

Phases in the bilateral relationship

On the all-important matter of convergence and divergence in our broader regional and global foreign policies, it is worth recalling that since 1945 Australia and Indonesia have experienced four very different phases of basic foreign policy orientation that have profoundly influenced the state of the more narrowly bilateral issues arising between us. Two of these saw strongly convergent trajectories, one was disastrously divergent, and the latest has seen a confused melee of policies and public opinion on both sides.

In the first phase of our relations with Indonesia, between 1945 and 1949, Australia's support for Indonesian independence put our regional policies on much the same track as Indonesia's, fortunately and somewhat fortuitously. It has come to be seen as an almost legendary time of good relations when Australian and Indonesian objectives were essentially convergent. Yet our knowledge of each other then was almost negligible.

In the second phase, between 1950 and 1965, when Sukarno was setting Indonesia's foreign policy trajectory and Prime Minister Menzies determining Australia's, almost the opposite was the case. We were on sharply divergent courses for most of the time, especially over the West New Guinea (Irian Jaya) issue and later over Indonesia's policy of 'Confrontation' towards Malaysia – which resulted at one point in Australian and Indonesian troops actually shooting at one other on the Sarawak–Indonesia border. There was divergence also, more fundamentally, over our basic attitudes towards Cold War alignments.

Australia's strongly anti-communist and anti-China policies led it into the ANZUS pact and SEATO. This put Australia sharply at odds with Indonesia's inclination towards non-alignment, anti-colonialism, and resistance to imperialist and neo-colonialist pressures on the newly independent nations. That was expressed most dramatically in the 1955 Bandung Conference of Afro-Asian Nations and the formation in 1961 of the Non Aligned Movement. The drift to the left in Indonesia's domestic politics under Sukarno's 'Guided Democracy' from the late 1950s to 1965–66 led to increasing alarm in Australia about the possibility of a communist Indonesia on our northern frontier. Despite frequent expressions of hope in both countries that policy differences over West Irian would not put the bilateral relationship in peril, there was little scope for significantly closer cooperation at any level so long as divergent attitudes to the presumed communist threat to Southeast Asia persisted.

In the third phase of the relationship, the pendulum again swung back the other way. After Sukarno was displaced by General (later President) Soeharto in 1966, we found ourselves again on basically convergent paths with regard to our broader international alignments. Although Soeharto was essentially a right-wing president, pursuing a strongly anti-communist course in both his domestic and foreign policies until being deposed in 1998, both Labor and Coalition governments in Australia found it beneficial to work closely with rather than against him on most issues, despite occasional disagreements over human rights violations and episodes like East Timor. Neither government wanted to allow these issues to grow into a major source of antagonism. And on several matters, such as the Cambodia peace initiative of 1989–91 and the formation of the Asia-Pacific Economic Cooperation (APEC) forum in 1989, the foreign ministries of the two countries cooperated very closely indeed.

In the fourth phase, since the fall of Soeharto in 1998, we have seen a reversion to unpredictability, ambivalence and mood swings on both sides, aggravated by the 1999 East Timor crisis and Australia's support for the United States on the 'war on terror' and the Iraq war, as well as Indonesian suspicions about Australia's defence policies and foreign policy rhetoric on 'pre-emption'. Howard's frequent references to 'values' as a key element in our foreign policy alignments have not been helpful either, since it cannot be expected that Indonesian and Australian values will be remotely similar at this stage in each country's history. The diverse policies of Indonesia's four presidents since 1998 have added to the uncertainties of this phase, although there has been a sharp turn for the better under SBY, especially as the tsunami elicited a very positive response from Canberra.

This is where the importance of our respective regional policies in and after the East Asia Summit comes into the picture. If we find ourselves pursuing essentially convergent trajectories with regard to the new balance of power in Asia, the results could be highly beneficial in much the same way as were our similar policies towards APEC, the Cairns Group and the World Trade Organization in the early 1990s. The more important issues are likely to take precedence over the more transient ones that are bound to arise between us from time to time. So the more closely we can keep in step on major issues the better. Yet there will inevitably be times when this does not happen.

Indonesia and Australia will therefore need to keep exchanging ideas about how we intend to cope with the rising power of China (and eventually India) over the next decade or more, and on Japan's role in the region – not to mention US dominance across the world – in an effort to resolve whatever differences of approach may emerge between us on those crucial matters. It will be essential for each country to understand and accept the reasoning behind the other's policy stance to the greatest extent possible.

To slip back towards the kind of fundamental divergences of the Menzies–Sukarno era by allowing the 'war on terror' to become a dominant issue between us in the way that communism was then would be a disastrous error. Much has been achieved since then to draw many elements of Australian and Indonesian society closer together, through commercial contacts, educational and cultural exchanges, and governmental and institutional links of an enduring (and often very valuable) nature. These are too crucial to be put at risk by sheer lack of foresight just to pursue some transient objective. It is essential that we continue to build on the progress that has been made while the political climate is as benign as it currently is. It may not always be so.

Assessing policy priorities

There are always bound to be major differences between the views of the Indonesian and Australian governments on various matters, not to mention the differences in the views of diverse societal groups such as the media, lobby groups, advocates of human rights and similar causes, and, most notably, our respective religious organisations, to mention only a few. Civil liberties advocates are rarely likely to see eye to eye with supporters of closer military cooperation, but the arguments on both sides deserve serious consideration. One has only to compile a brief list of the key principles and propositions that seem to warrant a strong claim to the highest priority in the formulation of any Australian statement of policy towards Indonesia to realise how inherently divergent or even contradictory some of them are. Consider merely the following list, which could easily have been made much longer.

•   Supporting the national integrity of Indonesia – and avoiding any actions or policies that might arouse suspicions to the contrary.

- Helping to maintain a strong, viable national government in Indonesia and avoid serious local disorder (while also backing effective decentralisation to regional bodies).
- Supporting efforts to strengthen human rights and civil liberties in Indonesia.
- Promoting trade and investment between Indonesia and Australia, an essential element in any strengthening of the bilateral relationship.
- Avoiding situations of potential conflict between the two countries as far as possible, at least on minor issues.
- Pursuing closer engagement in the widest sense, in whatever forms are feasible – with particular reference to people-to-people contacts, on which Australia's past record has provided some valuable comparative advantage, as in the pioneering life and work of Herbert Feith.
- Providing foreign aid as effectively and generously as possible to help relieve poverty and promote economic development.
- Developing educational exchanges and language training, in both directions, on both a governmental and private commercial basis.
- Promoting defence cooperation, including officer training (both ways).
- Seeking to enhance cooperation in areas where friction is likely to occur, such as fisheries and quarantine matters, maritime boundaries, illegal immigration, avian flu outbreaks and so on.
- Helping to strengthen democratic institutions and the rule of law, good governance and transparency in Indonesian institutions.
- Developing interfaith dialogue in and between both countries with the aim of bridging the gulf between the Muslim and Christian faiths and generating progress towards broader 'shared values'.

It is almost impossible to imagine how any set of foreign policy experts could bring a coherent ordering of priorities, or even balance, to such a list of objectives. Any such process would have to involve trade-offs or concessions of principle on both sides, in circumstances that would probably be constantly changing. So let us not delude ourselves that the relationship can be 'put right' simply by formulating some magical policy change or new balance of principles. Both governments will always have to keep juggling a diverse and sometimes conflicting range of policy objectives, principles and promises to their electorates. Contiguous countries all over the world are constantly faced by this sort of juggling act, often on issues that may seem irreconcilable at times. France and Germany have long been the most obvious examples of that, but even Canada and the United States are often caught up in very serious and tangled conflicts of interest. Australia was lucky to have had no need to bother about such problems between 1788 and 1945, and even since then its learning curve has not been a very arduous one. But Australia and Indonesia will both need to pay closer attention to the implications of contiguity in the decades ahead as contacts between the two countries proliferate and the communications revolution shrinks the distance between us.

Engagement – with Indonesia and with the region beyond

Ever since 1945, some Australians have seen that the ability to engage with Indonesia successfully was likely to be a litmus test of Australia's ability to achieve workable relations with the other newly independent nations of Southeast Asia. As that wise old diplomat Macmahon Ball put it in the 1950s: 'If we make a mess of our relations with Indonesia, we'll have little hope of being able to succeed with any of the other nations in our region'.

Closer Australian engagement with Asia, and in particular with Indonesia, was advocated strongly by Paul Keating in the early 1990s at a time when the booming economies of East and Southeast Asia seemed to be opening up limitless opportunities for Australian firms to expand into East Asian markets. His foreign minister, Gareth Evans, had earlier put great stress on the institutional and people-to-people contacts that would be central to any such process, in the hope of creating more 'ballast' in the relationship to prevent it from being upset by the squalls and storms that inevitably blow across the path from time to time. Unfortunately, the Howard government's lack of enthusiasm in its early years for anything like the kind of 'special relationship' with Indonesia that Keating had (allegedly) pursued, coupled with the economic setbacks resulting from the financial meltdown of 1997–98, put a damper on the hopes for a closer relationship that had been kindled in the boom years of the early 1990s. The tensions aroused over East Timor in 1999 and the 'war on terror' after 2001 marked a further turn for the worse, on both sides. And until the Indonesian economy regains the strong momentum it developed in the early 1990s it is unlikely that anything like the Keating-era enthusiasm for closer engagement with Indonesia will be rekindled widely in Australia.

Relations began to improve in 2004–05 as a result of the cordial relationship established between John Howard and SBY, followed by Australia's prompt and generous response to the tsunami disaster. But despite improved relations at the government-to-government level, enhanced most notably by the cooperation between the Australian Federal Police and its Indonesian counterparts after the 2002 Bali bombing, there are still serious problems at the people-to-people level, as the Australian media reaction to the Corby case revealed quite blatantly. Meanwhile, divergent attitudes in Indonesia and Australia to the threats posed by JI and Muslim terrorists continue to rankle in both countries. It is hard to imagine that there can be much improvement on that front so long as Australia is so closely associated with the United States in the 'war on terror', since Indonesian Muslims are, to say the least, greatly vexed about it all. So it is bound to remain a problem between us that will not easily be resolved by friendlier words between our prime minister and Indonesia's president.

Closer engagement with Indonesia may still be little more than a dream, but it is a dream worth cherishing – and even proclaiming forthrightly as the goal towards which we should be advancing. It does not greatly matter that the goal will probably remain forever just beyond our grasp. It is the direction that the dream provides that is crucial. For if two such profoundly different countries as Australia and Indonesia can go on creating the bridges to make such a dream appear attainable and desirable to us both, we will have achieved something unique in the modern world. Where else has anything comparable yet been seen?

GLOSSARY

ABC	Australian Broadcasting Commission
ABRI	Angkatan Bersenjata Republik Indonesia (Armed Forces of the Republic of Indonesia)
Abu Sayyaf Group	'Father of the Swordbearer'; a southern Philippines nationalist movement formed in 1991
ACICIS	Australian Consortium for In-country Indonesian Study
ADB	Asian Development Bank
ADF	Australian Defence Force
ADS	Australian Development Scholarship scheme
AEI	Australia Education International
AFP	Australian Federal Police
AIPRD	Australia–Indonesia Partnership for Reconstruction and Development
al-Qaeda	'the Base'; name of jihadist organisation formed by Osama bin Laden in the 1980s
AMS	Agreement to Maintain Security
ANU	Australian National University
ANZUS	Australia, New Zealand, United States Security Treaty
APEC	Asia-Pacific Economic Cooperation
APS	Australian Partnership Scholarship scheme
ASEAN	Association of Southeast Asian Nations
ASPI	Australian Strategic Policy Institute
AusAID	Australian Agency for International Development
Bappenas	Badan Perencanaan Pembangunan Nasional (National Development Planning Agency)

BNI	Bank Negara Indonesia (State Bank of Indonesia)
BPK	Badan Pemeriksaan Keuangan (State Audit Agency)
BPKI	Badan Penjelidik Kemerdekaan Indonesia (Indonesian Independence Investigatory Body)
BRR	Badan Rehabilitasi dan Rekonstruksi (BRR) NAD-Nias (Rehabilitation and Reconstruction Agency for Aceh and Nias)
bupati	head of a *kabupaten* (district)
CEO	chief executive officer
DFAT	Department of Foreign Affairs and Trade (Australia)
DIFF	Development Import Finance Facility
DPR	Dewan Perwakilan Rakyat (People's Representative Council); Indonesia's parliament
EAS	East Asia Summit
ELICOS	English Language Intensive Courses for Overseas Students
EU	European Union
FBI	Federal Bureau of Investigation
FDI	foreign direct investment
Front Pembela Islam	Islamic Defenders Front
FTA	free trade agreement/area
G8	Group of Eight (the United States, Japan, Germany, France, the United Kingdom, Italy, Canada and Russia)
G20	Group of Twenty (finance ministers and central bank governors)
G77	Group of 77 (developing countries)
GAM	Gerakan Aceh Merdeka (Free Aceh Movement)
GDP	gross domestic product
Golkar	Golongan Karya; the state political party under the New Order, and one of the major post-New Order parties
Guided Democracy	the Sukarno era
IELTS	International English Language Testing System
IMET	International Military Education and Training; military training program between Indonesia and the United States
IMF	International Monetary Fund
Interfet	International Force for East Timor
JI	Jemaah Islamiyah; terrorist organisation
Kadin	Kamar Dagang dan Industri (Chamber of Commerce and Industry)

KNKG	Komite Nasional Kebijakan Governance (National Committee on Governance Policy)
Kopassus	Komando Pasukan Khusus (Special Forces Command)
KPEN	Komite Pemulihan Ekonomi Nasional (National Economic Recovery Committee)
KPK	Komite Pemberantasan Korupsi (Committee for the Eradication of Corruption)
LAPIS	Learning Assistance Program for Islamic Schools
Laskar Jihad	'Holy War Fighters'; Indonesian paramilitary force formed in 2000 and disbanded in 2002
LKDI	Lembaga Komisaris dan Direktur Indonesia (Indonesian Institute for Directors and Commissioners)
merdeka	independence, freedom
MILF	Moro Islamic Liberation Front; southern Philippines organisation formed in 1978
MMI	Majelis Mujahidin Indonesia (Council of Indonesian Mujahideen), established in 2000
MOU	memorandum of understanding
NAM	Non Aligned Movement
New Order	the Soeharto era, 1965–98
NGO	non-government organisation
OIC	Organization of Islamic Countries
OPEC	Organization of the Petroleum Exporting Countries
OPM	Organisasi Papua Merdeka (Free Papua Organisation)
Parna	Partai Nasional (National Party)
PAS	Parti Islam Se Malaysia (Islamic Party of Malaysia)
PBB	Partai Bulan Bintang (Crescent and Star Party); an Islamic modernist political party
PDI-P	Partai Demokrasi Indonesia-Perjuangan (Indonesian Democratic Party of Struggle)
pembangunan	development
PKII	Partai Kemerdekaan Indonesia Irian (Indonesian Independence Party Irian)
PKS	Partai Keadilan Sejahtera (Prosperity and Justice Party)
PNG	Papua New Guinea
PPP	Partai Persatuan Pembangunan (United Development Party)
PPP	public–private partnership

RAMSI	Regional Assistance Mission to Solomon Islands; Australian force deployed in 2003
reformasi	reform
RSPAS	Research School of Pacific and Asian Studies
SBY	Susilo Bambang Yudhoyono, Indonesia's president
SEATO	Southeast Asia Treaty Organization
SME	small and medium-sized enterprise
SOE	state-owned enterprise
stabilitas	stability
TNI	Tentara Nasional Indonesia (Indonesian National Army)
ummat	the Islamic community
UNSW	University of New South Wales
US	United States
VET	vocational education and training
walikota	mayor
WTO	World Trade Organization

Currencies

$	US dollar
A$	Australian dollar
Rp	Indonesian rupiah

REFERENCES

Abbot, Tony (2005), 'Three's not a crowd in our Western alliance', *Australian Financial Review*, 6 August.

Aedy, Richard (2005), 'Indonesian media & the Corby case', interview with Krishna Sen, Media Report, Radio National, 2 June, <http://www.abc.net.au/rn/talks/8.30/mediarpt/stories/s1382786.htm>.

AEF (Asia Education Foundation) (2005), 'National forum: Engaging young Australians with Asia', Canberra, 21 June, <http://www.asiaeducation.edu.au/pdf/engagingyoungaustralians.pdf>.

Aguswandi (2005), 'Aceh's reconstruction clumsy and disorganized', *Jakarta Post*, 18 October.

Alatas, Ali (2000), 'Challenges to Indonesian foreign policy', *Jakarta Post,* 31 March 2000 and 1 April 2000.

Alcorn, Gay (2002), 'US push to Hunt Indon al Qaeda', *The Age*, 22 March, <http://www.theage.com.au/articles/2002/03/21/1016701778590.html>, accessed 19 May 2002.

Allard K. Lowenstein International Human Rights Clinic (2004), 'Indonesian human rights abuses in West Papua: Application of the law of genocide to the history of Indonesian control', Yale Law School, New Haven CT, April.

Amirrachman, Alpha (2005), 'The humanistic character of our southern neighbor', *Jakarta Post*, 1 April.

APSC (Australian Public Service Commission) (2005), 'Connecting government: Whole of government responses to Australia's priority challenges', APSC report, <http://www.apsc.gov.au/mac/workingtogether.htm>.

ASAA (Asian Studies Association of Australia) (2005), 'After the tsunami: The urgency of maximizing Australia's Asia knowledge', submission to the 2005–06 Federal Budget, <http://coombs.anu.edu.au/SpecialProj/ASAA/Budget/ASAA-budget-sub-2005.doc>.

ASEAN (Association of Southeast Asian Nations) (1997), 'ASEAN Declaration on Transnational Crime, Manila, 20 December', <http://www.aseansec.org/5640.htm>.

ASEAN (Association of Southeast Asian Nations) (2001), 'ASEAN Declaration on Joint Action to Counter Terrorism', Bandar Seri Begawan, 5 November, <http://www.aseansec.org/5620.htm>.

ASEAN (Association of Southeast Asian Nations) (2002), 'Joint Communiqué of the Special ASEAN Ministerial Meeting on Terrorism', Kuala Lumpur, 20–21 May, <http://www.aseansec.org/5618.htm>.

AusAID (Australian Agency for International Development) (2005a), 'Australia's overseas aid program 2005–06', budget statement, 10 May 2005, <http://www.ausaid.gov.au/publications/pdf/budget_2005_2006.pdf>.

AusAID (Australian Agency for International Development) (2005b), 'Indonesia: Analytical report for the white paper on Australia's aid program', Canberra, September, <http://www.ausaid.gov.au/publications/pdf/indonesia_report.pdf>.

Balint, Ruth (2005), *Troubled Waters: Borders, Boundaries, Possession in the Timor Sea*, Allen & Unwin, Sydney.

Banham, Cynthia (2005), 'Bilateral bond a thin veneer over suspicion', *Sydney Morning Herald*, 25 July.

Beazley, Kim (2005), 'Address to the Lowy Institute', Sydney, 18 April, <http://www.alp.org.au/media/0405/spefll180.php>.

Boediono (2005), 'Managing the Indonesian economy: Some lessons from the past', *Bulletin of Indonesian Economic Studies*, 41(3): 309–24.

Bonay, E.J. (1984), 'Sejarah kebangkitan nasionalisme Papua' [History of the emergence of Papuan nationalism], unpublished manuscript, Wijhe, Netherlands.

BPS, Bappenas and UNDP (Statistics Indonesia, National Development Planning Agency and United Nations Development Programme) (2004), *Indonesian Human Development Report 2004. The Economics of Democracy: Financing Human Development in Indonesia*, Jakarta June, <http://www.undp.or.id/pubs/ihdr2004/ihdr2004_full.pdf>.

BRR (Rehabilitation and Reconstruction Agency) (2005a), 'Working together for a better Aceh and Nias', 4 October, <http://www.e-aceh-nias.org>.

BRR (Rehabilitation and Reconstruction Agency) (2005b), 'Aceh and Nias one year after the tsunami: The recovery effort and way forward', <http://siteresources.worldbank.org/INTEASTASIAPACIFIC/Resources/1YR_tsunami_advance_release.pdf>.

Cai Bing Kui (2004), Keynote address to the ASEAN–China Forum, organised by the Institute of Southeast Asian Studies (ISEAS), Singapore, 23 June; also p. 27 in Saw Swee Hock, Sheng Li-jun and Chin Kin Wah (eds) (2005), *ASEAN–China Relations*, ISEAS, Singapore.

Chauvel, Richard (2003), *The Land of Papua and the Indonesian State: Essays on West Papua, Volume 2*, Monash Asia Institute, Monash University, Clayton.

Chauvel, Richard (2005), *Constructing Papuan Nationalism: History, Ethnicity and Adaptation*, Policy Studies 14, East-West Center, Washington DC.

Chow, Jonathan T. (2005), 'ASEAN counterterrorism cooperation since 9/11', *Asian Survey*, 45(2): 302–21.

Cook, Ivan (2005), 'Australians speak 2005: Public opinion and foreign policy', Lowy Institute for International Policy, Sydney, <http://www.lowyinstitute.org/Publication.asp?pid=236>.

Costello, Peter (2005a), 'Australia–Indonesia Partnership for Reconstruction and Development: Joint ministerial statement', 6 September, <http://www.treasurer.gov.au/tsr/content/pressreleases/2005/077.asp>.

Costello, Peter (2005b), press conference, Jakarta, 7 September, <http://www.treasurer.gov.au/tsr/content/transcripts/2005/131.asp>.

Cotan, Imron (2005a), 'Indonesia in 2005 and beyond', speech delivered in Sydney, February 2005.

Cotan, Imron (2005b), 'Indonesia–Australian relations: East Timor, Bali, Tsunami and beyond', speech delivered in Canberra, March 2005.

Dagg, Christopher (2001), 'Religion and politics in Indonesia', paper presented to the Canadian Consortium on Asia Pacific Security 9th Annual Conference, University of British Columbia, 7–9 December.

Daley, Paul (2004), 'Breach of trust', interview with Imron Cotan, Indonesian ambassador to Australia, *Bulletin*, 14 April.

de Castro, Renato Cruz (2004), 'Addressing international terrorism in Southeast Asia: A matter of strategic or functional approach?' *Contemporary Southeast Asia*, 26(2): 193–217.

DFAT (Department of Foreign Affairs and Trade) (2004), *The APEC Region Trade and Investment*, Canberra.

DFAT (Department of Foreign Affairs and Trade) (2005a), *Education without Borders: International Trade in Education*, Economic Analytical Unit, DFAT, Canberra.

DFAT (Department of Foreign Affairs and Trade) (2005b), 'Response of the Australian Government to the report of the Joint Standing Committee on Foreign Affairs, Defence and Trade "Near Neighbours – Good Neighbours: An Inquiry into Australia's Relationship with Indonesia"', September, <http://www.aph.gov.au/house/committee/jfadt/indonesia/indonesia.pdf>.

Dibb, Paul (1986), *Review of Australia's Defence Capabilities*, AGPS, Canberra.

Dillon, Dana R. and Paolo Pasicolan (2002), 'Promoting a collective response to terrorism in Southeast Asia', Heritage Foundation Executive Memorandum No. 825, 22 July, <http://www.heritage.org/Research/AsiaandthePacific/EM825.cfm>.

Dodd, Tim (2002), 'Shadow of doubt frustrates Al Qaeda connection', *Australian Financial Review*, 30 January.

Downer, Alexander (2005a), 'Australia–Indonesia Partnership for Reconstruction and Development: Joint ministerial statement', 17 March, <http://www.foreignminister.gov.au/releases/2005/jointms170305_aus-ind.html>.

Downer, Alexander (2005b), 'Joint press conference Australian Indonesia', 17 March, <http://www.foreignminister.gov.au/transcripts/2005/050317_joint_press_conf_aust_indo.html>.

Downer, Alexander (2005c), 'Australia–Indonesia Partnership for Reconstruction and Development: Third joint ministerial statement', 7 December, <http://www.ausaid.gov.au/hottopics/aiprd/pdf/min_3rd_state_dec05.pdf>.

Drooglever, P.J. (2005), *Een Daad van Vrije Keuze*, Boon.

Emmerson, Donald K. (2001), 'Southeast Asia and the United States since 11 September', statement prepared for a hearing on 'Southeast Asia after 9/11: Regional Trends and U.S. Interests' organised by the Subcommittee on East Asia and the Pacific, Committee on International Relations, US House of Representatives, Washington DC, 12 December.

Foreign Affairs Subcommittee (2004), *Near Neighbours – Good Neighbours: An Inquiry into Australia's Relationship with Indonesia*, report of the Foreign Affairs Subcommittee of the Australian Parliament's Joint Standing Committee on Foreign Affairs, Defence and Trade, 31 May, <http://www.aph.gov.au/house/committee/jfadt/indonesia/report.htm>.

Forrester, G. (2005), 'Staying the course: AusAID's governance performance in Indonesia', Lowy Institute Perspectives paper, Sydney, April, <http://www.lowyinstitute.org/Publication.asp?pid=257>.

Giay, Benny (2000), *Menuju Papua Baru: Beberapa Pokok Pikiran Sekitar Emansipasi Orang Papua* [Towards a New Papua: Some Principal Thoughts on the Emancipation of the Papuan People], Deiyai/Elsham, Jayapura.

Giay, Benny (2001), 'Towards a new Papua: When they hear the sacred texts of the church, Papuans see a better future', in Theo P.A. van den Broek and J. Budi Hernawan (eds), *Memoria Passionis di Papua* [The Collective Memory of Suffering in Papua], Lembaga Studi Perkembangan Pers, Jakarta.

Gyngell, A. and M. Cook (2005), 'How to save APEC', Lowy Institute Policy Brief, Sydney, October, <http://www.lowyinstitute.org/Publication.asp?pid=305>.

Hamilton-Hart, Natasha (2005), 'Terrorism in Southeast Asia: Expert analysis, myopia and fantasy', *Pacific Review*, 18(3): 303–26.

Hartadi, Kristanto (2005), 'Keterlibatan internasional di Papua tak terelakkan' [International involvement in Papua is unavoidable], *Sinar Harapan*, Jumat, 16 September.

Hatta, Mohammad (1979), *Mohammad Hatta Memoir* [Mohammad Hatta: Memoir], Tintamas, Jakarta.

Hill, Robert (2005), 'Combined defence exercise with Indonesia', media release, 13 April, <http://www.minister.defence.gov.au/Hilltpl.cfm?Current Id=4774>.

Howard, John (1999), 'Joint press conference with His Excellency B.J. Habibie, President of the Republic of Indonesia', Bali, 27 April, <http://www.pm.gov.au/news/interviews/1999/bali2704.htm>.

Howard, John (2005a), 'Australia–Indonesia Partnership for Reconstruction and Development', media release, 5 January, <http://www.pm.gov.au/news/media_releases/media_Release1195.html>.

Howard, John (2005b), 'Address to the nation', 9 January, <http://www.pm.gov.au/news/speeches/speech1202.html>.

Howard, John (2005c), 'Joint press conference with His Excellency Dr Susilo Bambang Yudhoyono, President of Indonesia, Parliament House, Canberra', 4 April, <http://www.pm.gov.au/news/interviews/Interview1300.html>.

Howard, John (2005d), 'Address to parliamentary luncheon', Parliament House, Canberra, 4 April, <http://www.pm.gov.au/news/speeches/speech1298.html>.

Howard, John (2005e), 'Increase in overseas aid', media release, 13 September, <http://www.pm.gov.au/news/media_releases/media_Release1561.html>.

Huang, Reyko (2002a), 'In the spotlight: Jemaah Islamiyah', *CDI Terrorism Project*, 1 April 2002, <http://www.cdi.org/terrorism/ji-pr.cfm>, accessed 31 May 2002.

Huang, Reyko (2002b), 'Al Qaeda in Southeast Asia: Evidence and response', *CDI Terrorism Project*, 8 February 2002, <http://www.cdi.org/terrorism/sea-pr.cfm>, accessed 29 May 2002.

ICG (International Crisis Group) (2002), 'How the Jemaah Islamiyah terrorist network operates', ICG Asia Report No. 43, 11 December.

ICG (International Crisis Group) (2003a), 'Dividing Papua: How not to do it', Asia Briefing No. 24, Jakarta/Brussels, 9 April, <http://www.crisisgroup.org/home/index.cfm?id=1764&l=1>.

ICG (International Crisis Group) (2003b), 'Jemaah Islamiyah in Southeast Asia: Damaged but still dangerous', ICG Asia Report No. 63, 26 August.

Jones, Sidney (2002), 'Indonesia: The fear factor', *Le Monde Diplomatique*, internet edition, November, <http://www.mondediplo.com/2002/11/04indonesia>, accessed 19 January 2003.

Keating, Paul (2002), 'A time for reflection: Political values in the age of distraction', Third Annual Manning Clark Lecture, delivered at the National Library of Australia, Canberra, 3 March.

Kent Hughes, Sir Wilfred (1950), 'Indonesia might as well claim Holland as Dutch New Guinea', *Melbourne Herald*, 2 January.

Kerin, John (2005), 'Australia "will sign" pact with ASEAN', *The Australian*, 26 July.

Krastev, Nikola (2002), 'Indonesia: Radical Muslim groups elude easy classification', Radio Free Europe, October, <http://www.rferl.org/features/2002/10/17102002161557.asp>.

Liddle, Bill (2005), 'Year One of the Yudhoyono–Kalla Duumvirate', *Bulletin of Indonesian Economic Studies*, 41(3): 325–40.

Maarif, Ahmad Syafii (2002), 'Islam and the challenge of managing globalisation', paper presented to the Trilateral Commission Task Force Meeting on Islam and Globalisation, Washington DC, 6–7 April.

McAllister, Ian (2004), 'Attitude matters: Public opinion towards defence and security in Australia', Australian Strategic Policy Institute, Canberra.

McAllister, Ian (2005), 'Representative views: Mass and elite opinion on Australian security', Australian Strategic Policy Institute report, Canberra, 15 June.

McVey, Ruth (2003), 'Nation versus state in Indonesia', pp. 11–27 in Damien Kingsbury and Harry Aveling (eds), *Autonomy and Disintegration in Indonesia*, RoutledgeCurzon, London.

Media Watch (2005), 'Give Malcolm a microphone and away he goes', ABC TV, 23 May, <http://www.abc.net.au/mediawatch/transcripts/s1369667.htm>.

Murdoch, Lindsay (1999), 'Timor "timetable to disaster"', *Sydney Morning Herald*, 29 April.

Netherlands Government (1960), *Annual Report to the United Nations on Netherlands New Guinea, 1960*, The Hague.

Netherlands–Indonesian Union (1950), *Rapport van de Commissie Nieuw-Guinea (Irian) 1950* [Report of the New Guinea (Irian) Commission], Vol. 4e, Nederlands-Indonesische Unie, The Hague.

North, D. (2004), *Understanding the Process of Economic Change*, Princeton University Press, Princeton NJ.

Novotny, Daniel (2005), 'The threat of (from?) misperception', *PostScript*, 2(6): 19–23.

Nurdi, Herry (2005), 'Dosa-dosa Australia pada Indonesia' [Australia's sins towards Indonesia], special investigation, *Sabili Cybernews*, 3 June, <www.sabili.co.id>.

Olson, M. (1965), *Logic of Collective Action: Public Goods and the Theory of Groups*, Harvard University Press, Cambridge MA.

Pew Global Attitudes Project (2005), 'Islamic extremism: Common concern for Muslim and Western publics', 14 July, <http://pewglobal.org/reports/display.php?ReportID=248>.

Poulgrain, Greg (2005), 'US pulls plug on Papuan independence hopes', *Courier Mail*, 2 August.

Prasetyono, Edy (2005), 'Next steps in ASEAN–Korea relations for East Asian Security', paper presented at the ASEAN–Korea Conference organised by the Institute of Southeast Asian Studies (Singapore) and the Institute of Foreign Affairs and National Security (South Korea), Singapore, 15 September.

Republic of Indonesia (1995), *Risalah Sidang Badan Penyelidik Usaha-usaha Persiapan Kemerdekaan Indonesia (BPUPKI)*, Panitia Persiapan Kemerdekaan Indonesia (PPKI), 28 May 1945 – 22 August 1945, Sekretariat Negara Republik Indonesia, Jakarta.

Rosihan Anwar (2005a), 'Akibat Corby dihukum' [Results of the Corby verdict], 6 June, *Waspada Online*, <http://www.waspada.co.id/>.

Rosihan Anwar (2005b), 'Tabiat jelek Australia' [Australia's bad character], *Waspada Online*, 13 June, <http://www.waspada.co.id/>.

Rosihan Anwar (2005c), 'Bang Bam', *Waspada Online*, 20 June, <http://www. waspada.co.id/>.

Samudra, Imam (2004), *Aku Melawan Teroris* [I Fight Terrorists], Jazera, Solo.

Saraswati, Muninggar Sri (2004), 'Court issues unclear ruling on Papua', *Jakarta Post*, 12 November.

Saraswati, Muninggar Sri (2005), 'Indonesia: Forum seeks public debate on Papua', *Jakarta Post*, 7 September.

Schulze, Kirsten E. (2002a), 'Militants and moderates', *World Today*, January.

Schulze, Kirsten E. (2002b), 'Laskar Jihad and the conflict in Ambon', *Brown Journal of World Affairs*, 9(1): 57–70.

Seccombe, Mike (2005), 'Relationship must be built on optimism as well as tragedy', *Sydney Morning Herald*, 5 April.

Shergold, Peter (2005), 'Bringing government together', speech delivered by Dr Peter Shergold, Secretary of the Department of Prime Minister and Cabinet, at the conference 'Creating a Culture for Success', Adelaide, 8 April, <http:// www.dpmc.gov.au/speeches/shergold/together_2005-04-08.cfm>.

Sheridan, Greg (2005), 'Bambang can be our best friend', *The Australian*, 7 April.

Singh, Daljit (2003), 'ASEAN counter-terror strategies and cooperation: How effective?', pp. 201–20 in Kumar Ramakrishna and See Seng Tan (eds), *After Bali: The Threat of Terrorism in Southeast Asia*, World Scientific and IDSS, Singapore.

Swanström, Niklas (2005), 'Southeast Asia's war on terror: Who is cooperating across borders?', *Harvard Asia Quarterly*, 9(1&2): 4–11.

Walters, Patrick (2004), 'Closer, yet still distant: Indonesia – a special country survey', *The Australian*, 30 August.

Wanandi, Jusuf (1984), 'Security issues in the ASEAN region', pp. 297–308 in Karl D. Jackson and M. Hadi Soesastro (eds), *ASEAN Security and Economic Development*, Research Papers and Policy Studies No. 11, Institute of East Asian Studies, University of California, Berkeley CA.

Wayoi, Herman (2002), 'Quo vadis Papua: Tanah Papua (Irian Jaya) masih dalam status tanah jajahan' [Quo vadis Papua: The land of Papua (Irian Jaya) still has the status of a colonial territory], pp. 59–68 in Agus A. Alua (ed.), *Dialog Nasional, Papua dan Indonesia 26 Februari 1999, 'Kembalikan Kedaulatan Papua Barat, Pulang dan Renungkan Dulu'* [National Dialogue, Papua and Indonesia, 26 February 1999, 'Return West Papua's Sovereignty, Return to Basics and Reflect First'], Seri Pendidikan Politik Papua No. 2, Sekretariat Presidium Dewan Papua dan Biro Penelitian STFT Fajar Timur, Jayapura, December.

Wing, John and Peter King (2005), 'Genocide in West Papua?', Centre for Peace and Conflict Studies, University of Sydney, Sydney, August.

Witoelar, Wimar (2005), 'Changing perceptions of Australia post-Corby trial', *Jakarta Post*, 9 July 2005, <http://www.perspektif.net/article/article.php?article_id=58>.

World Bank (2004), *Indonesia. Averting an Infrastructure Crisis: A Framework for Policy and Action*, World Bank, Jakarta and Washington DC.

World Bank (2005a), 'Indonesia: New directions', Report No. 31335-IND, January, <http://siteresources.worldbank.org/INTINDONESIA/Resources/Publication/280016-1106130305439/CGI_Indonesia_New_Direction.pdf>.

World Bank (2005b), 'Rebuilding a better Aceh & Nias: Preliminary stocktaking of the reconstruction effort six months after the earthquake & tsunami', June, <http://www-wds.worldbank.org/servlet/WDSContentServer/WDSP/IB/2005/11/09/000160016_20051109121239/Rendered/PDF/328930Replacement0aceh16months.pdf>.

Yamin, Mohammed (1959), *Naskah-Persiapan Undang-undang Dasar 1945* [Manuscript of the Preparations for the 1945 Constitution], Jajasan Prapantja, Jakarta.

Yudhoyono, Susilo Bambang (2005a), 'Speech by His Excellency Dr. Susilo Bambang Yudhoyono, President of the Republic of Indonesia', Parliament House, Canberra, 4 April, <http://www.kbri-canberra.org.au/speeches/2005/050404e_PresRI.htm>.

Yudhoyono, Susilo Bambang (2005b), speech given at a gala dinner for the American Indonesian Chamber of Commerce and the United States–Indonesia Society at the Pierre Hotel, New York City, 15 September.

Zhaoxing, Li (2005), press statement issued at the ASEAN+3 meeting in Vientiane, August.

INDEX

JI, *see* Jemaah Islamiyah
Joint Commission, *see*
    Australia–Indonesia Partnership for
    Reconstruction and Development
Joint Standing Committee on Foreign
    Affairs, Defence and Trade
    (Australia), 118
Jordan, 17
journalism
    see media commentary; *see also*
    exchange program

Kalla, Vice-President Jusuf, xviii, 146
Keating, Paul, 2, 15, 33n, 34, 35, 37, 41,
    43, 47, 166, 172, 174, 182
Keelty, Mick, 166
Kelian Equatorial Mining, 154
Koizumi, Prime Minister Junichiro, 12,
    25, 26, 27

Laskar Jihad, 59
Learning Assistance Program for Islamic
    Schools (LAPIS), 141
Lee Kuan Yew, 63
Leighton Contractors, 152–3
Leunig, Michael, 80, 81, 83n
'Little Boy from Manly', 85
Lowy Institute, 74, 166
    survey, xvi, 2, 14, 173

Mahathir, Prime Minister, 4, 12, 14, 76
Majelis Mujahidin Indonesia (Council of
    Indonesian Mujahideen), 59
Malaysia, xix, 4, 12, 13, 14, 17, 20, 22,
    23, 25, 46, 74, 81, 149, 160, 174, 178
    Indonesian students, 87, 96, 98–101
    students in Australia, 91
    and terrorism, 59, 60, 61, 63
Mas Selamat Kastari, 57
media commentary, 2, 6, 16, 18, 35, 36,
    37, 38, 70, 71, 135
    Australian press, 38, 79–80, 123, 172
    globalisation of news, 73, 83n
    Indonesian press, 73, 74, 75–6, 144,
    146
    political cartoons, 81, 84–6, 177
Menzies government, 106, 113, 178, 180
Mexico, 155n
money laundering, 16, 18

Moro Islamic Liberation Front (MILF),
    59, 61
Muhammadiyah, 59

National Asian Languages and Studies in
    Australian Schools strategy, 3
National Committee on Governance
    Policy, 149, 150
    performance indicators, 151
National Institute for Asia and the Pacific,
    xv
National Statement for Engaging Young
    Australians with Asia, 3
Nauru, 141n
Netherlands, 15, 101, 102, 111
    agreement on cooperation with
    Australia, 114
    and Papua, 106, 108, 109, 113–16,
    118, 120
New Zealand, 12, 15, 24, 158
Newmont, 154–5, 155n
Nias, xx, 15, 136, 141n
Non Aligned Movement (NAM), 21, 22,
    179

oil,
    declining production, 147–8, 154
    exploration, 147
    imports, 147
    price rise, 146–7, 149, 154
Organization of Islamic Countries (OIC),
    21
Organization of the Petroleum Exporting
    Countries (OPEC), 21
Osama bin Laden, 58
    support for, 30

Pacific War, 12
Pakistan, 17
Palar, L.N., 112, 124n
Pangestu, Mari, 7n
Papua, 5, 38, 106–28, 172, 174
    Act of Free Choice, 107, 108, 109,
    110, 124n
    Australian attitudes, 113–14
    Freeport mine, 109
    future, 122–3, 178
    history, 111–14
    human rights abuses, 119–20, 123,
    125n

INDONESIA UPDATE SERIES

Indonesia Assessment 1988 (Regional Development)
edited by Hal Hill and Jamie Mackie

Indonesia Assessment 1990 (Ownership)
edited by Hal Hill and Terry Hull

Indonesia Assessment 1991 (Education)
edited by Hal Hill

Indonesia Assessment 1992 (Political Perspectives)
edited by Harold Crouch

Indonesia Assessment 1993 (Labour)
edited by Chris Manning and Joan Hardjono

Finance as a Key Sector in Indonesia's Development
(Indonesia Assessment 1994)
edited by Ross McLeod

Development in Eastern Indonesia
(Indonesia Assessment 1995)
edited by Colin Barlow and Joan Hardjono

Population and Human Resources
(Indonesia Assessment 1996)
edited by Gavin W. Jones and Terence H. Hull

Indonesia's Technological Challenge
(Indonesia Assessment 1997)
edited by Hal Hill and Thee Kian Wie

Post-Soeharto Indonesia: Renewal or Chaos?
(Indonesia Assessment 1998)
edited by Geoff Forrester

Indonesia in Transition: Social Aspects of Reformasi and Crisis
(Indonesia Assessment 1999)
edited by Chris Manning and Peter van Diermen

Indonesia Today: Challenges of History
(Indonesia Assessment 2000)
edited by Grayson J. Lloyd and Shannon L. Smith

Women in Indonesia: Gender, Equity and Development
(Indonesia Assessment 2001)
edited by Kathryn Robinson and Sharon Bessell

Local Power and Politics in Indonesia: Decentralisation and Democratisation
(Indonesia Assessment 2002)
edited by Edward Aspinall and Greg Fealy

Business in Indonesia: New Challenges, Old Problems
(Indonesia Assessment 2003)
edited by M. Chatib Basri and Pierre van der Eng

The Politics and Economics of Indonesia's Natural Resources
(Indonesia Assessment 2004)
edited by Budy P. Resosudarmo

Different Societies, Shared Futures: Australia, Indonesia and the Region
(Indonesia Assessment 2005)
edited by John Monfries